# I'd Rather
# Be
# Right
# Than
# Happy!

# I'd Rather Be Right Than Happy!

## The Perfect Formula For Failure

Dr. Theresa M. Benjamin

Coda Publications
San Marcos, California

*I'd Rather Be Right Than Happy:*
*The Perfect Formula For Failure*

By Theresa M. Benjamin, Ph.D.

Published by Coda Publications
P.O. Bin 711, San Marcos, California 92079

LC #00-135111
ISBN 0-910390-66-5

*Printed in the United States of America*

# Contents

**Preface** . . . . . . . . . . . . . . . . . . . . . . . . . . . . . . . **ix**

Why You Want To Read This Book. . . . . . . . . . . . . . . . . . . xiii

**Foreword** . . . . . . . . . . . . . . . . . . . . . . . . . . . . . **xvii**

**Acknowledgments**. . . . . . . . . . . . . . . . . . . . . . . . . **xxi**

**Introduction** . . . . . . . . . . . . . . . . . . . . . . . . . . . . **23**

Creating The Problem . . . . . . . . . . . . . . . . . . . . . . . . . 24

Where You Have The Problem . . . . . . . . . . . . . . . . . . . . . 25

Frequency Of The Problem . . . . . . . . . . . . . . . . . . . . . . . 25

Intensity Of The Problem . . . . . . . . . . . . . . . . . . . . . . . . 26

Length Of Time You Keep The Problem . . . . . . . . . . . . . . . . 26

Why You Have The Problem . . . . . . . . . . . . . . . . . . . . . . 26

Summary . . . . . . . . . . . . . . . . . . . . . . . . . . . . . . . . . 27

## CHAPTER ONE

**Balancing Love, Quality And Money** . . . . . . . . . . . . . . . **29**

What Is Love?. . . . . . . . . . . . . . . . . . . . . . . . . . . . . . . 30

What Is Quality? . . . . . . . . . . . . . . . . . . . . . . . . . . . . . 34

What Is Money? . . . . . . . . . . . . . . . . . . . . . . . . . . . . . 37

Summary . . . . . . . . . . . . . . . . . . . . . . . . . . . . . . . . . 41

## CHAPTER TWO

**Identifying A Problem** . . . . . . . . . . . . . . . . . . . . . . . **43**

First Degree Problems . . . . . . . . . . . . . . . . . . . . . . . . . . 44

Second Degree Problems . . . . . . . . . . . . . . . . . . . . . . . . 47

Third Degree Problems. . . . . . . . . . . . . . . . . . . . . . . . . . 48

Summary . . . . . . . . . . . . . . . . . . . . . . . . . . . . . . . . . 49

## CHAPTER THREE

**Loving Your Problems** . . . . . . . . . . . . . . . . . . . . . **51**
   Process vs. Content . . . . . . . . . . . . . . . . . . . . . . . 59

## CHAPTER FOUR

**You Better Be Right — Or Else** . . . . . . . . . . . . . . . **63**
   Belief Systems That Pay A Price. . . . . . . . . . . . . . . . 71
   Belief Systems That Limit Your Success. . . . . . . . . . . 72
   Limiting Love. . . . . . . . . . . . . . . . . . . . . . . . . . . 73
   Limiting Quality . . . . . . . . . . . . . . . . . . . . . . . . . 74
   Limiting Money . . . . . . . . . . . . . . . . . . . . . . . . . 76
   Contaminated Dollars . . . . . . . . . . . . . . . . . . . . . 76
   Summary . . . . . . . . . . . . . . . . . . . . . . . . . . . . . 78

## CHAPTER FIVE

**Perceptions Are The Way You See It** . . . . . . . . . . . . . **79**

## CHAPTER SIX

**The Traditional vs. The Today Relationships** . . . . . . . . **87**
   The Today Relationship . . . . . . . . . . . . . . . . . . . . 93
   Context. . . . . . . . . . . . . . . . . . . . . . . . . . . . . . . 99
   Contaminating The New Context . . . . . . . . . . . . . . 102

## CHAPTER SEVEN

**Formula For Failure** . . . . . . . . . . . . . . . . . . . . . . **107**
   Anger . . . . . . . . . . . . . . . . . . . . . . . . . . . . . . . 108
   The Gossip Game. . . . . . . . . . . . . . . . . . . . . . . . 112
   Ending The Gossip Game. . . . . . . . . . . . . . . . . . . 116
   Guilt . . . . . . . . . . . . . . . . . . . . . . . . . . . . . . . . 117
   Your Non-Resolution Self . . . . . . . . . . . . . . . . . . 120
   Your Retaliatory Self. . . . . . . . . . . . . . . . . . . . . . 123

## CHAPTER EIGHT

**The Clock To Failure.** . . . . . . . . . . . . . . . . . . . . . **131**
   The Degree Of The Payoff . . . . . . . . . . . . . . . . . . 137
   Frequency Of The Payoff . . . . . . . . . . . . . . . . . . . 138
   Length Of Time In The Payoff . . . . . . . . . . . . . . . . 138
   Dr. Benjamin's Clock To Failure. . . . . . . . . . . . . . . 140
   Summary. . . . . . . . . . . . . . . . . . . . . . . . . . . . . 144

## CHAPTER NINE

Our Two Selves . . . . . . . . . . . . . . . . . . . . . . . . . . . . . 145

    Saints And Devils. . . . . . . . . . . . . . . . . . . . . . . . . . . . 149

    Summary. . . . . . . . . . . . . . . . . . . . . . . . . . . . . . . . . 151

## CHAPTER TEN

The Genesis Of All Games . . . . . . . . . . . . . . . . . . . . . . 153

## CHAPTER ELEVEN

The Game Of Living Or Dying . . . . . . . . . . . . . . . . . . . . 159

## CHAPTER TWELVE

The Games Of Life . . . . . . . . . . . . . . . . . . . . . . . . . . . 165

    The Abuser Personality . . . . . . . . . . . . . . . . . . . . . . . 166

    The Abused Personality. . . . . . . . . . . . . . . . . . . . . . . . 167

    The Abuser Solution . . . . . . . . . . . . . . . . . . . . . . . . . 168

    The Abused Solution . . . . . . . . . . . . . . . . . . . . . . . . . 168

    Summary . . . . . . . . . . . . . . . . . . . . . . . . . . . . . . . . 169

    Front Seat Drivers vs. Back Seat Drivers. . . . . . . . . . . . . . 170

    Front Seat Driver Personality . . . . . . . . . . . . . . . . . . . . 172

    Back Seat Driver Personality. . . . . . . . . . . . . . . . . . . . . 173

    Front Seat Driver Solution . . . . . . . . . . . . . . . . . . . . . . 174

    Back Seat Driver Solution. . . . . . . . . . . . . . . . . . . . . . . 174

    Summary . . . . . . . . . . . . . . . . . . . . . . . . . . . . . . . . 175

    Givers vs. Takers . . . . . . . . . . . . . . . . . . . . . . . . . . . 176

    The Giver Personality . . . . . . . . . . . . . . . . . . . . . . . . . 177

    The Taker Personality . . . . . . . . . . . . . . . . . . . . . . . . . 181

    The Giver Solution . . . . . . . . . . . . . . . . . . . . . . . . . . . 184

    The Taker Solution . . . . . . . . . . . . . . . . . . . . . . . . . . . 187

    Summary . . . . . . . . . . . . . . . . . . . . . . . . . . . . . . . . 188

    Frigid vs. Impotent. . . . . . . . . . . . . . . . . . . . . . . . . . . 190

    The Frigid Personality . . . . . . . . . . . . . . . . . . . . . . . . . 193

    The Impotent Personality. . . . . . . . . . . . . . . . . . . . . . . 194

    The Frigid Solution . . . . . . . . . . . . . . . . . . . . . . . . . . . 194

    The Impotent Solution . . . . . . . . . . . . . . . . . . . . . . . . 195

    Summary . . . . . . . . . . . . . . . . . . . . . . . . . . . . . . . . 196

    Talkers vs. Silencers . . . . . . . . . . . . . . . . . . . . . . . . . . 197

    The Talker Personality. . . . . . . . . . . . . . . . . . . . . . . . . 198

    The Silencer Personality. . . . . . . . . . . . . . . . . . . . . . . . 199

    The Talker Solution. . . . . . . . . . . . . . . . . . . . . . . . . . . 201

The Silencer Solution . . . . . . . . . . . . . . . . . . . . . . 201
Summary . . . . . . . . . . . . . . . . . . . . . . . . . . . . . 202
Waiters vs. Laters . . . . . . . . . . . . . . . . . . . . . . . . 203
The Waiter Personality . . . . . . . . . . . . . . . . . . . . . 204
The Later Personality . . . . . . . . . . . . . . . . . . . . . . 204
The Waiter Solution . . . . . . . . . . . . . . . . . . . . . . . 205
The Later Solution . . . . . . . . . . . . . . . . . . . . . . . 206
Summary . . . . . . . . . . . . . . . . . . . . . . . . . . . . . 208

## CHAPTER THIRTEEN

**Formula For Success** . . . . . . . . . . . . . . . . . . . . . **209**
Attitude — The Second Healer . . . . . . . . . . . . . . . . . 214
Communication — The Third Healer . . . . . . . . . . . . . . 217
The Art Of Avoiding Answering A Question . . . . . . . . . . 220
The Art Of Not Being Heard . . . . . . . . . . . . . . . . . . 221
Empathy . . . . . . . . . . . . . . . . . . . . . . . . . . . . . 224
Transactional Analysis . . . . . . . . . . . . . . . . . . . . . 227
Parent . . . . . . . . . . . . . . . . . . . . . . . . . . . . . . 227
Adult . . . . . . . . . . . . . . . . . . . . . . . . . . . . . . . 229
Child . . . . . . . . . . . . . . . . . . . . . . . . . . . . . . . 229
Summary . . . . . . . . . . . . . . . . . . . . . . . . . . . . . 230
Motivation To Change - The Fourth Healer . . . . . . . . . . 233

## CHAPTER FOURTEEN

**The Clock To Success** . . . . . . . . . . . . . . . . . . . . . **237**

## Illustrations

*Here And Now* . . . . . . . . . . . . . . . . . . . . . . . . . *55*
*Belief Systems* . . . . . . . . . . . . . . . . . . . . . . . . . *70*
*Emotional and Physical Feelings* . . . . . . . . . . . . . . . *84*
*The Clock To Failure* . . . . . . . . . . . . . . . . . . . . . *141*
*The Process Of Empathy* . . . . . . . . . . . . . . . . . . . *225*
*PAC Ego States* . . . . . . . . . . . . . . . . . . . . . . . . *228*
*Communication Preferred* . . . . . . . . . . . . . . . . . . . *232*
*The Clock To Success* . . . . . . . . . . . . . . . . . . . . . *238*
*Success To Infinity* . . . . . . . . . . . . . . . . . . . . . . *246*

# Preface

Dear Friend:

Thank you for your interest in my book and I imagine that, like my other friends, you're somewhat curious about the second part of the title, "The Perfect Formula For Failure."

My years of questioning and listening to beautiful loving people telling of having stupid arguments on subjects of no importance completely amazed me. Most of all, when I found that same madness in myself and noted that 98% of my arguments were pure "junk."

In the process of observing these phenomena I soon realized that the "why" of a disagreement is not important. How to prevent and stop such interruptions to love was far more relevant and vital to a happy life.

This self-analysis brought back the memory of what my mother often said. "If one person gets mad at you, that's too bad. If two people get mad at you, that's sad. When three people get mad at you, look into yourself."

I've now revised my mother's comment to become "If you are waiting for someone to change so you can be happy, you are truly insane. Change yourself and get a life." This is my Philosophy of Joy and what this book is all about.

The foundation of any problem is usually your own anger seeking a place to go, a situation which destroys relationships. Decide today to never again lay your anger on another human, nor give others the power to anger you. Settle "junk" arguments with Love and understanding. Cast your anger to the sky to get it off the earth and let's leave each other in peace. This is the foundation of my thinking and philosophy that I invite you to adopt in place of the disastrous roles we play with such vigor.

*There is no right or wrong, there is no good or bad, and no blame or fault. Believe in the goodness of human beings and share that belief.*

Now, Dear Friend, writing about the beginnings of this book brings me to what was my most important personal-solution step. That was the day I asked myself, "What are you going to do about anger?"

Further exploration brought me answers, which I pass on to you and your friends. Though, as you can imagine, the best answer didn't arrive until I asked another simple question. "What will I do the next time I become angry at someone or allow someone to anger me?"

The first thing that would happen to me as I entered my sad Formula For Failure was a feeling of righteousness and I would begin mentally criticizing the other person. I'd say to myself, "What a stupid thing for her to say." Then I gossiped to others about the situation and explained what stupid things the other person had said. Today, it's obvious to you and me that I was on my way to failure; totally unaware of doing the same thing as the person I was criticizing.

It was at this point that I learned to hear the alarm going off in my head. "Stop!" That was when I really needed to interrupt my thought processes. But what should I do? All I wanted was peace. What brought peace to me? The ocean. So I put on my bathing suit, drove to the nearby beach and lay in the surf. Each time an incoming wave washed over me I'd say, "Bring me peace." When the water flowed toward the ocean I'd say, "Take my anger. We don't need it here on earth." After peace and calm came over me, I went home, called the person I was directing my anger toward and made peace. She was surprised and so was 1. For that, and more reasons, I now view anger as a poisonous serpent. It may mean well, and believe it is needed for survival, but it can and will kill happiness and any kind of success in Love, Quality and Money, all of which are essential to our life.

This episode went a long way toward diminishing my anger sprees that were so devastating to others. Best of all, it lead to a supporting drama that validated the power to interrupt anger in others. While lying in the water one day, I felt someone poking my shoulder. I opened my eyes to find a young surfer leaning over me. He asked, "What are you trying to do, lady, drown yourself?"

I laughed and sat up. "Do you really want to know?" I asked him.

"Yes . . . I see you here all the time, just lying in the water," he replied. I was still explaining about throwing my anger out to sea to get it off the earth and out of my body, when he interrupted with "Lady, teach me." And so I did.

Months later I found him lying in the surf as I often did. I snuck up behind him, poked his shoulder and said, "What are you trying to do, kid, drown yourself?" We had a good laugh and hugged. A few years later I learned that lying in the surf had become his method of getting off drugs. Another proof that all of us can make friends with anger and turn it into Love.

After similar adventures, I reached the conclusion that there is only one problem in human relations. That is Anger, with a capital A. It is the root and stalk of our relationship problems, the basis of divorce, being fired from a decent lob, losing a friend, breaking the law on purpose, and forms of abuse up to and including killing.

Though we all can't lie on a beach, there are ways that you too can redirect your anger to a distant ocean or vacant planet. Here's a simple method I teach to children who usually respond with excellent redirection. They are told that when signs of anger appear they are in the first stage of their Formula For Failure. They are instructed to telephone me before letting another person know they are angry. When they call, we talk until I can lead them back to their loving self and their Formula For Success. After this is accomplished I pay them two dollars. In effect, a very good anger "break" for children to love their angry self too. Love cures all!

Do-It-Yourself is another way to diminish anger no matter where you are. Just relax your body. Swing both arms loosely and take deep breaths. Do not speak as you release your anger each time you slowly exhale to calm both body and mind and bring home your loving self.

This is simple and effective. Try it.

Another form of self-help is to add numbers. Emotion comes from the right side of your brain where there is no logical thinking. When you concentrate on adding 21 and 36, you have to use the left side of your brain. The normal logic that does not exist in the right brain will return as you count and you will be able to talk lovingly to yourself about allowing your anger to evaporate. You will now be able to think of your many wonderful deeds. Once you accept your loving self, you will be able to balance the logic from the left brain and the Love from your right brain to achieve the peace you want, as the anger is now gone.

You now know something about the dangers of anger and how to redirect it, so read on to make your every relationship a superior situation, as you love one another because you are breathing. This does not mean you do not seek to resolve a problem. But it does mean you reach each resolution with Love and affection. For example; I often say to my grandson, "John, I love you because you are breathing."

Nevertheless, a few years ago he stole from me. I immediately called the police. He whined, "But Grandma, you said you love me because I am breathing."

"I do, John," I replied. "And I love myself in the same way and will not allow you, or anyone else, to abuse me." When officers arrived they could not get over seeing John and I hugging each other and laughing.

One of them said, "I see you have already resolved the issue," as they left.

Most importantly, John has never stolen from me since.

Reinvent your world with my book's many ways of handling situations that invite anger. Soon you will be using the true Philosophy of Joy and have a more loving life. All you need to do is love others because they are breathing . . . and include yourself.

## Why You Want To Read This Book

Why would you want to read this book? What will it do for you? Here you will learn how to go within your inner self for the peace and serenity that a part of you craves. You will find answers to win and in the Love we all desire in life. And you will learn that waiting for someone else to change, so you can be happy, is futile.

Change yourself first and the rest will follow! My eight years of research led me to this conclusion, especially when I learned how to apply it to myself. All of us on earth are born with a certain amount of anger; most of us won't "own" it and definitely won't love it. I call my own little angry self my "Little Beastie." I have learned to love it deeply. Loving your little Beastie is the way to overcome expecting others to be the way you want them to be. It will lower your expectations of what one is to do, say, or act. If you have discussed any negative issue more than three times, accept that they are not going to change. They may when they decide to, but rarely will they when someone insists on it.

My purpose in writing this book is to invite each person on earth to be in charge of his/her anger. It will always be there, but if we redirect it elsewhere, we will never put our anger on another human being. You will also discover how to never give another human the power to anger you.

You will learn that every time you fight to be right, you will lose something in Love, Quality, and Money. You will learn how to settle your problems and gain positive results using your loving self. You will back it up so the other person knows that you mean business and they cannot get you angry. You will love yourself too deeply to allow this.

In this book, you will learn your Formula For Success and your Formula For Failure, and you will look within yourself to analyze how you win and succeed in your undertakings. You will also learn, in the same way, how you lose. Study both results to recognize, as soon as possible, if you are on the road to losing. If so, make the switch to winning a better lifestyle today..

When I teach this to children, I tell them that if they get angry and call me before they let anyone in the world know they are angry, I'll give them two bucks. This is successful and it works.

At one of my therapy sessions, the parents stated that their child broke everything he got hold of.

I asked the child if he knew why he did it, and he answered, "No, Theresa, I don't know why I do it."

When I eventually learned that breaking things began when his parents were constantly yelling, the child said, "They yell at the dog, yell at the cat, yell at me and my brother, and they yell at each other."

I taught him how to relax his body when he heard them start to yell and remember the times when they were fun and made him laugh. One day he came in with a big grin on his face. I asked, "Hey, Amigo, what are you so happy about?" He laughed and replied, "Theresa, guess what: I know what to do now."

"Tell me about it."

He said, "Whenever I hear yelling, I stop and be quiet like you told me. Then I play the matador game."

"What the heck is that, Amigo?"

He replied, "I pretend I am a toreador and have a cape in my hand. I take a deep breath and when the yelling comes my way, I take my hands and swing the cape to my side and I let it go by."

I said, "What do you mean you let 'it' go by? You let the 'bull' go by?"

He started to laugh and told me, "Yea, Tree, that's what it is, huh? It's bull!"

We laughed. I told him, "Yes, honey, that is what it is. All anger is bull. Don't ever let it get to you."

Read this book and find your way. Mine was to lie in the ocean and relax. When a wave rolled out to sea, I would say, "Take the anger out to sea. We don't want it here on earth." When the wave rolled in over my head, I would say, "Bring the Peace." This worked for me. I'm confident that you will find your own solutions to make peace within and that this book will help guide you to this experience with Love.

So, next time you feel a stir of anger, ask yourself, "Do I want to be right, or do I want to stop this nonsense and be happy?" Make a selection. I hope your answer is, "Yes, I want the peace and happiness that is available to all of us."

Read my book. Make the change to the good life.

*Theresa*

# Foreword

I feel privileged to write a Foreword for Dr. Theresa M. Benjamin's very special book. I have had the good fortune to know Dr. Benjamin as a client, student, colleague and above all a friend for over twenty years. Over these years, she has taught me a great deal and, wonderfully, she credits me with having taught her. When I was working with her in therapy, I was always amazed when I recommended a book and found that she had obtained it and read it by the next therapy session. I never had a client like that before and have not had one since. Her book will be one that I will add to my recommended list.

As I read the draft of her book, I was struck with how she has truly lived what she is teaching. There is no "Ivory Tower" theorizing here but a practical guide that will help people in all walks of life and in all life-styles. Often I have read self-help books that would be helpful to me if I had an extra three hours a day to implement all of the suggestions. This book is for the every day living of people who are busy working, raising a family, and getting along with their partners, be it business or marriage.

After reading the section, "You Better Be Right — Or Else," I realized a person can read any chapter that seems to address the questions that come to mind relevant to his/her particular problem or interest. This is not the kind of book that I would recommend sitting down and reading cover to cover, but to read relevant chapters and think deeply about the contents in relation to yourself. It is making a decision to invest the energy into implementing the subtle changes on a day-to-day basis. As I was reading the draft, I thought of all the people I would recommend it to. For example:

**Business People:** People in business, whether company presidents, managers or employees, will all benefit from this book. The section on balancing Love, Quality, and Money, Chapter 1, will help any person who wishes to expand the successes in their life in these three areas. I definitely agree with Theresa that many, if not most, people believe that they must sacrifice one or the other if they are to be a success. Theresa points out that we can have loving relationships with every person in our lives; we can create Quality of life in our work and social lives and we can have the kind of financial success that will allow us to enjoy the other two successes. She makes practical suggestions to help us overcome our beliefs and our practices that hinder our achieving success in these three areas.

**Families:** Be they married partners, parents or children, all will enjoy and benefit from the entire book but especially from the sections on communication, relationships and belief systems. By insisting that we are right, we often push others away. Theresa points out how we do this, why we do it and how we can reframe our beliefs and our practices so that we can get what we really want; Love with intimacy, a special Quality of life, and the Money to do it with. Success is not being right but being effective and happy.

**Individuals:** This book is also for the individual who wishes to grow as a person. Theresa has distilled a great deal of wisdom from organizational development, psychology, and true common sense that will be helpful to persons of any sex, age or marital status. "Know Thyself" and "To Thine Own Self Be True" are sayings that many of us have heard for years. This book puts meat on the bones of these sayings. It tells us how we give our power away without knowing it or wanting to give it away. She tells how we can keep our power and still develop loving relationships and have success in our careers.

There are many things I have enjoyed about Theresa over the years. One of the most important, for me, is her no-nonsense approach to life. If something is not working for you in your life, she will often ask, "What are you going to do about it?" I don't recall her ever saying something like, "Oh, you poor dear, you need to find someone to fix it for you." This is not to mean that she does not have compassion, but that her compassion is empowering rather than rescuing. She wants us to grow in self-awareness and to share our creativity and our happiness with others, not to try to make others happy or to rescue them. The only person we can make happy is you. We can share our happiness with others but we cannot *make* them happy.

There were many profound concepts Theresa projected those I felt needed emphasis because of their impact on our thinking. I recommended that she box them in to guide you to them and for you to ponder. I hope that you will enjoy and benefit as much from this book as I have. Happy reading!!

Dr. Donald F. Hanley

# Acknowledgments

I wish to thank Dr. Donald Hanley, my psychotherapist, guide, model, and best friend for all the years of being there for me and gently opening my mind to see all the good things in it. Without his ability to build the trust I needed to look within, I would continue caged and lost.

And thank my daughter, Lorri Benjamin, for her tenacity and patience in typing and typing and typing and reading and reading and reading this book. Her insights and suggestions have been invaluable. In using her to relate incidents to explain my concepts, she did not hesitate to tell me her version and my involvement. With her candidness and acute insight, I found she was the only person I trusted to change dialogue and improve on what I had written.

The feedback I received from my son, Richard Benjamin, has enabled me to find other dimensions to many of my concepts. He was not afraid to challenge or speak up on any concept I developed, and his astuteness in dissecting these concepts was profound.

My thanks also extend to all my patients and friends that were dissected in the name of research. Their patience and Love was always there with a support I could not have done without.

Most of all, thanks to the mind for being here. I love the mind more than anything else and believe it is our true essence of existence.

# Introduction

My life search to understand why we need to be right started many years ago when my husband and I played a game called, "Is there anything wrong with a person?" Whatever one of us came up with, the other would say, "No, that is not wrong because...." Twenty years later he asked, "Theresa, did you ever find a wrong in a person?" I told him I had not. Thus, I concluded there is no right and there is no wrong. My philosophy extended to there being no good and no bad. There is no blame and no fault. We just are. This was borne out when a young couple came to see me for therapy, and prompted my title of this book.

I sat there as though I was watching a ping pong game swiveling my head from one person to the other hearing, "It was Wednesday." "No it wasn't, it was Thursday." "I know it was Wednesday because that was the day Marion came over." This exchange came about when I asked what their purpose was in coming to psychotherapy and what did they wish to accomplish. It was at that point that the wife said sweetly, " We want to keep our marriage, do a good job raising our children and to be happy and that is why I called you Thursday." and he immediately countered with "No, it was Wednesday." This escalated into a restrained conversation, or war. Both were presenting proof and incidents to prove that the day each recalled was the right day and that they were right and the other person was wrong. I finally interrupted the conversation and asked, "What is more important; to be right or to be happy? Choosing to be happy did not enter the minds of either one of these young people during their dialogue.

This exchange prompted me to explore the minor areas people invest energy into being right. In almost every argument I explored in ten years, both parties believed they were right and were devastated when they were confronted with unquestioning proof that they were wrong.

I noticed conversations where people argued about who was right and I tracked these conversations. I found that more time and energy went into proving who was right than locating what the problem was and how to resolve it. One of the main shifts necessary to attain resolutions and happiness is to give up the need to be right and the need to change another person.

Pondering why this couple put so much energy into being right about something of no importance and nothing to do with the conversation, led to my investigation of HOW you create the problem, **WHERE** you elect to have it, the **FREQUENCY** that you repeat these problems, the **LENGTH** of time you stay in it, the **INTENSITY** you play the game and, finally, I pondered **WHY**. Tracking the frequency a problem occurs, the **LENGTH** of time it is held, the **INTENSITY** the game is played, will tell the health of a person, relationship or office.

### Creating The Problem

I looked for **HOW** people kept their problems and got themselves into positions that made them leave their good common sense behind and pursue the need to be right. My exploration of the painful games people played, led me to discover that all people have a Formula For Success and a Formula For Failure. These are maps of the process illustrating precisely how we talk and act to achieve the end result of being happy or being right.

I found that each of us has out own unique pattern of five steps within our Formula For Failure. The first is feeling angry which usually results in defending your position. This proceeds to the second step of amassing proof by gossiping to anyone that will agree with you.

This justifies a confrontation and you go into the third step and start feeling guilty. This increases the anger and projects you into step four and you enter your non-resolution self. This occurs when the other person does not change his/her behavior and you believe that change is your only solution. Last, but not least, is the fifth step where you now feel justified and bent on retaliating and getting back at the person no matter the consequences. You have just completed your Formula For Failure.

*Awareness of the "hows" and the "whys" of your Formula For Failure prepares you to look for, create and integrate your Formula For Success in all areas of your life.*

Whatever pattern we use, no resolution is possible since the argument is now regarding who is or who is not right. This is now the problem. The problem that prompted the argument is no longer under discussion. All defenses, excuses, gossip, etc., digress from the original problem resulting in no resolution.

## Where You Have The Problem

The next thing that puzzled me was **WHERE** people elected to use their Formula For Failure. They may elect to use their Formula For Failure at home and their Formula For Success at work, or vice versa. This way they can say, "I don't have a problem in the office." Thus they blame the ones at home for creating the problem. They cannot make the connection that each time they fail to resolve an issue, they are using their own process to do so. Rarely do other people, especially in minor problems, cause anger. Early belief systems and decisions, and the perceptions that resulted from them determine where and with whom you will have the problem to expiate your anger.

## Frequency Of The Problem

After learning about the **HOW** and **WHERE,** I became interested in the **FREQUENCY** they used their Formula For Failure to prove they are right. How often they use it was directly related to how often they were used in childhood by their parents, whether it was the passive or aggressive role. People usually use their Formula For Failure only ten percent of the time. However, if they persist in arguing daily about petty things that are of no importance, this ten percent can contaminate the good, happy ninety percent where they use their Formula For Success. This ten percent is what results in a divorce, losing a job or alienating a good friend.

### Intensity Of The Problem

The **INTENSITY** of the problems encountered has been broken down into three problem areas classified as First Degree, which is the primary focus of this book. This is where there is no tangible harm or loss to self or others. Second Degree problems are where they experience tangible harm, but are reversible. Third Degree problems cause tangible harm to self and others that are irreversible. My experience has been that Second Degree and Third Degree problems are handled better than the minor problems of life that make up their daily lives.

### Length Of Time You Keep The Problem

The **LENGTH** of time people elect to keep the problem also reflect the health of relationships. The longer they stay angry or retaliate, which keeps the problem going on, the unhealthier they are. Arguing about anything year after year guarantees you stay within the limits you have set for yourself in Love, Quality and Money.

### Why You Have The Problem

**WHY** do they need to prove they are right regardless of the price they pay to argue about minor problems of no importance? Take the case of the young couple above, arguing about what day the wife made the call. Was her disclosure of wanting to keep her husband and be happy too intimate for them and their discomfort erupted into an argument? This was my first clue to the why. I pursued this little argument to see what brought about their need to be right.

The way you handle any situation is determined by the inner attitude you developed toward people or events, and the values developed from birth through your belief systems and early decisions. These were passed on to you by your family, church and society and generally set by age ten. This is when the limitations in Love, Quality and Money are set and you will not go above these limitations without conscious awareness. When you do, you will have your argument to be right and fall back to your comfort level.

## Summary

The way your Formula For Failure consists of five elements: "Anger," "Gossip," "Guilt," "Non-Resolution," and "Retaliation." Your Formula For Success has four: "Love," "Attitude," "Communication," and "Motivation." Love replaces the Anger, Attitude changes the Guilt to peace, Communication stops the Gossip, and Motivation is then created to resolve issues and cease any retaliation. All of these ingredients are present when you use your Formula For Success no matter what situation you apply it too.

Throughout this book, I have used many of my own experiences and other poignant examples of clients, neighbors, friends and family. My philosophy is that there is no right or wrong, there is no good or bad, there is no enemy, and there is no blame. Our Formula For Failure is our inner being that acts out its childhood decisions no matter how negative or destructive they are to us. It is all of our negative behavior and beliefs that obey our inner dictates with a tenacity that defies our sensibilities.

You will find the first sections of my book outline the importance of balancing Love, Quality and Money. It then outlines how to detect your Formula For Failure and how to turn it into your Formula For Success anytime you want to. So read on and go for it!

*Chapter One*

# Balancing Love, Quality And Money

All successes fall into three areas: Love, Quality, and Money, and all are equally important in contributing to purpose and the total success of your life and existence. The fulfillment of self is to evolve to being responsible for you and accepting the ability to create these three successes within yourself as an individual. The power is in changing yourself and become what you want, find happiness and become financially successful, instead of expecting others to change.

*Two healthy-minded, resolution-oriented people create a healthy, loving relationship. They are together simply because they want to be, not out of need, expectation or commitment. This brings joy, and love becomes infinite.*

Over the years of searching for a purpose for everything, I wondered what the purpose was for wanting to be successful. I concluded it was because I existed. This purpose was to have a Quality life with Love and the common sense to add the Money to compliment the other two successes.

Since I have a body, I will make it comfortable and healthy. For Quality, I concluded that since I can see, I will make my surroundings aesthetically pleasing. With Love, I decided that since I live side-by-side with my fellow humans, I will Love and accept them as they are. The ultimate is to Love someone simply because s/he is breathing. To do this, you need to Love yourself first by trusting you will never allow someone to abuse you verbally, mentally, emotionally and physically. Most of all, while I exist, I have a mind and can think. I will use it to create a purpose. Money made it so much easier to reach these goals. Rene Descartes, known as the Father of Philosophy, claims that thinking is the only evidence we have that we exist. If there is a purpose for my existence, it will call and I will fulfill it. Victor E. Frankl put it this way:

> *For only to the extent that we have fulfilled the concrete meaning of our personal existence will we also have fulfilled ourselves. . . . The meaning, which a being has to fulfill, is something beyond self. It is never just self.*

To balance Love, Quality, and Money in your life, become a resolution person. You will then automatically achieve positive results. You Love and receive Love in return. Your Quality is reflected in your honesty, integrity and trust, and invites people with the same traits. When you are comfortable with financial success, you will have as much Money as you want. You will also encourage others around you, including your children, to do the same.

Your belief systems dictate the limits of these successes, and select the level of success you will experience all your life. Your comfort levels will affect the decisions you make, whether it is making Money, getting an education, or living in an elegant home.

The laws of the universe indicate that when everything is in balance, you attain perfection. You are aware that if you do not have enough water, you die. If you have too much water, you die. In balancing and expanding the three successes, you attain happiness and peace of mind through enriched relationships and ability to Love unconditionally. This assuredly improves the Quality of your life, and automatically increases your capacity to earn Money to live to the fullest.

## What Is Love?

Love is an event that occurs spontaneously and when genuine, brings joy. It is a warm personal attachment or deep affection for yourself as well as others. Love involves only self at the moment of birth. I believe, unless intervened, the circumstances you were born into at your conception create the degree of self-Love you sustain throughout your lifetime. In Joseph Chilton Pearce's book, *Magical Child*, he makes a basic premise. He says that when children are safely and lovingly bonded to the mother from the beginning, they will bond well and love in all other types of relationships.

Love is something outside your own being, and you can't make yourself Love or stop loving someone. It is an entity that transcends all reason. It makes no difference how the person treats you, who the person is, what race s/he is, or whether s/he is male or female. It is indeed a mystery and you want Love with all its wonders. It is an independent happening. It takes its own time, goes at its own pace and makes up its own mind regardless of the people involved.

In searching for the answer to "What is Love?" I delved into every explanation and theory I could find. Some were based on using our common sense, the religious experience, the primitive feelings, etc. It was elusive, unknown and mysterious. One day, as I was contemplating what Love was, it struck me. It made so much sense, and was so simple. Abraham Maslow explains a Peak Experience as having all five senses enhanced simultaneously. He claims that when you recall a past event with all five senses, it is more likely to be realistic. This removes the distortion of memory by recalling with only one or two senses Asking people what happened to them when they were in Love, they invariably related the pleasure of all five senses. Thus, Love is the epitome of all five senses simultaneously. You like what you see, a beautiful smile or gentle brown eyes. You hear a voice or the way a person laughs. You are thrilled at the way you feel within as well as feeling a loving hug. The two most important are smell and taste. If these are violated, generally the relationship ceases or it has a built in reason to not become fully intimate. The more your five senses are pleased, the more you are in Love and want to keep what you are experiencing as in Maslow's Peak Experience.

The way you start falling out of Love is when one of your senses is violated, and the Love starts shifting and diminishing. At this point you start to criticize the person you Love. She either doesn't say something right, didn't use good taste in dressing, or you will go as far as to say she has a "funny" walk, which I heard from a patient. Caring is different from Love. It is the way you express the Love you have within yourself to others. Love and caring, is knowing in your heart that you can help others without becoming part of the problem. When you know when to stop helping, you have become a true caring person. Learn to give, share and help others sensibly. Refrain from using other people to fill your noble purpose in life. This is when I use my refrain, "He who helps others often hinders."

*Love is an intangible and ethereal feeling that is not vital to survival. Money is tangible and necessary to survive on this earth. Quality, then, is the balance between Love and Money.*

The games we play, which are elaborated on later in this book, are used to keep us from successfully fulfilling our potential in Love, Quality, and Money. An example is when someone loves you beyond your comfort level, you will create a stir that will cut the Love off and reduce the intimacy. The loss of intimacy can be created with an argument, or getting physically or emotionally ill. You may also upset the other person thus creating the necessary distancing to return to your comfort level.

I watched very carefully whenever any of the three success areas: Love, Quality, and Money, exceeded the patients' comfort level either in degree or longevity. The sabotaging and set backs would begin when it went above or below their comfort level. When it went below their comfort level, they started rallying to return to feeling loved again. They do this by being exceedingly sweet, attentive and charming to beckon and receive Love and attention they need.

The following incident shows how early in life you learn to get people close or to distance them. I had a five-year-old boy in therapy and his mother said he was a "bear" all week. Asking him how he was a "bear," he screwed up his faced and let out a loud, menacing growl. I asked, "Why do you do that?" He said, "People leave me alone." I asked, "Do you know how to get people close?" He nodded silently and created the sweetest, angelic smile and said, "Like this."

I learned how my limit in Love was established through my religious belief system. As a Catholic, a person has only one husband until he dies. My husband disappeared, and I was not supposed to go with other men. After living alone for several years, I thought, "What a ridiculous rule." I decided to start dating and as a result, every time a man kissed me goodnight, I got the hives. They became so intense that I actually was twice pronounced Dead On Arrival at the hospital. Can you imagine the power of our belief system? Changing this belief system finally released me of the guilt that I used to limit the Love in my life and the hives disappeared forever. There are all kinds of beliefs we have that limit Love. When you have discarded the belief systems that limit Love, you will automatically expand your belief system to receive and sustain Love.

You are capable of Loving and being loved when you have made peace with yourself and the world. Anger or unhappiness is used to prevent you from giving or receiving Love that goes beyond your comfort level. You start to believe if you only found someone to love you, this would resolve all of your problems. When you do, abatement of your anger and unhappiness is temporary. The first time you doubt Love, all your fears will return and will destroy a beautiful relationship. A loving relationship doesn't change you or make you happy. You change and make yourself happy and you will then invite a loving relationship.

Success in Love is knowing what you specifically need to feel loved, and what the other person needs to feel loved. The next time you feel deeply loved, explore if it is the way the person looks at you. Is it what you hear, such as tone of voice? Check if you need people to talk to you and share their feelings, or need touching, hugs, or affection to satisfy your feeling self. Once you locate specifically what you need to feel loved, take the responsibility to tell your loved ones. In turn, ask your loved one what they need to know that s/he is loved and then give it freely and often.

I recall getting off the telephone with my daughter annoyed at something she said. I went out to my friend, Eldon, and said, "That Lorri really gets to me some days." He came over and put his arms around me and said, "Did you know I Love you?" The anger that flooded my body was surprising to say the least and I said, "What does that have to do with Lorri's telephone call?" Suddenly, the whole concept struck me. When I am upset or emotional, I need someone to discuss the problem with me, not touch me. I also knew from what Eldon's reaction was, that when he was upset he needed hugging and touching with no discussion. He did to me what would have comforted him, and I remembered and provided hugs and touching when he was upset. I also asked him to let me discuss my problems when they occurred, and when I have talked it out, then give me the hugs and affection.

Accepting and giving Love that is unconditional, is the ultimate in the success of Loving as long as you refuse to accept abuse in the process. We have not been taught how to show our Love and be loving and ask for what we want at the same time. This is indicative of loving yourself at the same time you love others. This is unconditional Love. When you Love and speak up lovingly for yourself, you give up the fear of Love. Your primitive mind will not allow you to attain something that it believes will hurt you.

When my grandson was two years old, he "painted" my white couch with a red highlighter. When I saw it, I felt no upset or need to scold him. It was unconditional Love and the couch was unimportant. I asked him, "Were you making it pretty for grandma?" He nodded his head solemnly. He said, "Yes, it makes it pretty." This does not mean that I will not feel anger at him another time. It was the acknowledgment that I was capable at that moment of experiencing unconditional Love. It was a high!

### What Is Quality?

Quality encompasses the values in your life and the pride in your work and profession. Quality is the day-to-day happiness you create for yourself. In your personal life, it manifests itself in many ways. One way is how long you have permission to be happy. Is it four days or three weeks? You will not live happily with someone if his/her happiness period is for four days and yours is three weeks. As in

Love, when the length of time you are happy exceeds your comfort level, you will find some trivial event to complain and argue about.

The Quality of your life considers the condition of your mental, physical, emotional health and being happy. You will remain happy until you exceed your comfort level, or remember the fear that you may lose the happiness. You will then have a compulsion to mess the relationship up again. This is more comfortable than living with the uncertainty of exactly when this happiness will end on its own. To use mental and physical conditions to deliberately end happiness gives you a measure of control over it. This, of course, is illusionary, as you create the very situation you fear. If you fear losing happiness, you may just bring it about.

Not staying physically, mentally or emotionally healthy is often an "escape hatch." You relinquish responsibility for your own happiness when you believe someone owes you something. You will think at some level within you, "It's now my turn to collect. I supported my family all my life and it is time I am taken care of." You will use illnesses and accidents to limit your success in Love, Quality, or Money to pressure someone to take care of you. Being successful in Quality, including health, Money and Love provides no reason for others to care for you. Being taken care of is interpreted as being Loved. This is not necessarily true. Either or both parties develop, many times, a deep animosity.

The Quality of your life is also having a moral value system. This is set early in your life and conveyed in many ways. The most powerful way is modeling. My neighbor modeled a type of Quality for his son without knowing it. He could not understand why his son stole as his whole family was honest. He was a marine and I pointed out all the items in his garage he took off the base. He immediately defended himself saying everyone did it. He explained how he had it coming because of his low pay, etc. All his justifications were irrelevant. He "stole" and bragged about it in the presence of his son. He modeled the boy without even knowing it.

Quality is also the sureness of self that builds your self-esteem. It allows you to look at yourself, to see what works and to change what does not. It is growing mentally by thinking and resolving problems. It is growing emotionally by living all your life without remorse or guilt. It is also knowing that mistakes present an opportunity to learn and nothing more. You will be congruent with your ideal self, perform work tasks well, live in good health, and enjoy each day of your life. This process helps you to accept there is no blame, no right or wrong or good or bad in day-to-day living. You have to reach extreme samples of abuse to prove something is right or wrong, good or bad. These extremes are not what everyday life is all about.

Quality is your honesty and integrity that gives you the self-respect you need, to lend credibility that invites loving relationships and financial success. You achieve the Quality of your life when you take full responsibility for your own happiness. This includes having all the comforts you need for a good life and attaining peace and serenity. You can offset adversities, and Love others unconditionally. You can do this and live a Quality life whether you are or are not receiving Love from others. Quality comes from within you. You, also, will not go below your Quality level. If you are an honest person, no one could persuade you to steal, cheat or do something below your value level that dictates the Quality of your life. You would experience extreme discomfort.

An important area that contributes to the Quality of your life is the way you manage your time. In business, time is the difference between a healthy net profit and loss. It is also a major factor in relationships and can enhance them or provide a passive tool for retaliation. You will use the withdrawal of time to punish someone or to keep from getting closer and more intimate than you are comfortable with in daily living.

I recall the day a couple came in for psychotherapy. She wished her husband stayed home more often. His reply was, "I'm working late to make more Money to provide you and the children with a better way of life. You are lucky I am not out with another woman or in a bar drinking." She gave him an answer that he least expected. She said, "I would rather have you home than have more Money. I don't care if you are sitting in church. I am still lonely." It is difficult to know what this man's reason is for working late every night. Whether his story was accurate or there was another reason, like avoiding intimacy, it does eventually show itself.

Look into how you are living your time. How many hours a day are you happy and what activities contribute to it. Expand your "happiness time" beyond your comfort level and experience longer periods of happiness than you are currently accustomed to having. The length of time you can sustain happiness determines to what extent you limit the Quality of your life. Your parents, society and church taught you very early in life that happiness was fleeting. An excellent gauge to use is how often you complain, criticize, or gossip. Once a week is healthy and rare. Gossiping is an addiction and often used on a daily basis.

Quality is having aesthetically pleasing surroundings such as a beautiful home, lovely furniture, clothes and jewelry. It is eating excellent food and driving a first class automobile. Quality is paying your bills on time every month, which has a direct affect on whether or not you will have money.

**What Is Money?**

Of these three successes, Love and Quality are acceptable traits in our society. These verify our purpose and existence in life. However, Money, the third success, is often viewed as too lowly a commodity to lend purpose. It denotes greed, and the reason why people are not caring and loving.

In debating the importance of Money with a friend, he said, "Caring for one another is far more important than Money. Look what Mother Teresa did in her lifetime." My rebuttal was that she needed other people's Money to do it. She had a charisma that invited people to give their Money to a good cause. There would not be any hospital or medication without Money, it matters not whether she received it directly, earned it or inspired people to spend it. She conveyed a feeling of trust that the Money would go to the recipients. Her Love and Caring were ethereal, but without hard cold cash, nothing would have been accomplished. It is irrelevant who provided it. We are on earth and no amount of Love will bring medicine and food to those that need it without someone paying.

For many people Money is a difficult success to accept and put on a par with Love and Quality. Therefore, I will put emphasis on its value. The negative ways used in the acquisition of Money over-shadow the positive ways it expands the Love and Quality in our lives. Often we are consciously unaware of the extent that lack of Money negatively affects Love and Quality. In reality, Money defi-nitely contributes to the Quality and Love in your life along with the sky, the land and the sea.

Socially, you have permission to make a comment on the capacity people have in Love or the Quality of their honesty and integrity. However, you must be careful how you address people about their Money. You know that you cannot ask how much someone's salary is or what s/he paid for an item. Society forgets that it uses this very same Money it sneers at to measure success. The church and society blame Money for the ruination of relationships as well as the ills of society and the "Root of All Evils." To the contrary, lack of Money adversely affects the Quality and Love in a relationship and often creates a strained and stressful existence.

A doctor had his perception of Money affect the Quality of his life by living in an extremely modest home, driving an old car and looking like he was in constant need of help. On hearing a remark referring to "A rich doctor . . . " he became incensed. It was difficult for him to under-stand that most people are not going to believe he did not have Money. He was ashamed of making so much Money and feared what others would think and say about him. To play the role of a poor man, he kept himself and his family in constant stress and turmoil and was unable to give his staff a raise. Once he became aware of the more positive results his Money brought, he was more comfortable with it. He provided twenty people with jobs, which included medical insurance that, with-out money, would not have been possible under other conditions.

Measuring peoples' comfort level in Money is most interesting. In my workshops I ask the audience to write down the increase in in-come they would like next month. The answers never ceased to amaze me. They ranged from $25 to $25,000. I asked myself, "Why? What makes them decide what figure to write?" How did they calculate the figure? Where in their head was this information accessed from?" Some struggled with this for some time. However, I pressed them to write down a figure. Then, as though they raised a curtain to some memory, they wrote a figure. This exercise is very uncomfortable for some people as they insist Love and caring is more important. They cannot write a figure down without scribbling, "This would enable me to help others." Women more often write this. Men automatically accept they are expected to give their Money to others dependent upon them.

When I go into an office and see they are producing $32,000. a month, I ask, "What would be a comfortable amount for you to make?" If the answer is $40,000, I know it will be a snap to reach. After attaining the $40,000, s/he will ask, "Can I go to $50,000?" I know this amount is attainable. However, if I provide information that his/her office has the potential to make $65,000, there is a shift. You see a definite discomfort, disbelief and resistance to this amount. To take people, even $2,000 a year, over their comfort level is a task that takes diligence.

Limitations in Money prevent you asking for a salary commiserates with your skills, as you will undersell yourself. If you praise your good points, society labels you conceited and self-centered and asks, "What makes you think you are so good?" If this discomforts you, you may use it to cut off your success. You may assume anyone exceeding the amount that constitutes greed to you got their Money by cheating, etc. It is irrelevant if it is $1,000 or $10,000 or $1,000,000.

While consulting in a dental office, twenty-three options were presented to five hygienists on how to make the hygiene department profitable and they turned all of them down. They felt the options either discounted the patient or did not show caring. They implied that it conveyed that the doctor's interest was in making a profit rather than caring for the patient's welfare. They did not consider that the doctor could give top care and receive top dollar.

However, on saying to the hygienists, "You seem to believe that there is no way to make the hygiene department profitable without offending the patient. Since you are all so caring, do you care for the doctor as well as the patient? If you do, this can be shown by sharing in his loss by taking a lesser salary?" Only one hygienist responded. She said, "Now, I feel like the doctor." The rest of the hygienists were upset. They had to face that their belief that Money was not as important as caring, whether for the patient or doctor, did not stand up in the face of this solution. Not caring for the doctor and not willing to take a cut in pay, put them in the same position they were accusing the doctor of being with his patients. This awareness created an entirely new picture when asked to share in the loss and four out of five of them did not like looking at that part of them.

*This reminds me of another one of my mother's sayings. She said if a man makes a dollar an hour and spends a dollar and one cent, he is a poor man.*

Another reason why you do not earn Money to your potential or keep what have you earned after making it, is when you have "Contaminated Dollars" which will be detailed later. You will limit your success if you have any resentment about where your hard earned dollars are going without thanks and recognition. Explore if you have any resentment and toward whom. Take several days to ponder this because many times you are not aware of these resentments. You may not have permission from yourself to quit your profession or ask for recognition and appreciation for the contribution made to your family or employees.

My observation has been that when you complain about Money, do not pay your bills or fail to pay them on time, you relinquish responsibility and will rarely make more Money without incurring more bills. This clearly demonstrates the evil of not having Money, and the stress it creates in every ones life. You are unaware of how you create situations that either prevents you from making Money or making and losing it. In the process, you ruin the Quality of your life by losing your job, being fired and alienating your friends, thus losing Love. You may also use a recession in the economy, which is a wonderful excuse to use for not being financially successful. It provides an excellent reason for your business declining, and not taking the responsibility of how you are doing it. It adds credibility when you find others making the same observation. It's bringing in the troops for confirmation that you are not totally responsible for your failures. You fail to consider the hundreds of honest businesses that are growing and are extremely successful in the same economy, and often the same neighborhood.

## Summary

The goal is to start changing your behavior, feelings and perceptions about Love, Quality, and Money that limits your potential for success. Explore your belief systems that keep you from expanding the limits in these three areas. If you like your life the way it is, you do not have to change anything. However, if dissatisfied, then search your belief systems, and change the ones that are not working for you. This exploration will open doors to your potential rather than waiting for someone to 'give you a break' to become more successful. Take responsibility for today's happiness by refraining from using yesterday's memories or tomorrow's worries to tarnish today's sunshine and your future.

Start looking for your sabotages to success and degree of severity, and determine to intercept and reverse the negative results of your Formula For Failure. The next time you have a setback, in Love, Quality, or Money, check to learn if you are blaming others or convinced there is no resolution. These are two flags that indicate you are employing another sabotage to success.

A common place to sabotage Love, Quality, and Money is often seen on vacations. I wrote an article called, "The Bickerson's Vacation Syndrome" wherein I followed the stories of hundreds of couples going on vacation. This study showed how being on vacation created an intimacy that became uncomfortable when it passed their limit in Love. As a result, an argument usually occurred before, during, or after returning from vacation that guaranteed the distancing they needed to be comfortable.

A couple told how they ruined every vacation for nine years. The assignment I gave them was to avoid arguing for one week before their vacation, during the vacation and one week after they arrived home. There were to be no surprises such as, "I didn't want to say anything before the vacation but I am leaving you."

They adhered to this agreement. However, both said it was the most difficult experience they ever had. They kept catching themselves getting angry or righteous and experienced a good deal of emotional turmoil in not ruining their vacation. The arguing they experienced on their vacations had affected their Love, the Quality of their time on vacation as well as the Quality of their relationship, and definitely cost them a lot of Money.

The degree of success you experience is in direct proportion to the amount of energy you invest in finding and implementing a solution or idea. Success in all three areas: Love, Quality, and Money are vital to your life and work when they are in balance. Thus, learning the self-imposed limits you have in your head will free you to expand these limits. It will enable you to enrich your life and partake of the abundance that is available to you. You are the only one that limits your potential and success. Learn how to tap into your natural talents and creativity, and learn to bring them to fruition. When you do, trust you will allow yourself to collect the rewards of Love, Quality, and Money and know the sky is the limit.

*Chapter Two*

# Identifying A Problem

Tangible And Intangible Problems defined themselves while listening to patients over the years when I found very few come in with real or tangible problems. They are totally unaware that griping about unimportant things is a habit and as strong an addiction as you will find anywhere. To convey to my patients and have them understand what "real" problems are, I give them three pieces of information. One is to determine if the problem is Level 1 or Level 2. The second is to locate if the problem is tangible or intangible, and the third is to check if it is a First, Second or Third Degree problem. Once these three concepts in defining a problem are understood, you will go about resolving a problem in an entirely different way.

The first concept is that every problem falls into one of two levels. Level 1 is when you do not have the information, knowledge or tools to resolve the issue. If you stay in Level 1, you will seek this knowledge, apply it, and resolve the problem. This may involve asking a friend, attorney, doctor, consultant or psychotherapist for the information. However, if you do not seek the information needed, or seek it and fail to use it when you get it, for whatever reason, you have gone to Level 2, which involves your emotional attitude.

Tangible problems are at Level 1, and can be brain stormed for a resolution. They are analytical and do not involve emotions. The energy goes into analyzing the problem and achieving a resolution, and is not wasted on emotional issues, that occur at Level 2, to prove who is right. You look for what the problem is, make it tangible and put your energy into how to fix it rather than argue about who did something wrong. You want to resolve the problem, not change the person. People are generally okay the way they are.

An example of an intangible problem at Level 2, is a doctor who had a nurse that would periodically not come to work. She said her son would unexpectedly become ill and she had no one to watch him. This left the doctor with no one on hand to help with the patients. Determining how to resolve the tangible part of the problem, we asked if she could find a back-up baby sitter that can be called on a moment's notice when her child became ill. This would prevent making her personal problems the doctor's business problem. She said, "That is impossible. I have no husband or family here and no sitter will take a sick child." This is not a logical conclusion, but an emotional one with no solution.

At this point, I assumed she did not have the information to find a back-up baby sitter. Several options were given to her such as putting an ad in the paper or contacting various agencies. She said, "I never thought about those options." We made it a tangible, and reached a resolution. Aside from the power it wields, the fact she makes it known she has no family or husband goes back to her belief system which is, that if you are bereft in any way, someone owes you consideration and should help you or excuse you. This belief will keep her from looking at what she may be doing to keep her problem, and she may never resolve it. This is intangible and irresolvable.

To help put problems in their proper perspective, I have broken down all problems that have a negative end result created by belief systems, to First Degree, Second Degree and Third Degree.

## First Degree Problems

The First Degree is the one most people experience. You can learn to avoid these or accept them calmly. However, if you persist in feeling annoyed, they will become a source of constant complaining and gossiping. Since most of your day-to-day living is First Degree, this book will concentrate on this and elaborate on how to detect, resolve and make your peace with them. First Degree issues are a process of living without harming self or others. They have no adverse or lasting affect on you or your life. They are reversible and solvable and not important. If you need to discuss them or want support when they occur, ask for it. Some examples of First Degree situations are:

- Being late.
- Coming home late.
- Missing your airplane.
- Burning dinner (even with company).
- Children fail to clean their room.
- Forgetting to pick clothes up at the cleaners.
- Changing jobs, or being fired.
- Failing to keep an appointment.
- Minor accident: a car dent, spilt milk, etc.
- Swearing, failing in school, etc.

An example of a First Degree problem is when a husband is late getting home. Be it from work, poker game or out with a friend. The wife will look at the clock a couple of times before the husband was due. This is a start of a build up that will bring anger that will result in an argument, not speaking, or whatever punishment this particular couple uses with each other. When the husband does not arrive by the agreed upon time, the wife accelerates her anger and righteousness and will make it known when her husband arrives home.

*Identifying problems as First Degree, and becoming aware that they are not important, changes the perspective to being a resolvable problem. It's more important to be happy than right especially about minor incidents in life.*

This may result in them not speaking for the evening, a couple of days, or even a couple of weeks. It never dawns on either party that the reason for the argument isn't worth the misery that they have put into their life. I refer to these types of arguments as JUNK and made myself a promise to get all JUNK problems out of my life.

The results of one First Degree negative problem have ten times the impact of one positive act. You will remember and act on the negative ones when under stress or when emotional. I recall teaching this in a course several years ago which my friend, Melda, attended.

*The purpose of giving up annoyances and griping about First Degree problems is to have a happier life and be the kind of person you want to be. When you give up First Degree annoyances, and wanting to change another person, you will no longer have minor, daily problems.*

One evening, I was making a point to the students on how much more power negative remarks have over positive ones. I gave Melda ten genuine compliments, which she seemed to accept. Toward the end of the class, she started to speak. I said, "Will you please hold your remark until I hear what Allen has to say." She immediately said, "Oh, am I talking too much?" Her belief was that she did something "wrong." It was so strong that she became upset and inconsolable. The rest of the class immediately perceived what was occurring. They could see in action how negativity of any kind affects us. I asked her, "Melda, where did the power of the ten compliments I gave you go?" I emphasized how I was using this as a demonstration to show the power of one negative over ten compliments. With the emotions this remark stirred in her, she was unable to see it. A year later she asked me, "Did I really speak too much in your class?" Powerful!

To achieve a resolution or to make peace with an annoyance, you need to redirect the negative energy into positive channels. This develops the attitude necessary for resolutions. I recall when fourteen year old Marc called to talk to me. We went to lunch and he explained how upset he was and said, "Theresa, I feel so badly. When I got mad at Mom, I went to my room and punched my dog. I don't want to be the kind of person that punches a dog." Think how profound this is. He didn't say his mother caused it and had to change so he wouldn't hit his dog that he loves dearly. He simply did not want to be that kind of person. He wanted to know how to change. I told him, "Marc, you are taking the responsibility for what happened. You are not expecting your mother to change. Most of all, you don't want to be that kind of person. I doubt very much if you will ever punch any dog again."

In reducing and resolving First Degree annoyances I found that my expectations of other people changing went down as I realized this went nowhere. When I did think it, I asked myself, "Theresa, can you change and let that behavior stop bothering you?" I am unable to apply this in all cases but the less I used it the happier I found myself. What a wonderful experience to overcome my own self-defeating behavior that I used all my life on friends and family.

*Oddly enough, even at this First Degree level, if you prove your point and are assured you are indeed right, it will only bring temporary relief. The other person may decide to change and in time the cycle will start over with someone else.*

Consistently, feeling annoyed upset, jealous, critical or unhappy continually, indicates you are problem oriented and has nothing to do with the other person. We all know that changing yourself for other people is futile especially if it is to please them. This is an improbable, task as healing and happiness comes in changing yourself, and has nothing to do with external events or people. Having expectations of people that cannot or will not do what you want makes the relationship finite. The relationship will deteriorate to a point where you are either both miserable for years or you will part. Resolving and changing negative feelings, balances Love, Quality, and Money as your expectations of others decreases. Know that almost all First Degree problems are intangible. When tangible, of little consequence.

## Second Degree Problems

Important or "real" problems fall into the Second Degree level, which are reversible or correctable even though they had caused tangible or physical harm. You are still functional and able to lead a successful life. They encompass the following problems:

- Sexual violence.
- Grief—loss by death, illness, insanity, etc.
- Handicaps (loss of hearing or a limb, going blind.
- Physical and emotional abuse.
- Divorce.
- Serious accident.

These are devastating when they occur, but with fortitude and determination you can emerge to live a fruitful and happy life. This type of experience often leads people to becoming more compassionate. The more serious a problem is, such as Second and Third Degree class, the better you handle it. The First Degree problems are usually blown out of proportion and you react as though they are Second and Third Degree ones.

*You may look at losing a limb as Third Degree since it is irreversible. However, going on to live a full successful life is still possible.*

Years ago I read about Jim Abbot, the baseball player for the California Angels. He stated that he was glad the fans looked at the hand that he used in pitching that enabled him to receive an award, rather than looking at the hand that was missing. He then earned $185,000 yearly! Many examples of this type of reversal exist. When Louis Braille was nine years old and watching his father tool leather he, wanted to learn how to do it. Though following his father's instructions, the awl broke hitting him in the eye. He lost the eyesight in that eye and eventually the other eye. Years later, a friend was having Louis feel a pinecone. As his fingers felt its way around the cone the idea of the blind reading by Braille was born.

Second Degree problems are more tangible than First Degree, thus easier to resolve. We resolve "real" problems much faster than the everyday First Degree problems of no consequence.

### Third Degree Problems

Third Degree problems are irreversible, or make a person permanently non-functional. In listing third degree problems, there are so many variables. An example is listing the death of a loved one, who is ninety years old, as Second Degree. It is a natural process of existence. It will have its grief, but it is not a problem like a young child dying of leukemia. Grief is natural. Your grief is an expression of Love when you do not feel responsible for the person's death

*In reality, the average person in his/her day-to-day life experiences very little violence or reason to be angry, upset, judgmental or unhappy.*

or guilty or angry about your involvement with that person. You are then at peace with the death. It is a natural process and one that accept with peace and dignity. We have seen excellent examples of this with Jacqueline and Rose Kennedy losing loved ones.

When you feel responsible, angry or guilty, your grief is mixed with depression. Depression is a tangible diagnosis and subject to solution and can be overcome. Problems classified as Third Degree are:

- Suicide Death of a loved one.
- Severe Retardation.
- Terminal Illnesses.
- Homicide.
- Irreversible Insanity.
- Serious handicap (Total paralysis, a vegetative state, etc.).
- Severe Anger.

Third Degree problems rarely occur and are usually handled better than the minor First Degree ones. By age forty you have lived 14,600 days. Rarely do you experience five days of Second and Third Degree problems. That is less than one tenth of one percent, which represents fourteen days. Rarely do people have real tangible tragedies or problems fourteen days of their lives. The majority of people have 99.9% good days in their lifetime. This illustrates that life as you live it is positive and made negative by belief systems and early decisions.

## Summary

As explained in the Introduction, in addition to identifying if the intensity of the problem is First, Second or Third Degree, I look for the frequency the problem occurs. Identifying the intensity and frequency of a person's problem, determines the health of a person, marriage, partnership or corporation.

Becoming resolution-oriented involves accepting responsibility for making the necessary changes within you. It takes work, tenacity, and a deep desire to change yourself, so how can you expect it from another person? The other person's satisfaction with the way his/her life is, may preclude having any thoughts or desire to change. You need to accept that s/he may not ever see your side or perceive events as you do no matter how clear it is to you. This is part of identifying a problem if others do not change, to know that the problem is yours to resolve without the cooperation of the people involved. Accept that there is a part of you that wants to keep the problem regardless of your conscious intent. We dearly Love our problems at some level and will create and associate with people that will help us carry them out. Most of all, it prevents us from identifying what the problem is, who it belongs to, and how you will resolve it. The next section has to do with keeping and loving your problems. They are so difficult to stop discussing or conveying to others. We are all true died-in-the-wool complaining addicts.

*Chapter Three*

# Loving Your Problems

As a non-resolution person, you will Love your problems and tell them to everyone. A genuine addiction will be difficult to stop, as you will have a compulsion to relate them, unaware that others may not want to hear it. You Love to tell people what others have done to you, and elaborate on the unfair maliciousness you endured and how unreasonable everyone was. You will be totally unaware you are being malicious and doing the same thing by relating the problem to a third party. Many times, you cannot wait to tell another person what happened, especially if you can say, "Guess what. He did it again." The next time you are upset and have this need to relate it to someone, see if you can refrain from telling it. This means verbally and with body language. Note the turmoil and pressure you experience in not allowing yourself to relate what happened. The process is not much different from stopping any other addiction, like alcohol or drugs. It takes a lot of awareness and attention to learn to stop discussing your problems, which only confirms that you have a problem and will rarely produce a resolution.

*When you meet a new person and tell them about negative experiences from your former spouse, siblings, parents, etc, you are informing them how you live and instructing them how to treat you in the future.*

By becoming aware of my need to discuss my problems, I gave up my annoyance of First Degree problems. These are the daily gripes that harm no one. I concentrated on the beauty of living without Second and Third Degree problems that affect life and limb. This sounds so easy but the process took perseverance and determination. Tell your friends that you want to stop discussing your problems and to take a stand to not listen to you talk about the same problem more than three times. By doing this you are setting up some preventive measures to help you conquer your "griping" addiction. You do not help friends by continuously listening to their problems. In reality, you may be helping them to keep them.

*Giving up your problem is far more traumatic than most people realize. Somewhere within, you keep your problem for a definite purpose that achieves an end result that benefits and appears positive to some part of you.*

As a psychotherapist I allow patients to discuss their problems for a certain length of time depending on the severity. I feel an obligation to tell this to them. After that point, I am now helping them keep their griping addiction, thus, their problems. Further discussion of their problems after this date is gossip and of no use except to keep and expand them. I am continually surprised at the anger that is generated and directed toward me (transference) when I will not let the person discuss the problem again. An example is when I diagnosed three patients as hypochondriacs; two were in their twenties and the third was in her fifties. After calculating the degree of their hypochondria, I gave the first two women three months to discuss their illnesses. After that time, they were to discuss the resolution and not the problem. I gave the third woman six months. The anger that was directed at me at these time limits was astounding.

*God, grant me the serenity to accept the things I cannot change, the courage to change the things I can, and the wisdom to know the difference.*

The woman that had six months wrote a scathing letter telling me how she lost faith in me. She said, "I thought you were my friend as well as therapist." I called her up and said, "Gertrude, for heaven's sake that limit is six months away. Let's go to lunch and discuss it." All to no avail! She was inconsolable that I could suggest her not discussing her problem even if it was six months away. Interesting enough, two years later I ran into her and asked her how she was doing. She was all excited relating her open-heart surgery she had seven months ago! Oh, how she loved her problem.

The other two women were equally angry. I told them, "When you want to get well and give up your many ills and complaints, even the real ones, come back." One of the women did after nine months. She asked, "Can you really learn how not to get sick"? I said, "Who knows? However, if there is one chance in a million, what have you got to lose?" It took nine months of therapy to teach her the positive way. It has been three years now that she has remained free of the continuing bouts of illnesses that had plagued her since age four.

When you stop talking about your problem, such as illnesses, you learn what benefits you derive from relating them. Learn to get these benefits in a positive way and you will not use the illness to get what you want. It was quite by accident that I learned the benefits Gertrude got from her illnesses. I was at a party and heard a woman discussing Gertrude to someone behind me. She said, "Henry wants to leave Gertrude but he can't bring himself to do so with her being so ill." Somehow or other, Gertrude knew her getting well would result in her husband leaving her.

*To ruin today's sunshine, we either remember an unpleasantness of the past or worry about tomorrow's problems. How fortunate we are, that most days of our lives there are no real, tangible problems.*

Over the years I have found that when a person resolves and gives up his/her problem, within four to ten weeks there will appear some form of depression. , a nurse, was most unhappy because she had to be responsible for the inventory supplies. She complained and griped for months that she did not have the time and felt pressured. The doctor hired someone to take it over. In presenting this in the staff meeting, Leanne immediately said, "I'm not sure I can turn the inventory over to her right now. I have to get together the names of suppliers first." Asking her for a completion date, she said, "Oh, I don't know, probably a month." She finally decided she needed three months. I said, "Leanne, you have been griping and unhappy for two months to find someone to take over the inventory. Now you are down and unhappy about giving the problem up. What do I need to do? Put my foot on your throat and wrest it away?" Luckily, she realized what she was doing and eventually learned to laugh about the entire situation she had created.

Another illustration that showed wanting to keep your problem was when a patient called for her first appointment. She said, "Dr. Benjamin, can you cure me in one session." I said, "Absolutely! You tell me your problem and I will give you several solutions that will resolve it. You employ one of them the next morning without hesitation and you will resolve it." She never showed up for her appointment.

I designed the "Here and Now" poster (Illustration 1) on the following page. It gives you an excellent example of how you keep problems. The center shows you "Stuck In Your Problems." The main characteristic that keeps you there is projection and blame. If you make a decision to stop projecting and blaming others for your problems, your mind will immediately find another way to keep the problem. This is done by either going into the past, and blaming the circumstances of childhood, or jumping to the future and blaming worry and anxiety about what is going to happen. When you go to the past or future, you are blaming others and excusing yourself from the responsibility for creating your own problems in today. The need to blame is immaturity brought about by using old belief systems that result in failing to get a resolution to problems.

I learned that the language you use tells how you avoid the responsibility of resolving problems. You can catch yourself going into the past if you use the phrases such as "If only . . . " "When I was . . ." etc. If you stop discussing the past, you may block a resolution another way by discussing the future. This can be detected by listening to yourself say, "When I get a job . . .," "After my husband . . . ," etc.

A powerful way to resolve any problem is to decide to stop all the sayings in the last inner circle. When you hear yourself saying, "I can't..." "I am forced to...," or "I have to...," *Stop*! Become aware of your usage of words and phrases as "can't," "I have no choice." and

# HERE AND NOW

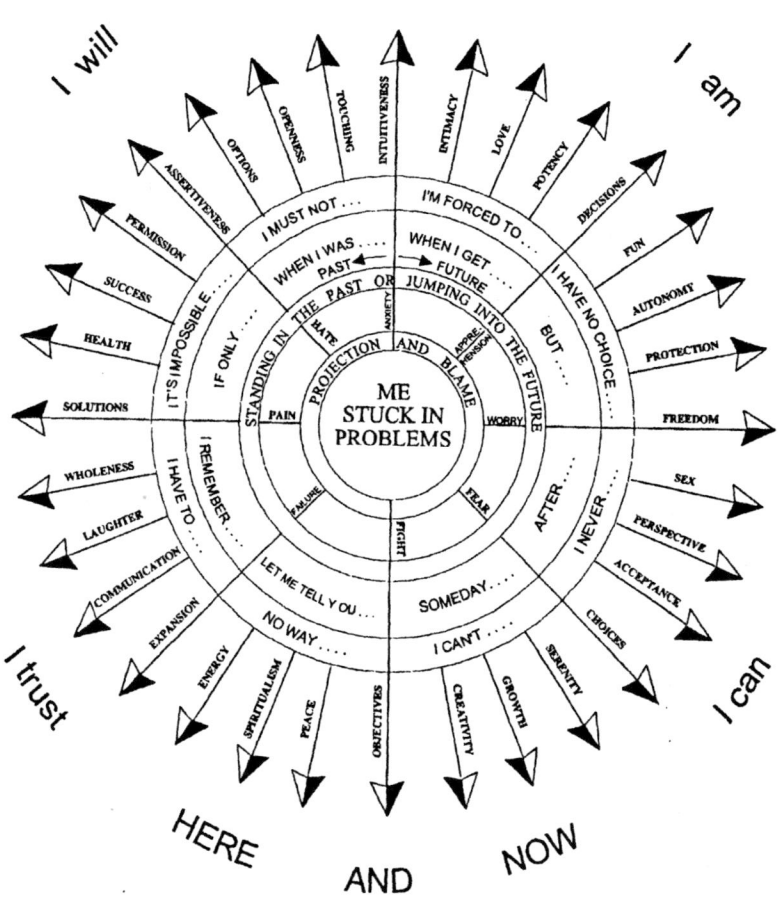

*Are you going to keep "Spinning Your Wheels"*
*OR _ _ _ _ _ Will you reach out?*
*Why settle for one winner once in a while, when you can have*
**The Whole Thing !!!!**    **Take the Right to Be !**

Illustration 1: Here and Now

use them as a clue to what limits you are subjecting yourself. Accept that your mind will obey these messages that are conveyed to us. You cannot pick up a cup without some part of you dictating you to do it.

*What will you do with your life if there are no problems in the world? What will you do that will lend meaning to life? Will you lose the purpose for existing?* These are your negative belief systems that prevent you from resolving any problem you may have. It is your need to prove you are right and the other person has to change to resolve the issue. Believing the problem is something outside yourself, allows you to keep it.

The limits within the circle in the poster impoverish your choices and options to achieve resolutions to deal with painful events in your life. Opening your world and expanding your limits brings all the good that is available to you. It brings you back from the past (which locks you in). It also brings you back from the future (which is a ticket to nowhere). Give up your minor problems, stop casting blame on others, and improve your relationships. This allows you to live in the exciting here and now. When you move to the "Here and Now," you stay in the present. It is your Golden Gate to all the wonderful gifts life has to offer that surround this circle. It is success into infinity. You will have many choices and options that you cannot dream of while living within the walls of this circle. Use words like, "I will," "I am," "I trust," "I can." This is when you know a person is healthy.

One of the reasons you need problems is that they provide purpose for your existence. Society, as well as out Belief Systems, base its needs on a grand and noble purpose for the importance of our existence. To fulfill these needs, you need the problems to help others as you were taught that was purpose to life. I gave up looking for this noble purpose. I decided it was enough to assume full responsibility to be happy, enjoy my family and friends, and Love my neighbors. Eventually, I will Love my fellow humans unconditionally. This often reminds me of Leo intuitive view of purpose in his excellent book, *Passions and Prejudices.*

*I cannot believe that the purpose of life is to be "Happy." I think the purpose of life is to be useful, to be responsible, to be compassionate. It is, above all, to matter, to count, to stand for something, to have made some difference that you lived at all.*

Is he saying that happiness has no purpose? This may be true, but once again goes back to the noble purpose. I want a simple purpose. Mr. Rosten wants a noble purpose. Use the one that works for you. I decided to take responsibility to be happy and not expect someone or something else to change. It was delightful to discover that those around me became happier and more relaxed. It is so much better to be happy than right. I tell my children to come see me when they want to, not because it is my birthday or a holiday. If they wish to be somewhere else on Christmas we can set another date. Celebrating in January will be just as much fun. Take the responsibility of not laying a trip on your loved ones. Just think how much happiness you will generate in the world. Can you imagine the stress it would remove from everyone around you? Start with yourself. That's a noble enough purpose and project. It will take a lifetime to stop the negative effects of petty annoyances and achieve accepting others without rancor. My favorite saying to all those I Love is, "I Love you because you are breathing."

*Being happy has made me more responsible and compassionate. I do not need to "stand for something" as I may discover in ten years it was not the stand to take. Few of us have the wisdom to know what to take a stand on.*

Noble purposes create drama. We all want drama in our life, and hold on to the most dramatic issues that occurred. If it happens to be negative, like being an abused child, it may take a lifetime to find a greater drama. We may never have one that will give us as much attention when relating it to others. If the old drama loses its power, we may be driven to create a new drama. When this occurs, we usually re-create a more severe abuse. When we get attention and Love negatively, we will create new negative dramas. The anger from our past negative experiences has us repeat them throughout our lifetime and is why people frequently have a

*Change "Horror Strokes" to "Honor Strokes" today. When you do, you will begin to heal. This is loving and honoring self and others no matter what happened.*

repetition of the same negative occurrences as they continue through what could be a better life.

They know of no other way to get Love. Negative drama does attract attention. I have used drama in the "stories" I weave throughout this book to get your attention. It was also done to reach another level in you that will help you understand yourself. Learning that these negative dramas are unimportant will help you give them up. I called my negative dramas "Horror Strokes." This is wallowing in the "poor me" attitude. You tell countless people what happened to you, and get all sorts of pity and support. You also prove how beastly and inconsiderate the other person was. You may also view life as cruel and unfair. I loved telling everyone that being the sixteenth of eighteen children piled miseries on me. What a wonderful Horror Stroke! Now I tell it with pride at what I learned experiencing this. Few people have that opportunity. I rarely received recognition since my mother was unable to always remember our names. It tickles me today to remember that and know I emerged happy. I accept it today as a positive experience. I tell this little drama without the negative emotions I used to attach to it

*People in psychotherapy dwell on their "Horror Strokes" thus taking years to work through a resolution. It takes a firm decision to stop dwelling on and telling your "Horror Strokes" which confirm you have the problem.*

most of my life. It is not important if I was one of eighteen or the only child. What is important is that I stopped talking about it negatively. More importantly, I learned that we are able to change our view of the past.

Start living in the here and now and create positive experiences for yourself. Get excited about today's living to the point that today is all you talk about. If you discuss a negative incident from the past, relate them by removing the negative energy. When you do this, ask yourself the purpose of relating it. A positive reason is for another person to learn from your experience. When you relate your experience positively, you are on the right road. Decide to create "Honor Strokes" and not amass "Horror Strokes." Do this by deciding to create dramas in your life that have positive results. This can be the enjoyment painting, sculpturing, having a child or expanding the imagination to bring joy. Any form of creativity will invite your "Honor Strokes"

## Process vs. Content

To give up creating and discussing your problems, it will help you if you understand Process and Content. All events in your life have a recurring theme. This is the Process that you developed early in life to handle people and situations. It is irrelevant whether it is a positive or negative Process. You will repeat it. This Process will determine how much or how little Love you will allow yourself to have. It will set the level of the Quality of your life, whether it is your value system, health, or the type of surroundings in which you live. It will also determine how much or how little Money you will have. Not only do you follow the Process in your own lifetime, but also there is evidence that you will pass it from generation to generation. This will generally be the same but the Content will be different. Each generation may have numerous illnesses, which are the Process passed on, but they may have different types of illnesses, which is the Content. I have had the opportunity to observe an unusual case that gave strong evidence of my theory that we indeed pass behavior on for generations.

My friend, Jensen, whose family came from Ireland had a Spanish surname, and his curiosity prompted him to have a genealogy chart done. It went back to the year 1100 and showed involvement in royalty in Spain and that they were quite prosperous. There was an overthrow and the family was exiled to Sicily without any possessions. They became pirates and took back their wealth. To make up the colony, they abducted

*Learning your Process, how it developed and where you use it is the most powerful way there is to give up your problems. Learn to Love yourself and your fellow man, and stop Loving Your Problems.*

women from Italy. The men on the mainland attacked, burned their ships and forced them out of Sicily and they migrated to Ireland. Once again they lost all possessions. Then Jensen's grandfather came to America and became a millionaire. Jensen's father lost all the Money in the 1929 crash. Jensen then went on to become a self-made millionaire in shipping and his sons have no interest in the business. The

Process in this family from generation to generation was to earn a lot of Money, become prosperous and lose it. The Content was how they made the Money or became prosperous. It was through the royal family, piracy, and shipping. Everyone in this family had the Process, or Formula For Success, to become wealthy and a Formula For Failure to lose it. In other words, they had permission to make Money, but not keep it. What Content they used was irrelevant. You can fix Content over and over and problems will continue to occur until you address and change the Process.

An example of Content is a wife complaining about her husband being away from home a lot. I can address the Content in two ways. I can ask the husband if he is willing to spend more time at home, or I can ask the wife if she can accept the situation as it is. I point out that her husband has many positive attributes and it is a minor problem. This may resolve a particular Content problem but the Process will remain and emerge another time with a new Content. A true resolution, is addressing the process of the need to create distance between them. The Process involves the underlying problem of the relationship. This is usually a "silent war." You can spend an eternity resolving "Content", as it will keep recurring if you have not resolved the "real" problem that is the Process. This is usually the main reason for long-term therapy. The Content may be the absence of your husband. The underlying Process may mean abandonment just like when your father abandoned you at eight years old. If you fear abandonment, you will constantly create situations where someone may be abandoning you. What you fear you create. This is precisely why you hear people say, "No matter what I do, I always end up losing someone I Love," (Process) and there are numerous ways to do this. (Content)

*Ideally, to change something within yourself that creates negative results, you learn you're the internal Process and externally, you change the Content. Internally, change your perceptions; externally, change your behavior. This is taking full responsibility for your life.*

I recall Marcia, who was upset with her husband, Martin. It soon became evident that her process to get anything out of her life was to criticize and pick on minor faults until Martin had enough and left.

Each cycle was a minor payoff resulting in temporary absences from each other either physically or emotionally. They are on their way to attaining a permanent separation, thus a more intense payoff. To achieve a permanent break, this process can take two to five years. It depends how many cycles of criticizing, picking and pulling apart whatever is said, and making up, are required by both of them to justify a separation.

It is simpler and less painful to be aware you want out of a relationship and leave the other person alone. However, the reality is that you will start to find fault and go through many of these journeys with repeated negative payoffs. In essence, you are building a case to convince yourself you are leaving because of these negative events unaware you are creating them to distance yourself and leave without guilt. Stop the process by exploring what end result you desire. Make a commitment to cease annoyance at minor refractions you are picking on and stop the retaliations. In the case of Marcia, in explaining her past, it became evident she did this process with high school friends, boyfriends, her children and now her husband.

This argumentative trip may take years with neither party aware of it. My friend, Leon, called me extremely upset. While on a business trip, his wife called him saying she had packed all his belongings and he was to move on his return. He was inconsolable and thoroughly shocked, stating he had no idea of any problems in his marriage. I said, "You may not know it, but I am sure your wife has been telling you about her unhappiness for one to three years. You did not hear her, or take her seriously until she resorted to this drastic method." In retrospect, he started hearing her complaints in his head of the things she was unhappy about. Somewhere inside, he also wanted the break or he would have heard her.

To change the Content of a problem, give an entirely different response to something that occurs consistently and bothers you. An excellent example is listening to a young woman who was relating the habit her husband had of lifting the covers off the pans to see what she was cooking (Content). He would peer in and make a face or a remark, such as, "Oh, that again." She would immediately defend why she selected this particular dinner. The Process was that her mother was highly critical of everything she did as a child and was unable to handle what she took as criticism from her husband. Her husband's process was that his Dad died and he believed if you got too close, you would lose the one you loved, and he was unable to see he was creating a comfortable distance through his criticism. She needed to learn how to change the Process of being sensitive to any action appearing as criticism toward her, and he needed to trust that he could get close to her and not lose her.

Discovering these beliefs was an internal process of change. The external Content was her reaction to her husband and how to change her response. Asking her what other way she could respond the next time it occurred, she was at a loss on how to change the Content. Her options were to burst into tears and run out of the house, fall to the floor laughing, or look up at him and say, "Gee, what beautiful eyes you have." In breaking your Process it is necessary to give a different or unexpected response. She chose to throw her arms about her husband's neck and say, "There are better things in life to look at." Three months later to the delight of both of them she said, "Thanks, Theresa, I'm pregnant." This changed the reaction of her husband peering into the pans, and he was unable to do it again without both of them laughing.

Experiencing the power to change the behavioral content of any problem encourages you to look at the Process within, creating the problem. Once you have learned your inner Process and changed your outer Content you have improved an entire segment of your life at home, work, and in relationships and expanded your potential for success. This is the most effective way I know of to change negativity, complaining or problems to a more positive way of life. Decide to remove as many of these annoyances as you can out of your life. It can be done with or without the cooperation of the other person.

*Chapter Four*

# You Better Be Right — Or Else

**O**ur Belief System distort our perceptions. They will affect our value system and contribute to our prejudices, assumptions and judgments we make on each person we encounter. Early teachings to be right, laid the groundwork for your belief systems and early decisions, and have a profound effect on your day-to-day life decisions. They determine your attitude and whether or not you will handle life positively or negatively, to what degree, and in which areas. They will dictate how successful you will allow yourselves to be in the three major success areas: Love, Quality, and Money. They will dictate how you will limit or lose in any of these three successes, as well as the price you will pay. You will obey these beliefs consciously or unconsciously. It makes no difference that they may defy common sense. Every aspect of our life is affected.

*Most parents fail to convey to the child the excitement of learning something new every day of his/her life. They also fail to assure the child that during each of those days, s/he is perfect.*

These teachings to do everything right creates a sensitivity to anything that appears to be critical, and to have hurt feelings which makes it difficult for you to learn anything new. The more no-no's you received, and the earlier in life you learned them, the more entrenched they become, and the more difficult they are to change. The more your parents taught you it was important to be right in unimportant areas, the less you learned to be happy, and developed a philosophy that it is better to be right than happy with your life.

When you look at all learning, growing instructions and criticisms from others simply as learning experiences, you will grow and give up the need to be right. You do not have to

*To prove you are right you will be willing to give up situations that extend from a pleasant evening to losing a loved one.*

feel you are being criticized or have done anything wrong, dumb or inadequate. When you learned to read in the first grade, it did not make you any better or worse a person than you were before you learned to read; you just learned something new. Belief systems and early decisions are both positive and negative. We are fortunate that most of them are positive, and this is why I believe in the goodness of humans as a whole.

People outside yourself set the belief systems and you adopted them. Your decision on how to handle situations is usually based on a survival issue at an unconscious level. Once the decision is made on how to handle a problem, you will adhere to it no matter how ineffective it is. As an adult, you are unaware that you still

*As an adult, even though there is no punishment for speaking up, you will still follow the same behavior as your belief system compels you to, and you will withdraw.*

handle situations based on these belief systems. They can be destructive and fail to provide the results you yearn for and desire.

I recall a seven-year-old boy who had an older sister that teased him unmercifully. He decided he would retaliate by withholding his Love. With this decision he very solemnly said, "I'll never Love my sister." This developed into a life long decision that affected all future experiences with women and Love. No matter how much he wanted to Love someone or be loved, the silent decision within his head prevailed. It took precedent over common sense and without awareness, he will obey it all his life. This is the power of negative beliefs.

I then delved into whether or not belief systems contributed to a person's physical or mental health, and made them accident-prone. As an employee of an insurance company I processed Workers Compensation claims. One of my responsibilities was to make up a Five Year

Experience report of all injuries. My findings amazed me because most illnesses and accidents over any five-year- period occurred to the same people. The ratio was that 20 percent of the people had 50 percent of the accidents. I learned it was a way of life for some people.

*The effect of an early decision is seen in people that have continuous illnesses or problems. They learned early in life that to have problems, be sick or unhappy brought them support and Love. As adults, they still believe that is the only way to get Love.*

My next-door neighbor, Alex, is an excellent example, as he had one accident after another. He had fallen off the roof and broke his ankle. He was on disability and doing chores limping around the house. He decided to chop up firewood and almost severed one of his toes. He then took up racing and got in a debilitating accident. It left his wife to care for him and three children and take on full financial responsibility. Is that what he wanted as a child?

I did not want my children to be compensated for the negative belief systems I gave them. As a result, when they became ill or injured, I did not shower them with Love or attention. If they sniffled, I said, "You better not get sick or I'll give you something that will make you sicker." There is no way of knowing if this contributed to both my children staying consistently healthy and accident free. My son had one accident when he fell out of a tree. My daughter had one accident when she broke her wrist. I said, "Don't you do that to yourself again or else..." Other than those two incidents, they have never been ill or in an accident since, and neither have I.

The most important and effective message to give a child is to not harm self or others: physically, emotionally or mentally. The rest of the no-no's are either not important or unnecessary. These "No-No's" are tools you use to avoid intimacy as adults. An example: You want to be close to someone and are adamant on how s/he needs to act and convinced you are right. This pushes her/him away. This is where you use the gauge of what is important. Ask yourself if it is affecting life or limb. The only fault that exists beyond harming self and others is what bothers you.

These belief systems and early decisions govern your life and become your Frame of Reference. Without conscious awareness, you refer to and rely on them the rest of your life to resolve situations and select which resolution options you will use. The dictionary defines Frame of Reference as:

*A standard or attitude against which actions or results are judged. The principles, circumstances, facts, values, etc. needed to inform or orient a person when thinking about judging or interpreting something.*

A belief is an acceptance of the truth or reality of something without proof or question. Most belief systems are very valuable and effective, such as honesty and integrity that makes up the Quality of your existence. You simply give the negative ones more power that they warrant. Minor negative events have a lot of power. Applying this to a physical level, you can see where 95% of your body is healthy but a little splinter will bug and distract you and get your entire attention.

When lecturing, some people in the audience get angry at my concepts. In the same lecture, others say I inspired them to change their lives. I did neither. I just talked. Everyone's belief systems and perceptions dictate how they accept or not accept what I said. The audience believes I made them feel angry or inspired. They were unable to understand that it was their own Process, or belief system, within that dictates what to accept and how to react.

*You will believe that your belief systems are the "right" ones and expect others to obey and live by them regardless of any common sense one may apply.*

If you have ever wondered why you said what you did, or acted in a way that you did not want to, read on. You are obeying some belief system or early decision that takes precedence over your common sense. It was difficult for me to believe that an early decision that I had no conscious knowledge of, may have caused me to lose my hearing. While taking a class to get my hypnosis certificate, we were asked what we would like to explore under hypnosis. I mentioned my hearing problem and the hypnotist asked me if I wanted my hearing back.

I answered in all sincerity from the depths of my soul, "I would give anything to hear again." and I believed it at all the levels I thought existed within me. Later in the class he hypnotized me and addressed the hearing problem. He asked the same question, "Would you like to hear again?" I'm glad it was taped because I would have never believed him or the forty students that heard it. My answer was inconceivable to me. I said, "No way. I like the silence when I remove my hearing aid. I like the attention I get when I act helpless and say, "I can't hear." It's also an easy way to turn off boring people or I can use it to aggravate someone that is annoying me." For weeks I asked myself, "Where did that information come from? Did I make myself go deaf?" If so, was it to find peace and quiet? If so, some part must view it as a hearing solution not a hearing problem. I explored the far corners of my mind and remembered how many times as a child I clamped my hands over my ears and said to myself, "Oh God, I wish I didn't have to hear this." "This" was ten children trying to get attention at the same time from overworked parents.

*Your belief systems from childhood are responsible for your anger, hate, joy and Love and the way you live.*

This led me to give credence to my theory that if you tell yourself something enough times, and it becomes part of your belief system, you will believe it, obey it and act on it automatically. It will manifest itself even though at another level you want the opposite results. This may be gaining weight, smoking or its possibly how I lost my hearing. Having good hearing does enhance the Quality of life.

To get an idea of what may be occurring at another level within us, watch the antics of a person under hypnosis following the dictates of a hypnotist. A hypnotist in San Diego had a young woman in the audience come up on the stage. He asked her, "Can you sing?" She said, "Oh no." After asking her what her favorite song and singer was, he put her under hypnosis. He told her to sing like her favorite singer. To everyone's amazement, she sang with her soul, belting out this song like a professional. He then took her out of hypnosis and she became consciously aware of her singing. She obeyed her inner belief that she did not know how to sing, and started mumbling and singing off key. She was unaware of the animated and professional way she had sung only moments before. Who within her told her how to sing or not sing? How many of us have talents repressed by belief systems? In Herman Hesse's book, *Steppenwolf*, he says:

> *In this way he was always recognizing and affirming with one half of himself in thought and act, what with the other half he fought against and denied. Brought up as he was, in a cultivated home in the approved manner, he never tore part of his soul loose from its conventional moorings even after he long since individualized himself to a degree beyond its scope and freed himself from the substance of its ideals and beliefs."*

When you change your attitude or belief system, it creates anxiety. It opens a whole new world that, up to now, has been alien to you. New worlds, thoughts or ideas, positive or negative, create discomfort. Without a decision to change, at the first sign of stress, you will revert to the old familiar ways even with the negative result. Have you experienced giving up the need to be right in a minor argument and telling yourself being right is not important and that being happy is? When you intercept these teachings and experience the tumult of emotions to reverse a negative outcome, you will know the power and beauty of achieving success. You have allowed Love and happiness (Quality) to conquer the need to be right.

*Even if these belief systems and early decisions are destructive, and they work against you, you will still obey them. These dictates are so powerful, you will go all the way to committing suicide or homicide.*

Explore these belief systems and early decisions and see if you can detect which ones contributed to the limits you set on the successes: Love, Quality, and Money. Learning what they are is the doorway to changing those that are not in your best interest. One way to do this is to fill out the Belief System form (Illustration 2) on the following page. Answer the questions as quickly as possible jotting down the first thought that comes into your head. Elicit as many answers as possible from your subconscious before contaminating it with your conscious self. Your ideal self finds it difficult to believe you obey such primitive commands. The first three beliefs are mine and affected me making Money for Quality of Life.

*Challenge yourself and expand your capacity to overcome early negative belief systems and decisions. Stop obeying those that limit your success and dictates that there is a price to pay. Go on to be successful in Love, Quality, and Money.*

Review your answers and ask others close to you for their feedback. When you do this, refrain from explaining, defending, denying or disagreeing. Listen carefully to what the person says. My experience has been that it takes about two weeks for a person to digest a new idea about him/herself. Remind yourself that you do not know all thoughts and beliefs going on inside your head at all levels. Study the answers and learn which ones lead to self-defeat. Check the results of these beliefs. Ask yourself if you are happy with them. Decide to change by stopping the behavior that put these beliefs into effect. If you put someone down, you will not succeed. An example is that if you believe people who are financially successful are crooks, you will not become financially successful. You will think people will say the same thing about you.

Your belief systems and early decisions keep you precisely where you are in your life. They are responsible for what education you have and what job or profession you choose. They dictate how much Money you will earn, how much you Love or are Loved, and what kind of value system and life you will have. The two main areas where they manifest themselves; believing there is a price for success, and the unconscious limit you have set on your successes. The belief of "paying a price" is that you will suffer for any success you achieve over your comfort level, especially Money. Start accepting that abundance is available to all of us. It is exciting to learn and incorporate into your life how to accept and balance Love, Quality, and Money. These challenge your creativity that brings positive people and events into your life that replace the negative ones that prevent you from achieving and expanding your much deserved success.

# BELIEF SYSTEMS

NAME _____ DATE _____

ADDRESS _____

Success comes in three packages: Love; Quality of life; and Money. These are governed by our belief systems and beliefs. IT IS BETTER TO BE RIGHT THAN HAPPY! Below is a list of some beliefs that keep us from success. Check the ones that may apply to you and write in what you know or can guess about your self.

| BELIEF SYSTEMS | NO | MAYBE | YES |
|---|---|---|---|
| 1. People that make money take it from the poor | | | |
| 2. People with money got it dishonestly. | | | |
| 3. People make money through other people's pain. | | | |
| 4. "Nothing can be done about my problems. That's the way it is." | | | |
| 5. The devil will come to collect. (If things go too good, something will go bad | | | |
| 6. I feel I don't deserve the good things in life | | | |
| 7. I remain dependent and want to be taken care of. | | | |
| 8. I enjoy suffering or showing how well I suffer. | | | |
| 9. I have a need to punish myself and others. | | | |
| 10. I'd feel guilty with all that money. | | | |
| 11. I like sympathy and for people to see how hard I try. | | | |
| 12. I don't want my parents to be happy or have credit for my success. | | | |
| 13. I don't want to give up my horror strokes. (childhood abuse) | | | |
| 14. Someone might take my money away from me or I'll lose it. (Alimony). | | | |
| 15. I can't say no when someone asks me for money, or I'll be a miser or selfish. | | | |
| 16 I'm comfortable with plush surroundings (butler, tuxedo, formal dinners). | | | |
| 17. Money is more trouble than it's worth with taxes, etc. | | | |
| 18. People don't like people with money. | | | |
| 19. If I have a lot of money, people will think I'm stuck up. | | | |
| 20. People making lots of money cut work quality and caring about others. | | | |
| 21. When someone loves me, it never lasts. | | | |
| 22. No one understands me. | | | |
| 23. I will be happy living in a seven bedroom house. | | | |

**Complete the following sentences to find your beliefs that hinder your success in Love, Quality and Profitability**

1. People with money _____
2. Happy people are usually _____
3. If I were more successful I would _____
4. I would be satisfied with $ _____
5. If I had all the money I wanted _____
6. When you are too happy _____
7. When I am highly successful, I will _____
8. If I had all the money I needed _____
9. A successful relationship involves _____
10 My mother made me _____
11. My father made me _____
12. I'm not as successful as I want to be because _____

13. I'm not as happy as I want to be because _____

14. I made my _____ angry by _____
15. The most significant thing I've done in the last 10 years. _____

16. I would be a greater success except for _____

Illustration 2: Belief systems

## Belief Systems That Pay A Price

Most people believe they must give up one of the three successes, Love, Quality, or Money, to succeed in another. They also believe there is a price to pay for any success they enjoy. It can be Love, where they make sacrifices, or earning Money without appreciation of how well they have supported their families. They may have also lived a Quality life of honesty, loyalty and integrity without recognition.

Over the years I have listened to people who believe they had to give up one success to attain another. This belief to pay a price is global. Many speakers emphasize this in their motivational tapes. A friend was listening to a motivational tape by a very famous speaker who invited his listeners to decide what price they are willing to pay for success. I instructed her to throw the tape away, as there did not have to be a price for any kind of success. My contention is that if you believe there is a price for success, you will pay it.

*Observe how all progress and inventions are made by people who dare to think differently and do not follow the rules.*

This belief alone affects the Quality of your life and you pay the price. To pay a price you need to have a war with ammunition to shoot each other down regardless of the type of relationship that is involved. The ammunition we use in the relationship war, Love (sex), Quality (time), or Money, coincide with the three basic fears: Unloved, Unwanted, and Unworthy. You punish yourself or each other by one, two or three of these, and believe you have no choice and pay a price. This may be seen twenty years later as "sacrifices" that no one appreciated. You hear people say, "I gave up a lucrative career for my family . . ." when they may have used this to avoid the risks of pursuing a career. With common sense and planning, you can have both and no one pays a price. The only way you pay a price for success is by keeping belief systems that dictates a price must be paid. If you believe this, you will automatically limit your success. When you are enjoying the journey through life no matter what you are doing, there is no price. Responsibility for attaining what you want is the true essence of freedom and assures that you are a free soul. William Ernest Henley (1849-1903) poignantly expressed this in the last stanza of his poem:

> *"It matters not how straight the gate,*
> *How charged with punishments the scroll,*
> *I am the master of my fate: I am the captain of my soul."*

The only price there is in life is the one you create in your head. You look at each day and check how you view it. Is your view of a half glass of water perceived as half empty, or half full? Wake up each morning and enjoy the good in your life.

## Belief Systems That Limit Your Success

Our belief systems and programming that has us pay a price for success also limits our success in Love, Quality, and Money. Let us follow the pattern of the development and results of our belief systems. When we are striving to reach these limits and learning something new that is within the comfort level of our environment, we receive a lot of support. This makes it a comfortable level to be at.

When we go above the limits of these successes and our friends and family start telling us we are greedy or think we are too good, we will sabotage ourselves until we drop back down to everyone's comfort level where we will receive the sympathy and support. This can be by getting depressed, ill, lose our job, get a divorce, etc. This prevents us from reaching our potential.

To go above our limits we need to be in the thinking part of ourselves. We are free of the emotional self that follows the childhood beliefs and brings us down again. Reaching or going above our potential that is out of the comfort limit of family and friends may even result in becoming an outcast.

*I have heard people say, "No matter what I do, I always lose." It is more effective to believe and say, "No matter what I do, I end up winning."*

When severe enough, we may even lose all, to get back the support and feel loved again. Each time we reach our potential, it creates a higher potential for us to go to in Love, Quality, and Money and it goes on and on to infinity.

Without conscious intervention of your self-imposed limits, you will repeat the pattern of going up to success, sabotage and come down over and over again whether it is with a relationship, position or money. Our awareness and decision to reach and go beyond our potential is always there. We need to know we are perfect at every level and that includes our ability to love and understand those that are unable to accept us at our new level.

To locate the repeat patterns of sabotaging that limits successes and how often they are used, I record my patient's name and date in each session on the upper right corner of a page. On the upper left, I write my initial reaction to the patient's mood and write, "Looks good," "Acts tired," etc.

I then ask and record how s/he perceives her/his own mood. This may be if happy or depressed or in the midst of a family argument. If it was the same as my observations, I know the patient is congruent and in touch with her/his feelings. If I see s/he looks depressed and s/he says, "Great!" I check for incongruencies that result in unhappy events. These were usually patients that will not admit to any feelings of anger. Once I locate what the incongruencies are, s/he can then know what to change and can now expand his/her limits in Love, Quality, and Money. Ask others how they view you, write it down and make no comment or defense. Study it in yourself and learn how you go about limiting yourself.

## Limiting Love

Love is expressed by the degree and level of intimacy one is able to give or receive. The intimacy level is one of the most difficult belief systems for us to locate. When someone gets close to your inner being and it exceeds your comfort level, you will create anything that will push the person back to a more comfortable distance. As I recorded information on my clients each week, I began to note when a patient was ready to build a case against her husband when the relationship got too intimate. Her belief system will dictate, "Do not let anyone that close," and she starts an argument. She is convinced that her husband doing something that annoys her does the distancing. She will go as far as to project a picture of being happy to prove that she is OK, it is her husband who causes the distancing, not her. However, I observe in her tension that she is not happy.

When the argument does occur, she then claims innocence. She uses the reasoning that she is happy until the other person makes her mad: the other person's action is what makes her withdraw. The reality is that she reaches or exceeds her level of Love or attention. She in essence obeys the dictates in her mind set of childhood at age 10 and creates the build up and argument that is necessary to create the distancing. This is a Formula For Failure.

The extent of their argument and degree of abuse shows me the intensity of their argument that they use to return to their comfort level. The argument may just involve some minor infraction that results in getting them upset or not speaking for a couple of hours. However, they may go to a higher degree over a minor incident where they get physically abusive, become depressed, have an accident or get physically or mentally ill. This shows an intense need to withdraw from Love and intimacy.

The second purpose of recording the date and the patients' moods is to discover the frequency with which these arguments or distancing occur. The dates will show the patients' time cycles of how long they can accept Love, Quality (happiness) or Money. Some patient's cycles reoccur every four days and others every four months. The time limit varies with each patient but once established occurs with consistent regularity. As a result, I am able to predict with unerring accuracy, the next time any particular patient will have an argument or set back in their relationships.

## Limiting Quality

The belief system limiting Quality can be the way you live, your health, honesty, integrity, etc. that makes up the Quality of your life. If you are uncomfortable in elegant surroundings or have anything that is above your comfort level, you will do something to regain your original position and become comfortable again.

As a child in the slums, a family won Money in the numbers game. I felt the excitement of their win and thought, "Good, they can buy a house and get out of the slums." Instead, they purchased an expensive Cadillac no one knew how to drive. In this way, they went through all their Money in less than a year. They then settled back and lived life as usual with the same struggle and poverty. The car sat in front of the house for years rusting away. They went back to their comfort level, obeying a belief system within their original status.

You will limit success when your loved ones ignore your success or are jealous. A friend came to visit me and found me in a happy and prosperous period of my life. I assumed he would be proud of me having attained my doctorate and building an excellent business. Instead I heard remarks about my "uppity" friends; I can only make friends in the country club, etc. It was enough to drive me to decide to have problems to appease him.

After several days, I addressed the issue and said, "You have been on my case for several days. I feel that if you had found me sick, broke and unhappy, you would have been more loving and supportive." He agreed to this and admitted he was unaware that he felt so hostile toward my success and that he was out of his comfort level at the Quality of the life I lived. It was enough for me to think about not being too successful or not to let anyone know.

I recall a dear friend that came to visit me and did not want to go into the Coronado Hotel in San Diego because it was too high class. I said to her, "Look, the people are in shorts and jeans." This was all to no avail. She believed that was above her. The discomfort was greater than her desire to go to a "nice" place for dinner.

Look around you, listen to how you speak, how healthy you are and acknowledge the honesty and integrity you have. Determine that you will expand all of these Qualities in your life. Learn to be comfortable in a hut and in a palace, in jeans, in furs, at a roadside stand or an elegant restaurant. True Quality is being comfortable no matter what you do, where you are, with whom, or when you are there.

## Limiting Money

In keeping track of the various ways people limited themselves in having Money in their lives, there were two things that contributed to this. The first, of course, is the belief system laid upon them from birth that affected how much Money they were allowed to earn or keep. Money was OK if you helped others.

Arguing about who is right also loses a lot of Money as well as your job, health, doctor bills, or provokes others to spend your Money foolishly. Know with a certainty that every annoyance, argument or dissatisfaction with no resolution will end up in you losing Money.

The limit on Money set at age 10 is the strongest belief we have and the most difficult to change. I asked 11 year old Kenny, a patient in therapy, "How much Money do you want me to pay you to change that behavior." You could see the turmoil he went through to answer me and said, "25 cents - 50 cents? 25 cents - 50 cents?" I finally said, "Ask for 50 cents." Kenny came from a poor family and in direct contrast to Dale who lived with wealthy parents. Asking Dale the same question, he immediately answered, "$2.00." Not only that, as he kept changing his behavior he asked me to pay him $10.00. I said "No way" and settled on $5.00. Listening to these two boys and how they handled Money, you can see that Dale will have far less problems asking for and earning more Money.

*In addition to your Belief System limiting your dollar potential, you have "Contaminated Dollars." This is resenting where your Money is going and sabotaging your efforts to earn or keep it.*

Removing your preset limit on Money definitely contributes to your receiving it. The limits are lifted when you become aware of the belief systems that keep you in the level you are currently in as indicated in the Belief System form in Chapter 3, "You Better Be Right—Or Else!"

## Contaminated Dollars

The second way you limit or lose Money is by "Contaminated Dollars." When I see people earning less Money than their potential indicates I ask, "Do you have any "Contaminated Dollars?" My records show that patients that broke themselves financially often revealed feelings of resentment about where their money was going. I met a psychiatrist one day and said, "I have fifty-two case histories of men that financially broke themselves after age forty-five. Are you experiencing this with your patients?" He stared at me a full thirty seconds and responding, "You just got your fifty-third case."

My exploration of why this was happening with such regularity, repeatedly showed there was contamination around where a person's Money was going. High on the list is paying alimony. Child support is a close second. According to current statistics, 72% of fathers do not pay child support after the fifth year of divorce. They wanted to give the Money but were unhappy not getting a return on it. In fact, there were complaints and requests for more Money from both the ex-wife, who may take him to court, or his children. They often believed the wife spent the Money in ways that did not benefit the children or themselves.

One common factor was that they felt taken, not appreciated, or discouraged and there was no end. When was someone going to start caring for them? To keep from paying, they would either not earn the Money, earn it and lose it, or become physically or mentally ill and cease working.

No matter how resentful you are about these dollars, your belief system that you should pay, will continue the game. It is at this point that you may financially break yourself rather than speaking up and having a candid conversation. Rather than saying, "I can't afford to give you any more Money", learn to say, "I do not want to give you any more Money." Look for options to paying or accept it and make peace with yourself.

*The acceptance that you have distorted perceptions and resentment of paying "Contaminated Dollars," opens new doors of communication to expand your success.*

The easiest areas to locate "Contaminated Dollars" in impersonal situations are:

- Paying large sums to the Internal Revenue with no say about how much they can take.
- Paying high interest rates for loans on homes, cars, etc.

In personal areas, you are more reluctant to admit you resent giving these dollars. This would be:

• Giving to your family or friends for years with no recognition, thanks or appreciation.

• Repaying school loans to your parents or a government who should have helped you.

• Not paying yourself in some manner a weekly, monthly or annual sum of Money that is exclusively yours for working whether it is savings or a special gift.

• Paying alimony or child support that is not benefitting you or the children.

• Paying employees' salary and benefits with no appreciation, and feeling dissatisfied.

### Summary

Amazingly, in spite of these negative beliefs, we lead good lives on a day-to-day basis. The negative results of belief systems only emerge when we are stressed or exceed our comfort level in Love, Quality and Money. Consciously becoming aware of your limits in these areas, gives you the opportunity to expand those limits. Change your perceptions about your belief systems and accept that the rewards in life are infinite. Break all the limits in your head. Accept Love openly with all your heart. Expand the Quality to increase your integrity, health, and way of life. Explode the barriers to Money knowing it means you will never be a burden to your loved ones or the Government. Now! This is living!

*Chapter Five*

# Perceptions Are
# The Way You See It

**B**elief systems and early decisions also color and distort perceptions. Of anything you see or hear, you will automatically make a judgment based on your teachings as a child. All memory affects our perception. It makes no difference if the memory of the event is erroneous or not, or whether it is sensible. This memory dictates how we react and handle situations when under stress. A client facing the fact that what she remembered may not be the way it was, said it was one of the most difficult and profound concept to accept. She could not believe that the way she remembered a past event was not the reality of other family members discussing the same event. Each person who recalls the event believes as strongly that his/her memory is the "real" one.

*People think their recollection of what occurred, is the true, and only reality. It is difficult to accept that their belief system, anger, environment, assumptions and prejudices, distorts facts.*

To get an idea how your perceptions of your belief system dictates your actions, think of an action that is unacceptable to you. Now picture yourself doing it and note what discomfort you experience internally. To give you an example, I will relate an incident that happened to me as a child.

As a Catholic, the church taught, therefore I perceived as truth, that eating meat on Friday would offend the Lord and all kinds of evil would descend upon me. I had vivid visions of what would happen if I dared such a sacrilegious act. At nine years old, two thoughts struck me about this belief. First, it did not sound right that God would concern himself with something so minor as His interest would be in how I lived my life. Second, my common sense said to me, "How can there be a day called "Friday" in Heaven? I planned eating meat on Friday to see what would happen. However, it took two years to have my emotional self give me permission. Finally, one Friday I walked to the beach and to the hot dog stand. In sheer terror, I looked up and down the street for someone or something to save me. With beating heart and much fear, I determinedly bit into the hot dog. I waited for a bolt out of the blue from God and the punishment. I instinctively knew that nothing could possibly happen. What if someone saw me and told my mother? I then realized I was far more fearful of what my mother would do than what God might do.

This was one of my first major lessons to change my perceptions of a belief that had no value for me. This became clear when I stopped thinking about what day it was when I ate meat. My comfort level expanded. I learned how I could take a false belief that was not comfortable, and apply my common sense until it was, thus changing my perception. An interesting aside was telling my brother about it ten years later. He was visibly shaken and upset. Such an act was inconceivable to him and outraged him. His belief about eating meat on Friday remained intact. I asked, "What if you just died. Do you think God would ask if you led a good life or if you ate meat last Friday? For heaven's sake, there isn't even a Friday in heaven." No matter what I said, his discomfort remained. Just think of the power of our perceptions and beliefs. Thousands of these early beliefs dictate to us in spite of common sense. We will obey them no matter how they affect us or our relationships.

If you keep your belief systems intact and do not change your frame of reference, you cannot change your perceptions. If you do not change your perceptions, you relive and re-create the feelings of being unwanted, unloved, and unworthy. This is evident when you hear someone that feels unloved say, "If they loved me, they wouldn't continue being late."

You can change your perception of Love by accepting that Love has nothing to do with what you do to one another. Each of you is acting out what you learned as a child and rarely has anything to do with the other person or Love. You may Love someone deeply but if you believe s/he deliberately hurt your feelings, it will trigger your negative emotions or fears into action. At some level you will retaliate and create harm to the person. This can be physical, mental, verbal or emotional. It can be severe, such as striking the person, or mild, like not speaking.

Parents who model the behavior you adopt set perceptions. You may act it out differently, but it will be the same degree of intensity (positive or negative). An example is having an alcoholic parent. The extreme of the parent's alcoholism will create the same extreme in the child. This may manifest itself by the child ending up drinking as much, or to the opposite extreme of never allowing it in his/her presence. Thus the depth of the problem will remain the same.

When parents feel their own behavior may not be exemplary, they get defensive and demand more of the child. This is when you hear, "Do what I say, not what I do." This creates the

*Change your own perception and refrain from expecting others to change theirs. This is expanding your limits in Love and Quality.*

split of the two levels you work out of. One is factual or analytical, the other emotional. The emotional right side of your brain distorts your perceptions. To change your perceptions you need to reconcile your emotional states. If you do not change your perceptions, it will be difficult to change the physical reactions you experience. This can be blushing or your hands shaking. The emotional response created by the stimulus can be anger or embarrassment.

An example is that you hear a loud voice say, "Get out of here!" Your perception may be that the person is mad at you. This is instant and this perception affects your central nervous system that makes your heart beat faster, which results in you feeling angry, nervous, etc. The rest of this person's sentence may be, ". . . the place is on fire."

Thus, your perception was inaccurate, but the resulting emotions linger. You went from feeling unwanted to feeling cared for which creates conflicting feelings. This all can happen in fractions of a second and not even be at a conscious level. Your perceptions register that fast. When this occurs in an ordinary conversation, you can see that the emotions can very well affect your response. Emotions prevent you from using effective communication and resolving problems. You need to take care of the psychological (emotions) first before you can communicate with the logical (analytical). When emotional, it is difficult to get or give factual information. Settle the emotional issues before addressing the analytical with its common sense.

One day I noticed how these emotions and judgments affected the interaction between shoppers and teenagers. I was at the mall where a group of young boys and girls clustered. They were wearing long earrings, black jeans, boots, and jackets with death's head on them or long loose sleeveless shirts. The girls' hair was long and wild, sticking straight out. The boys had the sides shaved with spikes of hair sticking out on the top of their head. Some were dyed a bright purple or orange.

I noticed that many of the people passing by them made loud derogatory remarks based on their perception of their appearance. The young people laughed aloud, making the people even angrier. These young people were saying metaphorically, "Look at me! Look at me!" I have had many young people in therapy and know what backgrounds many of them come from. It swings from the high academic expectations of parents, to coming home to an empty house, or to parents in a drunken or drugged stupor.

One of the young girls said in a very sarcastic voice, "What are you staring at?" I replied, "At someone who dares to be herself." Thus, I made friends with them. I cared for them being, not for what they were doing. If you find yourself bothered by this type of appearance, change your perception. Understand where they are coming from, look at them differently and give up your negative view. Why do you need that sort of irritation in your life? They did not cause it. Your perception and judgment caused your discomfort.

Using the Emotional and Physical Feelings form (Illustration 3) on the following page, locate and write any stimulus that creates your negative reactions. This can be a loud voice, someone wearing a low cut blouse or a child having a temper tantrum. Whatever occurs that has you think or feel negatively is due to the distorted perceptions given you as a child. Keep in mind that these actions harm no one.

As you can see on this form, what you believe will immediately affect your nervous system with electrical impulses. These then affect the glands and muscles in the body creating a physical feeling such as the blood rushing to your face. You feel warm and start to blush creating the emotion of embarrassment. It is only your perception of what you experienced that caused the reaction. If you do not change your perception, you will react to the same stimulus the same way for the rest of your life. Start changing perceptions that do not harm self or others and are unimportant. This will save you and those around you many hours of irritation, anger, and unhappiness. Your judgment of others on unimportant events, creates this chaos in your life, and has a negative effect on the person being judged.

An example of changing your perception occurred when Angela came in to see me. She suffered terribly from extreme shyness. I asked her what bothered her the most. She said, "When I walk into a room full of people I don't know, I feel like they are all staring at me and thinking something's wrong with me". At this point I changed her perception of shyness. I said, "You are projecting a perfect picture of the vanity of the shy person. What makes you think you are that important? The most you will get is a second's glance". She was taken aback at this picture of herself, thinking she was worth more than a glance. I then reinforced this by explaining to her, she did to the people in the room the same thing she accused them of doing to her. She said, "What did I do"? I said, "You made an assumption those people's looks were negative and putting you down. That's not fair to accuse others of doing this because they turned around when someone walked through the door. It's natural and they would do the same thing if it were a cat or a dog. In future sessions, she said she was unable to walk in a room again without laughing at her true vanity.

# EMOTIONAL AND PHYSICAL FEELINGS

When we talk about "feelings", we mean what most people call "emotions". This distinction between "emotional" feelings and "physical" feelings is not as easy as you might first think. This will help you explore the concept that emotions have a physical base or physical manifestation.

**STIMULUS**

i.e., angry words, room full of people, picture of loved one, being in a high place, etc.

Fill in your own stimulus:

_____     _____

_____     _____          **PERCEPTIONS AFFECT:**

_____     _____

| <u>Describing Feelings</u> | <u>Expressing Feelings</u> |
|---|---|
| **EMOTIONAL FEELINGS** | **PHYSICAL BODY STATE** |
| Anger | Heart Beats Faster |
| Hostility | Fists Clench |
| Hurt | Eyes Narrow |
| Shy | Jittering Hands |
| Anxious | Throat Tightens |
| Insecure | Higher Pitched Voice |
| Sad | Lump in Throat |
| Lonely | Tears |
| Terrified | Shallow Breathing |
| Apprehensive | Heart in Throat |
| Frightened | Overall Tenseness or Trembling Knees |

A feeling is a sensory experience. Our nervous system receives a stimulus (an angry word), sends electrical impulses along nerve fibers, and activates muscles and glands. Feelings touch off physiological chain reactions that change our body chemistry (our breathing rate, our heart beat, our muscle tone, etc.). These physiological changes alert us to the fact that we are feeling something emotionally.

Illustration 3: Emotional and Physical Feelings

The next time you are angry, annoyed or frustrated, write it on this form. Follow it through and locate the affect it has on your feelings. Make a decision to change it. The old saying is, "You catch more flies with sugar than vinegar." Think what your face looks like with a mouthful of vinegar. Now picture what you look like with a mouthful of delicious ice cream. Vinegar is the angry self within you. There is no need to use anger to get what you want or to create change. All negative feelings such as shyness, hurt feelings, fear, etc., are all forms of anger that you can dispense with.

Acknowledging your anger and learning what it does for you, positively or negatively, is your first step in changing your perception. Reduce your anger and attain what you want in a Loving straight, factual manner. Now that you are aware of the goal of this book and the positive, beautiful person you are, it is time to become aware of when you are acting on these negative beliefs that bring negative end results. Learning this process produces changes that give you positive end results in any discussion.

*Chapter Six*

# The Traditional vs.
# The Today Relationships

The Traditional Relationship sets the basis of your belief systems of the male and female roles you were destined to play. The expectations to play these roles were assigned to you by society, religion and family. These roles were specific and still have a strong pull on you. They contaminate your current thinking that prevents you from formulating your new role in "The Today Relationship."

"Traditionally," the successful man earned the Money and the successful woman provided the Love and care. This union in its finest form created the Quality. This combination of Love, Quality, and Money is the essence of a successful life. The roles were clearly defined. The man went out of the home to work, earned dollars and brought them home to support his wife and children. As head of the household, his word was law.

The woman's role represented Love, which was to have children and take care of her husband, and in return the man took care of her financial needs. She was to maintain the home by staying in it and 'ruling the roost' when the

*The women at the shower celebrated the bride gaining a husband with gifts to entice her husband or the home society expected her to set up. Men had a stag party mourning the loss of bachelorhood and got no gifts for the home. They did not celebrate a gain but had a wake for the man's loss of freedom.*

man was not at home. Her job was to see that the family got tended to, fed, cleaned and be caretaker whenever anyone was ill. She also saw to their religious and social needs. This combination created the Quality of their lives and was well protected by the marriage laws of the state.

In essence, the man traded Money for the woman's Love (which included caring and sex). The more Money the man had and the less sex or knowledge of sex a woman had, preferably none, the more valuable they were as potential marriage partners. Thus, if a man could not support a family decently or a woman was promiscuous, they were poor marriage risks. This would definitely affect the Quality of their lives and their children's lives. When a couple got married, the woman had a shower congratulating her on getting married. In this way she did not end up as a spinster or an "old maid" who was a disgrace unless she was a schoolteacher, nun, or taking care of her parents.

How did these "traditional" roles assigned to men and women come about? If we go back to the caveman's age, we can easily see how man's physical strength was necessary for survival. It was needed to forage for food, protect women and children from animal attacks, rape, and being abducted. The wife stayed in the cave and tended the children and the men went out into the world and risked their lives for provisions. These roles were established out of necessity and passed on for generations.

People, especially men, thought women as empty-headed and just prattling on saying nothing. This female role included playing helpless and being incapable of handling anything mechanical. Thus, the creation of the "dumb blonde" role came into being. As a little girl, women learned to hide their intelligence, knowledge or business talents in front of men. Sewing and cooking were acceptable.

Traditionally, if a woman broke any of the rules by not caring for her family, having an affair, getting pregnant out of marriage, or pursuing a career, society ostracized her. Surprisingly, it was the women in our society that meted out punishment rather than giving support. That is how well trained women were and still are. They did not support, or accept, each other's indiscretions as men did.

An example of this was an event that occurred while I was in high school. A student, Ramie, got pregnant. When she arrived at the football game, a group of girls hovered around her. One, in her most sarcastic voice, said as she tweaked at the girls sweater, "Is this wool?" Ramie said it was. The girl then said in her meanest voice, "Is it *virgin* wool?" strongly emphasizing the word, "virgin." At this point all the girls went off into gales of laughter jostling her between them. When Ramie went up to the bleachers to sit down, all the girls around her got up and walked away, including me. As I turned around, I saw her sitting all by herself with a frozen expression. She held her head high and stared straight ahead. After seeing her face, I went back and sat down beside her, neither of us saying a word.

*Yes, women punished their own as they followed the dictates of society and religion that failed us in many areas. How did our parents, society and religion teach such cruelty?*

For this act of kindness, the entire female students blackballed me for two weeks including my best friend of ten years. I cried a river and made myself go to school everyday. I endured these young women who got up from the table in the cafeteria whenever I sat down. They righteously walked away saying there was a bad smell at the table at which I was sitting.

Woman's child role to the male parent was immediately changed upon the man leaving the house as she had to take over the parent role with the children. An excellent example of this is when I was working with Marine wives at Camp . They had to constantly adjust to the changing roles they played. When their husbands went overseas and they were home alone, they were in charge of all aspects of the home, children, budget, etc. This was the parental adult role. When their husbands came home from overseas, the wives would abruptly give up command to the husband and be submissive. This was the child role and expected if they were to receive the husband's Money and Love. It was like living two entirely different lives. I admired all of these women for being so capable.   They handled all difficulties when their husbands went overseas and then made a complete change on their return.

Another instance of this dual role of women became apparent to me, when I was twelve years old, while visiting my sister. She was looking out of her kitchen window at the back yard for some time. She then said, "You know, Theresa, we could make an ice skating rink. All we need to do is cement in those two corners and move the rose bushes." The more she planned, the more excited she got. She called a construction company man out who gave her the statistics and costs.

That night when her husband came home, she sat him in the same chair so he would be looking out into the yard. She leaned over his shoulder and spoke in a sweet little girl voice. She said, "Do you think if we moved those bushes and put some cement... oh no, that's silly. Forget it." He said, "No, tell me what you were going to say." She continued, "Don't you think it would make a little ice skating rink? Oh, that sounds stupid." He assured her it could be done and told her how it was possible. I then heard her telling him how clever he was. She got all excited, hugged and kissed him and ran to the telephone and called her girlfriend. She said, "Guess what my husband came up with?" and went into a long dissertation of his cleverness in thinking of such a brilliant idea.

At twelve years old, I watched this fiasco. I wondered why you couldn't be yourself in front of men. My sister was like two different people. Watching this transformation was an amazing experience. It is a wonder more women didn't get schizoid or end up with a split personality. I felt this was losing self and promised myself I would never do what she did. She remained married sixty years by playing her role and I ended up divorced thirty-five years by deciding to change that role. I believe this is how "The Traditional Relationship" started to change. There is a twenty-year age difference between my sister and myself, and we represent two generations and the Traditional Relationship started to change. I was the only one in the family to get a divorce out of eighteen brothers and sisters. All my brothers were responsible men that provided financial protection for their families. All my sisters were responsible people who tended to their children, their husbands and their homes.

This constant role reversal in the Traditional Relationship got women the reputation of being, "dizzy dames," unable to decide, and not very responsible. You see it reflected today where the women want independence and at the same time want a man to pay, which, of course, is incongruent.

When either the man or woman stepped out of the stereotypical roles assigned to them, they became the butt end of all kinds of jokes and made to look silly or ashamed. These roles are portrayed as comedies in movies.

Traditionally, parents selected the daughter's husband and set up a formal betrothal without consulting the selection with her. They

| Male | Female |
|------|--------|
| Pacing the floor waiting. for baby's birth | Driving a car and unable to shift. |
| Changing a baby's diaper. | Playing the dumb blonde. |
| Playing with baby and making funny faces | Hammering a nail. |
| Putting an apron on. | Looking at a car motor. |
| Acting passive, dependent, or indecisive | Acting, aggressive, independent or decisive. |
| Out of work. | Working and earning much Money. |

went to the eligible young man's home to discuss with his parents the possibility of the union between these two eligible young people. The marriage was contracted for. The betrothed couple was not present and had no say in the matter.

My mother and father were betrothed when she was nine years old. This assured their parents that the marriage had all the ingredients they felt were important. They were the same race, nationality, cultural and social mores, religion, value systems and came from healthy families. It was an arrangement acceptable to both their parents and expected to last a lifetime. Love was of no consideration and the decision was final. Betrothal was a sensible union and made the family value system survive. Love was not sensible and did not contribute to survival. Love could lead to selecting a mate that created family, religious and social splits as seen in the Today Relationship society of current times.

*Security, was accepting* My sister dated a young man and they were
*that marriages lasted a* so in Love. She was not betrothed because my
*lifetime no matter what.* mother said she would not do that to us, how-
*Everyone ostracized* ever, he was betrothed to a young woman.
*those that did not com-* They did whatever they could to see each
*ply, male or female.* other. His mother came to see my mother to
urge her to keep my sister away from their son. His parents finally had him sent away until he was twenty-one years old and he was released marry someone else.

There were also marriage brokers that would seek a husband and wife for the young daughters and sons. This was to assure that the sons got virgin wives, and the daughters would be financially cared for by responsible men. The parents were responsible for fulfilling these areas for their daughters.

The "traditional" man worked all his life and gave his earnings to his family. Society expected him to go out in the world to earn a living, not only for him, but the entire family. This was a lifetime role with no escape. The expectation to be financially responsible for others, spanned his entire lifetime often without acknowledgment or appreciation. In fact, many times he was berated for not making enough Money or working long hours and neglecting the family. What often occurs, at some point in his life, is that he no longer can withstand, or want, the responsibility of the financial role. As a result, he either retires or gets physically or mentally ill. This forces the female to take the Parent role to care for him, often until either one dies. Thus, the male/female role is reversed in that the female is now dominant, caring for the "poor" male who is ill. It is an answer for a man to stop giving away every dime he earns for the rest of his life. His alternative is to leave. This is difficult as the "traditional" man that has supported his family for thirty or forty years is known as responsible and has a sense of obligation.

There were some women and men who had difficulty in adjusting to the "traditional" roles of submissive women and dominant men. They usually have a nature contrary to the "traditional" role dealt to them. If women displayed any traits of the left-brain man and spoke up for herself, she earned the name of "Bitch." The "traditional" male role did not allow for showing any emotions or crying but rather to project a picture of complete control and stoicism. It took me many years to recognize the beautiful depth of emotion inside a man. In the "traditional" model, he sublimated his feelings, as they were an admission of weakness. If he showed any emotion, he earned the name of "Wimp" and was considered "hen-pecked."

In addition to society and our parents passing on these traditional roles of women obeying, following and serving the husband were fostered and encouraged by religion. In Colossians 3:19:

*This means that the husband is to take the lead in the home, planning family activities and shouldering the responsibility for making final decisions.*

In Ephesians 5:23:

*Knowing how he made man, and the purpose he had in view, Jehovah recorded in the Word that a husband is head of his wife as Christ also is head of the Congregation.*

These roles were in essence that the man was the parent taking care of the wife who was a child. It worked beautifully for its time and place and many people, male and female, yearn for it.

**The Today Relationship**

These "traditional" traits were fine in an age where the woman needed a man's protection and financial security, but not in an age where she wants him just because she loves him. In "The Today Relationship," the Traditional Relationship is archaic, as the necessity for women to be protected by men no longer exists. Between the contexts of the traditional and today relationship, we have no rules or roles to play. Men and women have to make them up as they go, and are often ostracized for their stand. As a result we enter the "Valley of Discomfort" and lose the security we knew before.

What disrupted these roles that projected us into a world where there are no rules to follow in creating a relationship? This started the moment women were provided with the tools to move anything or to protect themselves, like the creations of an electric button and a gun trigger. Driving a car was one of the first major areas of independence for women. From that point on, females no longer needed the male's physical strength for survival or his protection. This made the status of men and women more equal.

These changes in our social structure changed the male/female role forever and the "war" between them started. We have a male/female role confusion and find many things we do are unacceptable to someone be it long/short hair, kind of jewelry, pants for women but no skirts for men. New generations are less contaminated by the Traditional mores and intermix of roles. Men are tending children more and women, becoming career oriented, often elect to not have children.

Today, parents have no thoughts of monitoring their sons and daughters. Though my mother did not pick our husbands, she did make it a point to monitor our dates. She either followed us or made sure we were chaperoned by a married couple. Today women find mates through advertising in the single papers or clubs. They go to bars, single parties, or ask friends to introduce them. The relationships appear transitory whether they involve marriage or not. Today's standards now accept families splitting, premarital sex, and having children out of wedlock. These changes have definitely affected the value system in Love, Quality, and Money in our lives. Not because there is anything wrong with them, only that we do not know how to integrate them. The new roles are still condemned by many, thus creating conflicts in families that prevent happiness.

Somewhere in the transition we have not learned or have lost the responsibility to monitor our sex lives. This is seen in the increase in abortions and not taking responsibility for having and raising our children to adulthood. I received a letter from a young woman that said, "My husband left me as he no longer wanted the responsibility of a family." This type of behavior in a traditional marriage would have brought the wrath of his family, friends and society. The family would have immediately helped in the raising of the fatherless children. Women are also leaving their husbands and children to pursue a career. We have no new roles to prepare for these situations.

You also see a change from the old "Traditional Model" of having children, to the new "Today Model" of electing not to. More and more, both men and women are remarking about not wanting children or glad their children are grown and gone. No one realizes what this does to the children that hear these remarks. I was discussing a boy's experience regarding his parent's divorce. I asked, "What bothers you the most, Nathan?" Expecting him to give an answer about the divorce, I was surprised when he replied, "Well, Theresa, you know how your parents take you places and you meet other grown ups? They say, 'This is my son Nathan.' Why do people always say, 'Isn't he cute?' Then you hear them say, 'I'm glad I don't still have small one's at home.'" He then asked, "What's wrong with kids? Why don't grownups like us or want us around?"

That is a far cry from the "Traditional Model" where four or five children clustered around their mother. It is heartening, however, to see more men alone with small children. Everyday you see them in restaurants, tennis courts and playing video games together. Most of us experienced our "traditional" fathers as vague figures and had little interaction with them.

My study of "The Today Relationship" showed men are sick and tired of paying for women and harbor a lot of resentment about it. Yet, when dating, men are still in the "traditional" role of paying for women. In marriages, women are confused about wanting the man to support them, and wanting to be independent. As a single woman, I have been paying my way on dates and supporting myself for many years. It is rare that I have dated a man that is comfortable with me paying. I recently dated a man who brought along another couple. We went to dinner and came back to my house to have an after dinner drink. I asked them what their experience was in dating today. The gentleman my date brought, jumped up with alacrity, reached into his pocket and dramatically fanned out some dollar bills. He shouted, "Money! Money! That's all women are interested in. They want to know how much Money you have. Do you own your own home? What kind of car do you drive?" I asked him to slow down a bit and asked, "Do you realize I put my Money out toward both of you five times this evening to pay for my dinner and neither one of you would take it?" From then on we had a sensible conversation of how both men and women need to settle who pays for what, and how do you want to go about agreeing on it. However, my date never asked me out again after telling everyone I should have passed the Money under the table.

Men need to decide if they want to play the "traditional" male role and pay which results in feeling resentful, or want to settle the issue with a woman before going out. No doubt this is an extremely difficult area for men to approach. The earlier in the relationship it is addressed, even before the first date, the more of a conversational tone it can take. They can say, "I am curious how you feel about paying on a date? Is it something that you will consider?" Women also need to decide if they want men to take care of them or want their careers and independence. They need to ask men if they are comfortable paying for the evening's entertainment and asking how she can contribute without offending her date.

*The Today Formula for relationships will have the three successes: LOVE, QUALITY, and MONEY, within each individual. Two successful individuals will create a successful relationship.*

In relating this incident to my grandson, John, I asked how it was in his 20 year old age group. He admitted he was tired of paying especially when some of the women made more than he did. I asked him what prevented him from speaking up and he said, "God, Grandma, they will think I'm a cheapskate." I told him he was then paying to project an image he was not cheap and not for the woman. This applies to many men.

We need to find a way to be more honest with each other and come up with some new rules that all will be comfortable with. I was working with six couples that were unaware of each other, and they each presented me with the same problem. Both husbands and wives were working. Two wives were making more than their husbands. The husbands all agreed they liked the added income because it afforded them luxuries and a home they could not otherwise afford. However, the husbands did not want to take on equal home responsibilities such as running the household, cooking, getting baby sitters, driving the children places and other "wifely" duties. All husbands admitted in one way or another that they knew it was unfair and still didn't want to do it. Out of the six men, two decided to take on some home responsibilities in the immediate future.

I followed these two couples to learn how they developed a different kind of relationship other than the "Traditional." They bore out my contention of what the most successful formula is to replace the "Traditional" of the man providing the Money, the woman the Love, which created the Quality. I learned both the man and woman needed to have the Love, Quality and Money to bring into a relationship. They will not need one another to fulfill any one of them. Two fully successful people create a successful partnership. and are together because they want to be.

*Women bring many positive traits into business and men bring many positive traits into the home. This will go a long way toward developing the new "Today Relationship" we are currently entering.*

These role conflicts are also affecting women in the business world. They are finding it difficult to reconcile to this new role in our society and mix their caring "Traditional" role with their professional "Today" role.

An example is when Dr. Ellen Quimby's secretary, Kelsey, started to have marital problems. The doctor and her staff gave Kelsey a lot of support and caring. When Kelsey got a divorce, she needed more Money and Dr. Quimby gave her a raise. When her car broke down, Dr. Quimby lent her one until she had hers repaired ending up paying for the repairs. Kelsey then had a baby sitter problem and the doctor offered her a baby sitter, and felt compelled to pay. Dr. Quimby used her caring self and did not know how to stop. She took on the responsibility that traditionally was the husband's role of supporting a wife and her problems.

In addition, some of the staff were starting to feel resentful as Kelsey was making more Money, getting more attention, excused from tasks, and taking time off to handle her problems. This put the burden of her work on the rest of the staff. The staff that were friends of Kelsey, started to feel resentment toward Dr. Quimby when she asked Kelsey to resolve her problems. What happened here is that Dr. Quimby allowed the employee's personal problems, to become her business problems. This is a common problem of women employers that have not learned how to professionally deal with staff.

Our cultural mores are currently in flux and this traditional success formula of enmeshing our lives are undergoing drastic alterations. In Herman Hesse's book, he says:

> Now there are times when a whole generation is caught in this way between two ages, two modes of life, with the consequences that it loses all power to understand itself and has no standard, no security, no simple acquiescence.

Hesse dramatically defined what occurs when society is caught between two contexts of cultural mores. Changes of this magnitude, create depression, which is why many people are experiencing depression today. He wrote this in 1929 and we are again between two ages; the "Traditional" marriage and the "Today's" relationship where working women bring Money home and men are house husbands.

*The belief, "If you Loved me, you would do what I want," is unrealistic and an illusion. The reality is that one has nothing to do with the other.*

"Traditionally," we believed success and happiness were provided by other people and if they loved you, they would make you happy by treating you well and doing what you wanted. You expected them to change what you didn't like and do what you think is right. Thus, they must act according to your beliefs and your value system. The "Traditional" relationship believes what the person you Love does, thinks and feels is your concern and business. What you do to each other has nothing to do with Love. You can Love someone deeply and still refuse to do simple acts to please him/her. You may know that a little act is annoying and no matter how much you Love that person, you will not stop the annoyance.

The "Traditional" model, which affected your belief system, still has a pull over our roles in society. These roles create havoc with our current thinking. This makes it difficult to formulate the new roles for "Today's" relationships especially when both parents are working. This is especially so when the woman is earning more Money than the man. The "Traditional" model has gone topsy-turvy, and no one has straightened it out yet. The financial responsibility went from the husband to the government. Welfare and housing was set up for families that had an irresponsible husband. The government then passed laws to make the employer responsible. This is in the form of health and dental insurance, retirement plans and currently there is a movement to provide baby sitters. The women who gave up the "Traditional" caring mother role, had the man look to his mother or sisters to take on the responsibility, or for a woman in the more "Traditional" role to raise his children. This is becoming more and more difficult to find. Fewer and fewer women want the role, and more and more men want the Money the new woman's role brings in.

### Context

Understanding Context will help us make the transitions that the current societies of the world are going through. On a personal level, each phase of our life is a context. We have a context called childhood. When we move out of it we need to leave childhood behavior behind. We have a context called single. When we move into the context of marriage, we need to leave the behaviors of the single life behind. The transition of moving in and out of each relationship, at home or at work, is a context. We are currently moving out of the "Traditional" to the "Today" context. Learning how to make these transitions as smoothly and quickly as possible reduces the stress in our lives. In each context you create a new environment with different friends and interests and will play another role. Throughout your lifetime you live within different contexts, or roles. Every change you make creates a new context to live in.

Throughout our lives, the contexts are:

| | |
|---|---|
| Being a baby. | Moving into your own place. |
| Growing to a child status. | Starting a new job. |
| Going to school. | Creating a career. |
| Being a teenager. | Getting married. |
| Becoming an adult. | Becoming a parent. |
| Entering the dating world. | Getting a divorce. |
| Being single. | Experiencing middle age. |
| Retiring. | Getting old, sick and dying. |

Look at all the moves, or contexts, we make through each phase of life. Think of the adjustments we need to make to go through these moves. All of them call for a different life style and we need to leave the old lifestyle forever. When you do not move forward, you will hear, "Start acting your age." In addition to personal contexts, we also have society's changing contexts.

In society the contexts are:

| | |
|---|---|
| Living in peacetime. | Going into an economic slump. |
| Experiencing a war. | Living the role of "The Traditional Relationship." |
| Living in prosperous times | Adjusting to "The Today Relationship" role. |

Changes are stressful, be it our own processes through life or changes in society. When we are between contexts, we go through what I call the "Valley of Discomfort" because we are in no-man's land. We can't go back to the old context, and aren't prepared for the new context. We have lost purpose and people cannot live without a purpose. The male has no one to protect, or need him or his Money. Females may want the Money, but they do not need it like the "traditional" women did. Each time you change context, you need to create a new purpose.

When we are secure in any one context, we have purpose and are fairly happy whether it is in a marriage or in business. This is especially so when you have the same goals. If you have different goals, you will eventually drift into different contexts. One mate may want to use the time and energy to become successful in business. The other may want to use the time and energy for having a family and enhancing home life.

You are now in different contexts and playing the roles you selected. In a "Traditional" marriage, these two contexts or goals were compatible. However, in "Today's" world you develop contexts that are not compatible. This occurs when a woman elects a career over a family, and her husband wants her to stay home and have a family or the woman wants to have a baby and the man doesn't. In a relationship, you want to create goals that are compatible and will benefit both of you.

*It is difficult to get back to the traditional formula, if not impossible, with no new formula to replace it. This creates a type of no-man's land that makes it difficult to find success and happiness in any relationship today.*

In this way, you maintain success in Love, Quality and Money. When goals are not compatible, accept the person with Love as s/he is; or decide to leave with Love.

You also will see the same format in business. If partners in a business do not have similar goals, the conflict of interest will put them in different contexts. An example is two doctors who were entering different contexts. One was planning to retire, and the other was building his practice as a new dentist who needed to pay off school and bank loans, and raise a family. He wanted to upgrade the reception room and invest in marketing to generate and keep new patients in the practice. The retiring dentist had already attained these goals and was moving on to his next context; retirement, and didn't want to pay for these items he considered to be unnecessary.

*Whether you are selecting a mate, or hiring staff, the relationship will be more effective if both parties have compatible goals. Working within the same context with similar goals makes your life more compatible (Love), more comfortable (Quality), and financially successful (Money).*

Sometimes when you are moving from one context to another, you may want to go to the other person's context and cannot. For instance, contemplating a divorce, you will change the context of your life to single. You may not want to hurt the person who wants to stay in the marriage context. However, once you have contemplated the move, something compels you. You must surely go forward and say goodbye no matter

*Moving between one context to another is a lonely journey and an existential place that elicits almost all depression as you feel you belong nowhere and to no one.*

how much the other person Love's you. Treating patients for depression revealed that often it is because they are between contexts. They are unable to stay in the one they are in and they are unable to say goodbye and go on to the next one. To avoid this lost and ambiguous feeling, they need to decide if they can live happily within the context. If they cannot, they need to leave everything behind and adjust as quickly as possible. The longer one stays in this nether land between contexts, the more difficult it is for all involved.

Learning to live happily within any Context, is learning to be successful in all the three areas of your life: Love, Quality, and Money. It can be done. This gives you the freedom and independence that makes interdependence of another person enduring and infinite.

## Contaminating The New Context

When you are ready to enter a new context be most aware of what you discuss or you will automatically set up the rules to have the previous context repeated. This can be when a woman meets a new man, she starts telling him of her unhappiness in previous relationships. This ensures it will be repeated in the new context. She is instructing the new man how to treat her. Leave the problems in the old context behind. One area of dispute that comes into the new context is the subject of having children. Working with children in therapy, they convey they can handle the divorce or separation. It is the bickering and fighting that the parents are using to get out of the marriage context that is painful and not knowing what to expect. The parents force the children to live between the contexts. This is a lonely place that is often hostile and inconsistent. They cannot go back to the old context, and the new context feels unfamiliar.

*The more detail you provide on how you were abused in past relationships, the clearer the message you convey to the new relationship how to treat you when you have a disagreement in the future.*

They start to feel that they belong nowhere. Each parent expects the children to take sides, which creates great stress and pain.

To avoid this stress for a child, have clear-cut information on how s/he will fit into your new context. Make a plan and inform the child of where s/he will stay, when and under what circumstances and conditions s/he will be living.

It is a beautiful thing to see children's loyalty regardless of how abusive or unhappy the situation is. Parents do not have this kind of loyalty for children. They want to tell how "bad" the child is, and get upset when not supported. It is important that all parties speak well of each other whether they are the parents, mother, father, stepmother, stepfather or stepchildren.

Remember, someone is changing the child's context without permission or discussion. You may Love another person in your next context, but that person is still a stranger to the child. The stress increases when the parent expects the child to Love and obey this stranger.

Leave the memories of other relationships in the context that created them. When I was unable to collect child support from my husband, I went to the District Attorney in Los Angeles. He was very supportive and urged me not to waste my time and energy pursuing my husband, as the chances of me collecting were slim. Giving this up without any rancor or ill will enabled me to keep from contaminating my current relationships.

*Leave your negative feelings of anger, hate or jealousy behind in the old context. Bringing these traits into your new context contaminates it and everyone within both contexts will be unhappy.*

A man paying alimony and child support is forced to bring the old context into his new context. You can easily see how the new life is contaminated and affected. Many men get angry and justify not paying the Money. In reality, they just want to escape from the effects of the old context and get on with their new life. This can create difficulties for all concerned in both contexts. This is when you learn how to settle with yourself and make peace with what is.

These are some of many areas affected by our new context of the "Today Relationship" as opposed to a "Traditional Relationship" that did not experience these particular problems. They are part of the transition that needs to be made if we are to create a successful "Today Relationship" and move onward with our life.

Death, as we know it, is the ultimate context. When you die, you cannot take the physical relationships or possessions with you. If there is no life after death, then that is indeed the ultimate context. If there is life after death, the only thing we can take into that context is what exists in the mind.

When a context changes, whether it is by choice or outside your control, decide to complete the change as fast as possible. The faster you make the transition and leave what you can't take or want, the happier you will be. The new context will have far less conflict and more peace of mind. Open your mind to all changes. The more open you are and the less you judge, the easier it is to move into the new context. Keep in mind that almost all relationship problems are minor or First Degree. Learn the following concepts and create an atmosphere to make new roles possible in "Today's Relationships."

- It is more important to be a person than to play a male or female role.
- What another person does is not your business as long as s/he is loyal and does not tangibly affect your life. It is not your right to tell others what to do or not to do. That is a privilege.
- It is okay to disagree, have other beliefs in religion, politics, food or entertainment, and have your own outside interests.
- Know that at the first-degree level, which is minor, the only thing that is wrong is what bothers you.
- Lower your expectations of what another person should be, do, give you, believe, etc, and
- Love the person as s/he is and because s/he is breathing.
- Accept that you are totally responsible for your own happiness as well as your anger. No person in existence or thing out there does it to you.
- Have a clear understanding regarding Money, who will pay for what, and how you want your assets (such as property, retirement income, etc.) distributed.
- Learn the following "Trusts" for healthy relationships:

• Trust you will handle anything that arises with common sense and settle it with Love.
• Trust the other person is faithful and never question it.
• Trust you will not accept any kind of abuse or put down.
• Trust you will live without judgment of others.
• Trust that you will clarify what you want in a personal relationship.
• Trust you will be sensible and not expect a person to change when they do not.
• Trust that if the relationship is not working or happy that you will support each other and separate with Love and dignity, especially when children are involved.

When you make peace with the context you are in and are happy, you will automatically enter into a new context as happy. To make peace with any context before moving on to the next is an invitation to the good life. It is indicative that you have broken a negative process in your life when you are able to do this. We draw people according to where we are. My belief is that, "Happy people draw happy people, troubled people draw troubled people." I say, "Like Attracts Like!"

These concepts are our Formula For Success where we can only win. By failing to apply them, while coping with the changing roles, we are more apt to use our Formula For Failure as outlined in the next chapter. Once you learn your Formula For Failure and become aware of the extent your belief system affects your relationship, doors will open for each of you to change to your winning Formula For Success.

*Chapter Seven*

# Formula For Failure

Your Formula For Failure is made up of five stages: Anger, Gossip, Guilt, Non-Resolution Self and your Retaliatory Self. To understand this formula and put its use in proper perspective, picture a box you go into whenever you get angry about something. This box has the lid securely nailed on. When you are outside the box, which fortunately is most of our lifetime, you have the world and its successes at your fingertips. This is when you are using your Formula For Success. You are a loving person, you have purpose and you help others with your wisdom. The creativity you access gives you numerous options to resolve any issue, be successful in your job and use your natural potential to achieve financial success. The Quality of your life knows no bounds as this part of you accepts Love and Money.

Picture this self that becomes annoyed, angry and unreasonable for the most minor reasons one can imagine. At this moment, you have fallen into a box and nailed the lid shut. You have lost all options available to you to resolve issues lovingly and feel stuck in your problem with no way out. The insistence that others need to change to resolve your problems and make you happy overwhelms you. Your common sense has gone to another planet. This is when you hear, "I feel so boxed in." True freedom is the ability to recognize you are in the box, kick the lid off, and come out and use all your beautiful qualities. You can do this by learning about your Formula For Failure that puts you in the box.

### Anger

Anger is the first stage of your Formula For Failure that drops you in the box and leads to the negative payoffs of life. Know it is the deciding factor on whether or not you will win or lose in any encounter. It is vital you explore the depth and extent of your anger that goes back to childhood, and is maintained by your belief systems, early decisions and maintaining your perceptions of them. If you fail to look at your anger and own it, you will consistently blame external circumstances and other people for it. The reality is that it is your decision to not look at how you create and keep situations through your own anger. You act out your anger by relentlessly pursuing the person that disagrees with you. You will not stop talking and demand the problem be discussed and settled now. This is the left-brained personality. The other way is the right-brained individual that withdraws and refuses to discuss the problem. It is a closed issue. This, of course, drives the left-brained individual mad. Either method constitutes the same problem of not achieving a resolution. I call it, "Angry Violent vs. Angry Silent."

One of the major reasons you limit your success and keep the anger is to harbor resentment toward your parents. Staying unhappy assures that they do not get the satisfaction of thinking they did a good job raising you. At some level in your head, you will be willing to forfeit success rather than letting your parents have a "win." This retaliation, which is acted out at an unconscious level, can be by showing constant distress, using drugs, alcohol or go all the way to suicide. This will prove to the world how badly your parents treated you as a child and punish them. Why would you want to make your parents happy when you are angry with them? This applies even when your parents are no longer living.

You cannot be angry with someone without it affecting your life and success in some way. Sometimes it is difficult to locate or acknowledge this anger. This unawareness results in sabotaging your ability to be successful whether in Love, Quality, and Money.

When your anger is blatant and conscious, it is far easier to look at and change. When it is subtle, you are not as aware of the anger within, whether it is toward your parents, God or existence. Here is an illustration of the extent you can go to deny your feelings of anger at your unconscious level. I had a patient that had been in prison for murder for many years. I asked him if he would kill again. He said in complete earnestness, "Theresa, I know I can never harm anyone again. Somehow or other when I killed that person, it expiated all the anger I felt and I am now at peace."

One week the signature on his check was so different it appeared signed by someone else. This triggered some doubt in me as to what he said and pursued it. On his next session, I said " I am going to deliberately provoke you." Taking notes in therapy, I put an asterisk beside every item the person told me that upset him/her. Remember, we are the only species that tells others what our weak and sensitive spots are. As I taunted him with these items, he assured me he was confident that he could not be tempted. On the ninth or tenth taunt, I saw the flare of anger in his eyes. I asked, "Kenneth, would you kill again?" His answer was, "You bet your sweet ass I would." It shocked him. I said, "Let's start there."

*When you are happy and successful, your parents immediately take credit for raising a child successfully. If you happen to be angry with your parents for past grievances, you will not want to give them this gift.*

It is this kind of insight into your unconscious anger that enables you to reach resolutions in your life. You need to transcend the anger and negativity toward anyone or anything. Changing your perceptions of your parents and the events that occurred with them does this. Create more positive pictures of who they are and the good they passed on to you which makes up ninety percent of your being.

This concept of owning your anger is the basis of Alcoholic Anonymous. You cannot recover until you own your alcoholism. After you own it, you can then consciously change the behavior that results in sabotages to your success in overcoming alcoholism. You need to notice what thoughts, behavior and patterns you exhibit that leads to drinking and once they are made conscious, you can change them.

Many people believe that it takes a long time to change, that you need to relate and live through the events again and again. They believe they need to work it out of their system or settle with the people involved. The subconscious has no time in it. It does not know the difference between one minute and one year. You can address your subconscious and picture working through your problem for years. In reality, one hour has passed and you can make your peace. You can do it in as brief a period as you believe and make your peace only when you decide to say goodbye to your problems. So do it today!

Another fallacy that prevents you from giving up your anger is the need to perpetually vent it on another person. This is especially true if it involves past infractions. Peace is within your self. Once you have made the decision to resolve your anger by yourself, it will not be necessary to say anything to anyone at anytime. What would be the purpose? You can ask for what you want with softness, Love and determination. Remember, you are anger looking for a place to vent. This occurs when you do not take the responsibility that it is yours. The more you deny your anger, the more you need to blame others for causing it. When you feel angry at what another person has said or done, often it is an act you fear you will do at some level with yourself. It can be an act modeled for you as a child by some member of the family that angered you.

One of the major ways anger shows itself is in hurt feelings. There is no doubt but that you are angry. My definition of hurt feelings is that it is a very effective manipulative tool that says, "You either say and do what I want or I'll fill you with guilt and make you suffer." Your hurt feelings will magnify the problem and definitely keeps you from achieving a resolution. It creates negativity and stress and the other person is at your mercy until they have done what you wished and you have punished them enough, and then you will emerge, forgive him/her and grant a smile.

Creativity and success occur when you stop filling your mind with negativity, be it hurt feelings or otherwise. I recall how anger and resentment were eating my grandson up and causing him to fail in school. We were driving down the street when he yelled, "There goes my teacher and I hate her." I said, "John, here you are hating her, and she doesn't even know you are alive. You can't do anything to her with your hate. You will only scar your own soul."

He adamantly insisted he did not care and was going to keep disrupting the classroom. I lovingly explained, "John, look at the trouble you are in with the teacher, the principal and your mother. Is it worth it? Don't decide now. Think about it for a couple of weeks and find a way to resolve it." I have found it is more effective if you do not elicit an answer from someone immediately. It usually takes two weeks to digest new information and the acceptance rate of achieving resolutions rises dramatically. Sure enough a couple of weeks later when I picked him up he jumped in the car and said, "Well, I resolved it." I asked him how he did it. He said he asked his teacher for an appointment to discuss the problem. Isn't that great for a twelve year old? In the meeting, he proposed the following solution. He said, "You stop swearing at me and putting me down in front of my friends, and I will stop cutting up in class." Up to this moment, no one had any idea what the problem was.

*To learn a resolution process and become resolution oriented, look at your negative beliefs, or Formula For Failure, that is responsible for you keeping the problem. Change these belief systems by giving up blaming and the need to be right.*

He also said, "Grandma, I followed what you said on how to seal a deal. When I shook hands with her I told her how you said never make a deal with people that smile when they shake hands on an agreement. So she shook my hand without smiling." After shedding his anger and resentment and getting a resolution, he put energy into his schooling. He became creative in resolving problems and did very well with his homework the rest of the year.

These examples are First Degree minor problems and do not tangibly harm self or others. When anger goes to the Second Degree level, you will most often see the pain and symptoms of depression. It is difficult to find anything more excruciating than the feeling of depression. It can drive you to suicide to relieve yourself of the pain. This then becomes Third Degree. Depression, in most schools of thought, is anger turned inward. If you have a clinical depression, somewhere inside of you there is a lot of anger.

This compulsion to repeat venting your anger and telling your problems confirms you have problems and anger. It actually becomes a habit and you develop an addiction to complain and gossip about how the other person wronged you and caused your anger. Learn to curb this need to gossip, complain and tell your problem.

### The Gossip Game

When you keep the anger you have identified in your Formula For Failure, it justifies your gossiping about the person and the problem. Gossip is a way to dissipate anger, ward off depression and keep your problem. It is healthier than abusing another human being; nonetheless, it can be destructive. Too often, it creates a lot of unhappiness. Gossip is the ultimate pastime to prove you are right. The main purpose of gossip is to have it reach the ears of the person you are discussing. In this way you have let s/he know what you are thinking and feeling. You may even rationalize that now that s/he knows, s/he will no longer do his/her dastardly deed and you did not have to confront him/her. However, the realization is, you have expanded the problem. Telling your problem to an unrelated party, without the express purpose of getting a resolution, is a decision to keep the problem. Gossip is destructive and has no other purpose than being a pure act of hostility.

You get others to agree with you to prove you are the one that is right. To achieve this proof, you will only gossip to people that support you, remain silent or make non-committal comments. Because you believe you are right and you need the proof, you conclude the person's silence means agreement. These people often feel righteous and justified in going back to the person to relate what you said. They are unaware their listening, taking sides, or telling the other person makes them as guilty as you are, as a gossiper.

I recall a friend who was going through a divorce. She related all the different ways her husband abused her that pushed her to divorce him. She believed that if he changed and stopped the abuse, she could avoid it, thus reasoned it was all his fault. I told her, "I Love you both and I do not take sides." This infraction of not taking her side got me an accusation of having an affair with her husband. It was also the end of a seventeen-year friendship. She said, in essence, "If you are not for me, you have to be against me." This is a prevalent feeling and why most people listening to gossip do not take a stand. Remember, the gossiper's purpose is to prove the other person wrong. The goal is to go back to the person you are talking about and say, "Everyone agrees with me that you are wrong." I call this, "Bringing in the troops."

Invariably, when you gossip, you have bought your own propaganda. You believe that what you are saying is accurate and the truth. It is difficult to accept that your perception of what occurred may not be what occurred. You gossip because you are upset and emotional. When you are emotional, there is distortion of what the other person said, did or meant.

You may feel that gossiping is a way to vent your emotion, anger or frustration. You often hear someone say, "I just needed to get it off my chest." If this was the only reason you are discussing a problem with an uninvolved person, you could go to a counselor or pastor and not expect someone to take sides. It is even better to sit on a park bench and confide to a total stranger. You can choose to resolve the emotion in yourself, and work on a resolution you can present to the other person involved in a positive and effective way.

If you share a problem to prove another person is wrong or look for someone to take your side, it adversely affects the relationships of everyone involved. It is discounting the person you are talking about and affecting that relationship. It is putting the person you are talking to in a difficult position of taking sides. If s/he does, s/he then needs to act unfriendly to the person you are discussing. Most of all, it is debasing yourself in the eyes of all concerned.

Think about discussing how thoughtful John was last night in bringing you flowers. He walks in at that moment. Everyone's reaction at his arrival will be one of smiles and relaxation. You will be happy to see him, smile and you will reiterate your conversation about him. Everyone ends up pleased.

Now imagine talking about Tyler in a negative and critical way. At that moment he walks in. The discomfort and tension are immediately apparent in the gossiper and listener. There will be quick, short movements of the body. You will see eyes shifting too rapidly to avoid looking directly at him. "Hi's" are muted in self-conscious voices. Both of you are trying not to appear too friendly and still speak. As the listener, you do not want to act too unfriendly since you know and like Tyler. You do not want him to know you were listening to negative talk about him, but he will pick up some kind of feeling as you are not as friendly as usual. As the gossiper, you will feel uncomfortable. However, your anger at Tyler can make you feel smug that he found you discussing him. Now the listener has been used and is aware of it somewhere inside with discomfort. This type of situation affects your self-esteem that is projected when you are discussing a person's good points. You can't be the open, self-confident person you usually are that achieves a resolution by going directly to the person involved.

When you are assured everyone you gossiped to agrees that the other person is wrong, even if it is only silently, it now gives you the permission to retaliate. This can be anywhere from a righteous confrontation to a divorce. Gossiping, or as some people disguise it, "sharing a problem," is habit forming and as strong an addiction as any drug can be. It does make for a more lively conversation than happy news that lasts about five minutes.

A friend, Aileen, and I recognized this addiction in ourselves and decided to stop gossiping about anyone and, in particular, the men we dated. We learned that at the exact moment we started to gossip about them, in reality, we truly wanted to break a relationship. We criticized and built up a case to justify "getting rid of him" by endlessly discussing his minor faults. We agreed not to do this again and if we wanted to break a relationship or retaliate for some minor infraction he did, we would catch ourselves, stop and lovingly make the break. Going through this exercise, we became aware of the difficulty of giving up gossiping. At first we did not know what to talk about when not discussing others adversely. No matter what we discussed, it would start having a gossipy tone to it. We would stop ourselves. It was difficult to recognize the shift into gossiping.

I was teaching Kerrin, an office manager, how to stop gossiping in an office to increase teamwork. On a recent visit, she related how well she handled the last gossip incident and was pleased with the results. Dorri, a dental assistant, came to her saying the doctor had criticized the front office, including the office manager, to an employee. Kerrin went to the doctor to tell him what she heard and he denied it. She felt she was open and straight forward discussing it with the doctor but failed to see she aided and abetted the gossip by believing that the doctor said it, without asking him.

The process was that she listened to Dorri unaware this was gossip. Dorri contributed to the gossip by telling Kerrin instead of the doctor about her discomfort hearing the front office being put down. An option was saying, "I'm sure the front office will want to hear what you are saying and correct it." In this way, the doctor either could not deny he said it or could tell the dental assistant that he was misunderstood. Kerrin also failed to pick up that she was listening and carrying on the gossip. She needed to say, "I'm sure Dr. Smith will want to know how you feel about this. Bring it up with him." She also missed that she then carried the story back to the doctor. This completed the gossip circuit.

You gossip to get a result. To stop the "Gossip Game" it will be important for you to check what this result is. It can be that you want to keep the problem to expiate your anger. You also may want to alienate a friend that hurt your feelings or break a relationship. Becoming aware of your "Gossip Game" prevents situations such as this.

I first became aware of my "Gossip Game" many years ago and resolved to stop it. I was an office manager and discovered there was money missing out of petty cash. At the next staff meeting I brought it up. The person who had not arrived yet was the culprit. Everyone agreed he probably was the one that took it. When he walked in with a big grin and said "Hi", I felt badly. I realized what I did. I said to him, "Marv, we were just talking about you. We surmised you may have taken the money out of the petty cash." My disclosure shocked everyone, especially my boss. I felt better after being honest. This developed into a an effective discussion about what may have happened and how to prevent it from occurring again.

### Ending The Gossip Game

This is the way I stopped myself from listening to gossip, which I like to do as well as anyone. I told each person I knew to not tell me one adverse piece of information about someone. I cautioned that if they did, I would go back and tell that person. Believe me, few people have gossiped to me in the eight years since I made this announcement. Today, I do not say that I'll go back to the person because I do not want to hurt an innocent party or have the gossiper use me to relay a negative message. I prefer taking a stand and stop the discussion in a loving way. I am willing to listen to someone if his/her mind is open to the other person's perception of what occurred. I also make it clear that in the discussion, s/he does not expect me to take sides. The express purpose of relating an incident without the person present is to resolve or release the pressure and stress.

To insure I do not take sides, I have made it a practice to open my mind to all aspects of the story. I do this by listening to the person's explanation of what occurred and simultaneously hear the other person's explanation in my head. I do not form an opinion or perception of the person discussed. There is always two sides to every story and both believe theirs is right while neither realize or will accept that they are both equally involved.

Use the following questions to help you diffuse listening to gossip. This is especially valuable and effective in business situations. When a person starts talking to you and criticizing another person, ask in as caring a way as possible:

- What is your purpose in telling me this?
- How is it affecting you or your job?
- What do you want me to do with this information?

To stop gossip, say in a kind, gentle and supportive manner, "I'm uncomfortable talking about Mary, while she's not here to tell her version." You also may say, "I'm willing to listen to you if it is to release tension. I want you to know I will support you both. I value my friendship with both of you." At first, this may be awkward but find what will be the most comfortable for you to say it. Practice inside your head for a while when someone starts to gossip and work up to saying it aloud. Gossip is insidious and corrodes friendships, relationships, and our country as a whole.

Gossiping is building a case that provides the justification to retaliate against those you are angry with and provokes feelings of guilt for both parties. Once you feel guilty, you no longer resolve issues and problems with common sense. It expands your Formula For Failure to its negative payoff. Giving up gossip ensures the use of your Formula For Success otherwise you go onto the next step of guilt.

## Guilt

The negative belief systems and early decisions made as a child distorts your perceptions and creates your anger. The anger causes you to abuse and retaliate against others and pressures you to gossip, which is a form of abuse. This abuse then creates the guilt. You can only resolve your anger or games when you decide to give up your anger, gossip and guilt feelings. Guilt distorts your thinking and has you help others in all sorts of ways to make up to people for what you have done, not for Love, friendship or common sense.

When my son and I discussed what I had done to him that created his anger toward me, he asked if I felt guilty. When I told him I did not, that I had given up feeling guilty, his outrage was evident that I was no longer using guilt to punish myself for my "sins" in how I raised him. However, the next Christmas when I gave him a gift, he said, "For the first time I feel you are giving me a gift out of Love and not out of guilt."

It is not uncommon to cover your guilt by overplaying the opposite role of caring. You may feel deeply resentful toward a person and act very loving and kind toward him/her. You may present gifts and services above and beyond the call of duty. The reality is you are try-ing to make up for wrongs and hurts you did to others that created your guilt. Freud refers to this as "Reaction Formation." This is where your behavior will be the extreme opposite of the one you are consciously aware of. L. P. Chaplin's Dictionary of Psychology, de-scribes it as follows:

> *Development of a personality trait which is the opposite of the original, unconscious, or repressed trait. Thus, an attractive young woman might show unusual solicitude for a crippled father for whom she must care for, when her real feelings express the unconscious wish that he would die so that she would be free to marry.*

This means that many times when you are doing a loving and kind act and helping others, there just might be a part of you that feels the exact opposite. You may feel a certain amount of resentment. This stems from the non-resolution belief that you are going to lose no matter what you do. As in the example above, the daughter can stay and help, and may lose the person she wants to marry. If she leaves and her father dies, she will be plagued with guilt. Finding a way out of this dilemma involves relinquishing your guilt.

We all know you cannot be happy if guilt is plaguing you. It in-vokes defensiveness that stops all communications. This defense cre-ates the games of "Abusers/Abused," "Waiters/Laters," "Gossiper/Listener" and other complimentary/negative relationships. Guilt drives you to punish yourself, which you transfer to others at an unconscious level, as some part of you believes you have sinned. Changing this belief and letting past negative associations go, helps you locate areas where you feel guilty when you have no idea what they are, be they minor or major incidents.

In going to a psychiatrist years ago, I surprised myself in discov-ering the amount of guilt I carried for many years unaware of what created it. To relieve myself of this guilt I constantly punished myself or got others to abuse me. Through my exploration, I discovered that when I was nine years old, I was playing with my nine-month old niece. She started to choke and she was rushed to the hospital where she died. I thought I did something that killed her and to avoid me more pain, the family said nothing. It was many years later that I discovered she had died of acute meningitis.

Two years after this incidence I wanted to stay at my sister's house because she had a new baby. She told me there was no room for me to sleep. Later she called and said her husband got a new job working nights and I could come over. I was so happy that he was gone. Later that night the police came and explained how a worker who was drunk dropped the crane on her husband killing him instantly. I did not consciously believe that I had the power to kill these people, however, while under hypnosis, other incidents of deaths were touched on. A car accident killed my nineteen-year-old brother when I was fourteen. My mother and father died when I was twenty. I revealed that I felt responsible for all five deaths. The guilt of these crimes created a need for self-abuse.

Not being aware of your constant need to punish yourself, you will blame circumstances and people for your "bad luck." This creates anger in you that you act out and dissipate in many ways. How you dissipate your anger is far more important than why it is there. Knowing how to do it allows you to reverse it. Many times in reversing your anger, the reason you feel guilty suddenly makes itself known.

Giving up your guilt is giving up your problems. Solving problems for other people is what you use to assuage your guilt. This lends purpose or meaning to your existence that holds off depression and loneliness that creates a deep void within. Your guilt will have you mull over the wrongs done to you or you did to others that makes it difficult to give up your Formula For Failure. This cycle of anger, gossip, abuse and guilt becomes part of your life and an addiction that leads to your non-resolution self and assures negative payoff. The freedom, joy and peace that comes to you when you relinquish your guilt, is a gift to yourself that expands the Love, and Quality of your life and for those around you. Know that the majority of your life, you are a loving, laughing, happy person and use your common sense. The Formula For Failure is used only ten percent of our time when we step out of our Formula For Success. Not giving it up propels you into your Non-resolution self.

## Your Non-Resolution Self

Your anger followed by gossip and guilt is your Formula For Failure that produces your non-resolution self. We live primarily in a non-resolution culture that is problem oriented. One of the reasons you become a non-resolution person is that you need your problems to vent your inner anger. You like to show how it's not you, and how you can suffer and play the martyr. Knowing you create problems and prevent resolutions is a difficult concept to accept, but it does exist. We love telling and hearing problems. Our entertainment in the movies, television and books is listening, watching and concentrating on people's problems. There are all kinds of mayhem and violence whether it is physical, emotional or sexual. At the closing, it shows there is no resolution or it has been miraculously fixed with a stroke of the pen. Someone usually dies or becomes a martyr. Once in a while, they will get a resolution and actually have a happy ending. All media became successful because they learned to elaborate on these non-resolution areas. The newspapers are the biggest offenders, being filled with doom and gloom.

Did you ever see the freeway blocked up for miles. Often it is just everyone slowing down to see what is going on. It can be an accident, a car pulled over, a police officer that pulled several cars over or someone getting a ticket. Everyone slows down to stare almost as though they are waiting to see some blood and gore. I call them "Gawker Blockers." (I include myself as well. I slow down and gawk too.)

Many times the resolutions we come up with are unrealistic; especially when it involves the other person changing so you can be happy. You believe this is the only solution but waiting for a person to change before you can be happy, is assigning yourself to a non-resolution position and an unhappy life. When expecting someone to change, ask yourself first if you can change and then accept the person as s/he is. This, of course, is if the problem is First Degree and there is no tangible harm to self or others.

Experiencing the difficulty involved in changing yourself will give you an idea of the difficulty of expecting someone else to change. This is especially true when the other person does not want to or does not consciously know they need to change. S/he is just as convinced as you that it is the other person's fault and believes s/he is a victim of circumstances.

Surveys show that people who live with negativity on a day-to-day basis get burned out. Dentists have the highest suicide rate with psychotherapists a close second. As a dental consultant and psychotherapist, I see dentists stressed. The cause is hearing patients express in some way or another, on a day-to-day basis, how they fear the dentist or pain. The dentist at some level within eventually takes this personally that the patient means him/her rather than their fear of the expected treatment.

In addition to hearing the negativity, "I hate going to a dentist," stress is conveyed through touch. This was borne out by studies made by Bandler and Grinder on Neurolinguistic Programming and my book *What's the Meta?* A dentist is touching a fearful and stressed person every hour of the day. The tension experienced by the patients, subliminally starts to manifest itself in the dentist. S/he eventually perceives that the patients really do hate and fear him/her. This results in stress and tension that affects the dentist's ability to re-solve problems and s/he becomes a non-resolution person.

In First Degree problems, a fault is often some trait that bothers you in another person and may be acceptable to someone else. There is no wrong in it. I often think of what "faults" I am willing to live with. I look for the petty actions of another person that bother me. I check out if I can release the irritation I feel. Without checking this you can keep the problem indefinitely. I recall a man I dated, Owen, relating to me about walking around with the laces of his high-topped sneakers trailing behind him and how it infuriated his former wife for 20 years. He was puzzled why it bothered her so much and she made it such a problem between them with her constant nagging." I looked him in the eye and said, "It will never be something that will bother me." In studying this minor incident, I noticed that on seeing the

trailing laces, I did feel irritation and annoyance. It was such a child-
ish act of defiance. I caught myself and cleared my head. I also knew

*My mother used to
say, "The only thing
wrong with a person
is what bothers
you."*

that would be the one and only time it would annoy
me or I would discuss it. Once he became aware
that his trailing laces would never bother me, he
never did it again. This was one of his ways to get
attention even when it was negative, and to create
the distancing when we became too intimate.

Owen and his wife had been married twenty-nine years and created a situation where there was no resolution. The wife would not
stop nagging about his trailing laces, and he would not tie them. Both
of them found it difficult to stop the power game between them where
both felt powerless. Either one of them could have stopped it immediately if they became aware of why they used it. Think of how many
times you have set up this type of non-resolution situation. One or
both of you can just look and laugh at the ludicrousness of it all.

Attorneys, doctors, therapists, etc., make a fortune on your non-resolution self. Your sensible side would never allow you to live with a
problem that was so minor and unimportant. Blaming others makes
sense of your decisions it is difficult to conceive that the problem is
that in certain areas you are a non-resolution person. If it is the other
person, why do you insist on staying within the context of such a relationship? Of all the excuses you can come up with, there are people
who would not live in such an environment. These are resolution-oriented people who have a greater Love (intimacy) level, who will accept the person to improve the Quality of or end the relationship.

There are resolutions. It is rare that you are genuinely stuck in a
problem especially those of such pettiness. You have the option to
change your attitude within the context and accept a person as s/he is.
If you can't find happiness within the context of the relationship, you
do have the option to leave.

In reality you need awareness, tenacity and the determination to
change yourself and your needs. You can learn to depend on resolving a problem within yourself. When resolving a problem outside
yourself by expecting the other person to change, you usually only

achieve a temporary solution. This gives you permission to call forth your retaliatory self and make them suffer when they "do it again."

## Your Retaliatory Self

When you elect to go to your non-resolution self instead of your resolution self, you will then retaliate. Depression is anger turned inward and has an entirely different thought process than our ideal thinking self. It is difficult to detect when you move from anger to depression, or back to your ideal self. It occurs in a flash of a moment and can be triggered by what someone said or any memory. When you feel this anger and depression, there will be distortion of what was said and done and you have a compulsion to gossip about it. This anger and gossip puts you into your non-resolution self that will justify and, most often, compel you to retaliate. In a relationship war, you "pay them back" by using "ammunition" from one or more of the three success areas: Love, Quality, and Money. You either withdraw one or more of these successes or attack the person for not coming up to your expectations in them. The ammunition was used in the following ways:

- *Love*: When sex was used, either party had an affair. Another way was for the female to become frigid or the male to become impotent. Either way, the sex was withdrawn. When the Love was withdrawn, they fell in Love with someone else. They may have flirtatious affair where they may or may not have sex. Flirting can be intangible because when confronted the person can say, "I was only fooling around."
- *Quality*: The Quality of life was affected by the absence of Love and/or Money. Not speaking to each other, criticizing, and not living within a value system also lowered the Quality of life. The women got sick, depressed, let the housework go to rack and ruin and picked on the children. The man withdrew, worked late or got sick.
- *Money*: Withdrawing Money and plunging women into poverty was a major weapon for men to punish women. The man withdrew his Money by either losing his job, having a heart

attack, making poor investments or becoming depressed.

Women retaliated by spending the man's Money foolishly.

The extent and frequency of retaliation is what I look for in relationships that are having problems to determine how healthy it is. Using Love, Quality, or Money to punish is in essence saying, "If you don't do what I tell you or fill my needs, I'll take away or attack you with one of them."

This is usually at an unconscious level as it is difficult for you to consciously believe you are the type of person that would deliberately retaliate. It is difficult to accept there is no just cause to retaliate, no matter what the other person has done. Retaliations put you in the same class as the person you are retaliating against, justified or not. To retaliate at a conscious level, you need to feel justified and righteous. When retaliating at an unconscious level, you have stopped your thinking process. If you consciously think about what you are doing, you most likely will not go through with it as we are basically good people. This is borne out by the minor retaliations we use. Accessing your conscious self brings the retaliatory act to your ideal conscious self that is unable to accept and do what the primitive part of you can easily do. You will look for a resolution instead.

What children do openly, adults do covertly. When children retaliate, it is direct as they are more honest with their feelings. When my grandson, John, wanted to use a typewriter I borrowed, he ran the gamut for getting his way. First, he used Love. He was very sweet and started to stroke my arm and asked if he could use the typewriter. He was so loving but when I said, "No, John, it's not mine. You cannot use it." He then went to phase two of whining and pleading and I repeated that he could not use it. He surprised me when he made his body rigid, gave out a loud wail and flung himself to the floor. This landed him halfway under my dining room table. I looked down at him and said, "That will not do you any good because you cannot use the typewriter." He then swore and I said, "Those are only words and don't mean anything to me." Following this was something that was profound as to how the mind works. It showed the determination he had to retaliate and destroy the Quality of the day. He said, "My other grandma gets mad." So I said to him, "You know what that tells me, John. It says that if you can't have the typewriter you want to get back at me by making me angry. Well, I am not going to get mad and you are not going to use the typewriter."

He then kicked me in the shin and I felt a wave of anger shoot through my body. I calmed myself and made sure I told him I felt the anger or he would have made a win. So I lovingly explained, "John, I almost got angry and I am telling you again, "I am not going to get angry and you cannot use the typewriter." He lay there for a few seconds and said, "Oh, Okay," and got up and ran outside to play.

You can see that he was half way to knowing exactly what process he was using to get what he wanted or to retaliate. However, he still played it out at an unconscious level. He was not thinking, "If swearing doesn't get her, I will try kicking her." He was no longer consciously thinking. He was acting out a process he learned to get his way or make the other person suffer.

To do something that is not acceptable to your ideal self, it is necessary to halt the process of your ideal thinking self which would not allow you to do negative or harmful acts. At this point, the patterned thinking from belief systems takes over. I track a person's thinking process when s/he consciously intends to do one action and ends up doing another.

To give you an example, Ellen came to me to quit smoking. When she started to smoke again, I asked her, "What happened just before picking up the cigarette?" At this point, without fail, the person's answer shows in one way or another that his/her common sense thinking stopped. Ellen's answer to the question was, "My mind went blank and before I knew it, I found myself smoking." I have also heard answers such as, "I can't remember," "I wasn't thinking," "It just happened," or "It surprised me to find myself smoking." There is a part of you that is stronger than the conscious intent of not smoking. It will instruct you to pick up a cigarette and smoke it and you will obey. Remember, you can only do what your mind or brain instructs you to do. Who or what is doing the instructing to smoke? It has to be some part of you. This led me to believe that no matter what your conscious intent is, the end result will be the true intent at an unconscious level within.

You have experienced times when someone does something and you get your feelings hurt. You sense or believe that the person did it on purpose. When you tell s/he this, his/her denial is genuine and shocked at your accusation. Can you recall people accusing you of doing something to them on purpose? You usually have no idea what they are talking about. It is difficult to accept that your retaliatory self can say or do anything that purposely harms someone else. You want to believe you are above such small acts of spite. Most times you are.

In the last fifteen years, I have recorded the results of moving patients' appointments. Within the next three appointments, they will cancel their appointment or be late. I will ask them, "Is there a connection between me moving your appointment and you canceling." There will be instant and adamant denial. They cannot see or connect a more base instinct within them that has a need to retaliate to even the score but the consistency that this has occurred over the years, bears this out.

An excellent example of this happened when I went into an office to resolve its emotionalism, resistance and complaining which made itself known with gossip. Twenty-three employees were individually interviewed. They all professed they had nothing to do with the problem. They were out of it, above it or not involved. In fact, some were righteously indignant that I would have such a thought. As individuals they all perceived themselves as innocent of any involvement in the emotional climate in the office.

After the interviews, at a staff meeting I brought up the phenomena of total innocence. I explained my philosophy that when there was dissension in the ranks, it involved all of them. Any group, in the office or home, was similar to a posse in that it developed its own unique personality. The individuals in the posse may not perform the task of hanging someone by themselves, but as a group, they are all responsible. It makes no difference what individual pulled the rope.

I asked the group, "Did anyone passively listen to or overhear office gossip without saying a word to stop it?" Many agreed they had.

Now, they did not perceive this as their contribution to the emotionalism. I pointed out that the Listener was as guilty as the Gossiper. The Gossipers then defended themselves saying, "I was only explaining this point . . ." In this way they consciously discovered their involvement. Up to that point, all genuinely believed they were innocent. Neither the Gossiper nor Listener were aware that both roles were acts of retaliation.

This brought me to the next step of a resolution: "What were they retaliating against?" The meeting revealed how all were unaware they were angry with the doctor. What happened was that the doctor had hired a young consultant who was given unlimited authority over the staff that had worked for the doctor for years. They retaliated by creating havoc in the office by resisting this young consultant, and got "back" at the doctor. The retaliation affected the Quality of the office staff and patients by creating a stressful atmosphere. This resulted in production going down which affected the Money for all of them. Most of all, the Love they had for the doctor and each other were put aside. This was all done at an unconscious level.

You will also use Quality to retaliate by becoming physically or mentally ill. This affects the Quality of your mate's life as well, if s/he needs to take care of you. If the unconscious need to "pay them back" is strong enough, this can sometimes last a lifetime and provide you with the excuse or "privilege" to retaliate. Whether you take care of someone, or put him/her in a position to take care of you, it is still exerting power over another person. It can lock both of you into a negative relationship for years affecting all aspects of your lives. People use their own favorite retaliation. If it is in the Love area, they will withdraw their Love or sex with impotence, frigidity or an affair. The Quality will be not taking the time to be with the person you Love. It is getting in a car and totaling it out and even harming yourself in the process. Retaliating with Money, involves losing your job, getting fired, investing and losing all of your Money. Fortunately, we stay in the first-degree level most of the time.

Not accepting your retaliatory self and noticing the negative actions it evokes, gives you the permission to abuse the other person.

You "punish" them in righteousness and justification. Accepting your retaliatory self in handling little minor snits is a major step in being resolution oriented.

When you cannot or will not conceive that you are capable of retaliating, you will use a passive method. This enables you to achieve the same result without conscious knowledge. A doctor going through a divorce became quite depressed. His wife asked for child support and alimony. The amount she requested increased his depression and started to affect his business. He asked me for a letter for his insurance company stating his depression was too severe for him to continue working. His depression was real. Unconsciously, his resentment was creating his depression to avoid or to reduce the amount of Money he had to pay in alimony. He was unaware that losing the Money was a way of retaliating.

He put his office up for sale. I asked him to hold off his decision until I ran up some figures for him that would show the results of this move. I made up a spreadsheet that calculated it would take him ten years before he would be able to recoup his current financial status if he went through with this plan. In the interim of compiling the figures, he had already sold his practice for $100,000 less than it was worth, and he was unable to reverse the damage. He was bent on financially destroying himself and believed he couldn't help it. After reviewing my calculated figures he made a turn about. He gave up this passive way to retaliate, talked to his wife and attorney and made a more equitable financial settlement. His depression lifted, he opened a new office and started a new life for himself.

Another way we use Quality to retaliate is by withdrawing time from people. You may become a workaholic, especially if you are a family provider. You are convinced that to earn enough Money to support your family in a manner acceptable to them, you need to work long hours. As a workaholic, you usually end up feeling like you paid a price by giving up Love and attention. The rationalization is that it is not possible to spend more time at home with this responsibility on your shoulders. Consciously, you believe you are doing your best and unaware you may be retaliating. This may be because you have not received the recognition or appreciation for giving your Money year after year to provide for your family.

Your anger and need to retaliate also affects the Quality of life for your children. One of the most difficult concepts to accept is that your anger can extend all the way to abusing your children. This can be First, Second or Third Degree. Your unconscious mind will push you to this extent to retaliate for the wrong doings affecting you as a child. No matter how much you profess you will not do what your parents did to you, the chances are that you will. You may disguise it use a different method, or marry someone that will do the abuse for you and you believe there is nothing you can do. Nevertheless, you will convey your anger, tension, etc. to your children.

When I had my children, I promised myself I would never put upon them the abuse I received as a child. My mother hit or gave me a beating on a consistent basis. I rarely hit my children while raising them. However, years later my daughter went to psychotherapy. She came home to visit one day and said, "My therapist asked me if I realized I was a physically abused child." I asked her why. She said it was the teasing, bullying, and hitting by her brother while I was at work. I was fascinated at how I unknowingly passed on the family trait of abusing children to my son. Thus, she still grew up abused. At an unconscious level, I believe I taught my innocent son how to abuse her for me. This was the way I abused both of them. I created an "Abuser" and the "Abused," and in the process remained "innocent."

My awareness from the above example prompted me to take the stand that when a parent physically abuses a child, both parents need to be prosecuted. This includes the parent that abused and the parent that allowed it to occur. Both have committed the crime and are equally guilty. One did the physical beating and the other gave up the responsibility to protect the child.

Facing that you can deliberately harm your children at an unconscious level is an extraordinary growth prospect. It is the hope for the end of abuse of the world's children. As long as you believe you are not responsible, you did not know, you could not stop it or you depend what you did for whatever reason, abused children will continue to be the recipient of their parent's retaliatory selves.

These three emotions: anger, gossip and guilt create a non-resolution self that results in you retaliating against anyone and is the essence of your Formula For Failure. When we are in our healthy good thinking self using our Formula For Success, we do not think of using our failure cycle. Fortunately, we use our Formula For Failure only about ten percent of the time. However, it can contaminate the other ninety percent where we are happy and at peace. To learn the details of how your Formula For Failure is used, study "The Clock" in the next chapter.

*Chapter Eight*

# The Clock To Failure

In the previous chapter, you have been introduced to the five components of the cycle that make up your Formula For Failure, namely: anger, gossip, guilt, non-resolution and retaliation. It's a process that creates negative results. I use "The Clock" in this chapter to illustrate how the cycle progresses. It swings from being happy and confident to being unhappy and back to being happy again. The goal is to remain in the happy and confident self that uses its Formula For Success, that communicates well, achieves effective win/win resolutions and attains positive payoffs. Once you learn how you begin your cycle that makes up your Formula For Failure, you will be able to intercept it and stop the negative payoff by consciously deciding to switch to your Formula For Success. To accomplish this, you need to be thinking. For negative behavior to occur, you need to shut off your thinking self, which acts, not reacts.

This first occurred to me when I was in training as a psychotherapist. One of my assignments was that the next time I became upset, I was to consciously reverse the reaction at the time it occurred. I put this in effect one weekend. On Friday night around ten o'clock my telephone rang and I discovered it was an obscene telephone caller. My first reaction was to gasp and slam the receiver down, which would be my Formula For Failure.

I stopped and made myself think. I said, "Theresa, those are only words. He can't hurt you as he is not in the room. Wait and handle it the way you want to; don't react" I waited until my shock and emotions calmed down. I brought up my Formula For Success that is my loving self and said, "I believe in the goodness of man. I am going to talk to you as though you are someone other than an obscene telephone caller." Now, this is an adult talking that is guided by a nurturing parent. There was a long pause on the other end of the wire and he started to cry and said, "I'm sorry lady." I told him we have all been there in one way or another. This led to a poignant conversation that revealed women made fun of him. I liked myself better after I stopped my judgments of this young man and handled the unusual situation in a more humane way.

The process in using the Formula For Failure Clock, shows that at twelve o'clock you are in the "Good Life." You are happy and enjoying your loved ones, job and life. You like yourself and feel like a winner. You balance logic and emotion to settle situations and discuss situations that bother you. To achieve this, you keep your voice calm and confident. You talk in an entirely different manner than when you are upset, angry, emotional or righteous. This is your resolution voice, and your attitude is one of common sense. You are using the positive sides of both sides of your brain simultaneously. We are fortunate that we are here most of the time.

Six o'clock is the place you go to get a "Negative Payoff," where your need to be right is strongest. These are periods in your life when you are a loser, and feel badly. You genuinely feel stuck in your problem with no resolutions possible. At the six o'clock position you deal out and receive punishment. You will convince yourself that you have the right to dispense this punishment or you will believe you deserve to receive it.

From the "Good Life" (twelve o'clock) to the "Negative Payoff" (six o'clock), the pattern of each person is unique. It is very much like a cassette that you put in your head that you play and obey without question. You repeat it over and over, most often at an unconscious level, and you believe another person causes it. As long as you believe this, you are at the mercy of that person. You will respond the same way and carry out the dictates of your inner pattern. You are waiting for someone else to change before you can be happy since that is the only solution you can see.

The dichotomy is that you do get happy again without the other person changing. You make up and then repeat your pattern again on another day. This occurs because after a bad payoff, you experience temporary relief whether the person "gives in" and admits s/he is wrong or not. The process around The Clock can take seconds or a year (or more) to build up a case to reach the "Negative Payoff" position.

To learn how you go into your Formula For Failure, first notice what puts you into an emotional state. Think of all the words and actions that upset you. It can be someone leaving a sweater over the living room chair, breaking a piece of china or some act, word or deed that is petty and not important. This stimulus is what prompts you to leave the good life. Refer to the Emotional and Physical form you filled out in Chapter 8 listing some of your annoyances. When these unimportant events occur and you express more anger than the offense warrants, you are either bringing anger from past memories, or worrying about what can happen in the future.

Put your list of what upsets you on your refrigerator, automobile, at work, etc. Look at it daily. Prepare yourself for the first stimulus that annoys you, and locate the first thought or emotion you experience. Slowing the process down and dissecting it, gives you the opportunity to intercept the anger and prevent you from acting on it. Learn this process starting with the first-degree level of problems and then progress to second-degree problems where there is tangible harm and loss, which is actually the minority of people.

**From 12 o'clock to 1 o'clock** When you have located what stimuli upset you, and you move out of the twelve o'clock into the one o'clock position, record your first thought or emotion. If you are right brain (emotional) you usually will get the feelings first. You feel hurt or resentful and are out of touch with your analytical thinking. If you are left brain, you will start making thoughtless remarks.

You will get adamant about explaining something trivial, and are out of touch with your feelings.

Check if your first clue in your Formula For Failure falls in one of the following categories:

- Physical: Where and what do you feel in your body? Stress? Tension?
- Emotional: What emotions do you feel? Irritation? Anger? Frustration? Hurt?
- Logical: What thoughts go through your head? Are you listing the wrongs experienced? To whom are you directing these wrongs? Are you being critical of that person?
- Behavioral: How are you acting? Are you withdrawing? Are you lecturing, criticizing or berating the person?

When you catch your cycle at this stage, you can go back to the "Good Life" position. You have an option of reversing the process and avoiding a negative payoff. You can look for whatever is bothering you and find what you need. You then go about fulfilling that need on your own and leave the other person alone. This avoids a negative payoff or damage to the relationship. This is balancing the right brain by changing the negative emotion to caring. It balances the left-brain that will resolve logically without caustic remarks or joking. Balancing the two sides produces positive results.

**Two o'clock:** If you fail to stop this process of sabotaging, you will go on to the two o'clock position. You will feel increased discomfort that may show in your body language with a frown or scowl. You may feel a stirring of resentment and find it difficult to talk to the person in a soft, loving voice. You are unable to tell her/him gently what you want or prefer. Your annoyance shows and both of you are moving toward a negative payoff. At this level of the pattern your emotions are more intense and it becomes more difficult to apply logic. However, it can be done and you can go back to the "Good Life" without a negative payoff. You can take a break, a brisk walk or a shower. Approach the person with a different attitude and tell her/him what you need. You are now changing your old pattern and stopping a negative payoff you really don't need.

If you do not return to the twelve o'clock position, you will start building a case against the other person by gathering information to show how s/he is wrong. You are using your negative critical thoughts to justify your position. If you do not stop this process, the natural step is to proceed to three o'clock, which is the gossip stop. Gossip is any negative remark, implied or otherwise, about another person. Know that gossip is an addiction.

**Three o'clock:** You may find yourself making short retorts or sarcastic remarks about the person to someone and then laugh and say you are joking or you don't mean it. This is a sure way to know you do mean it at some level or there would be no need to say it. Remember, gossip, no matter how you disguise it, is intended to get back to the person. Some part of you feels resentful and this is a negative way to let the person know what it is, hoping s/he will rectify it. S/he may, but it will be at a price since the resentment also reached the person who is now angry. You did not go to them directly and discuss it with Love and respect and you let others know the negative things this person did; real or imagined.

Of course, you will only go to a person that agrees with you, even if it is by remaining silent. You accept her/his silence as concurrence. You go and tell everyone that will listen or will give you some confirmation that you are right whether it is one or ten people. Heaven help the people who say a good word about the other person. Your need to be right supersedes all logic and you now want to keep and expand your problem. It will take awareness and determination to stop and reverse it. Admitting to the person that you are gossiping can do this. You can say, "Hey, I just realized I am putting Kevin down and I feel badly about that. It's unfair since he is not here. I don't expect you to take sides. I know you like him and it is not fair for me to put you in this position. If you can tell me of a way I can resolve it, I will appreciate your feedback."

In essence, what you are doing is owning your anger rather than letting your anger own you. When your anger owns you, it tells you what to do and say, and when to do it, and to whom. Owning your anger allows you to resolve the problem and go back to the twelve o'clock position with a small negative payoff, as the chances of gossip getting back to the person is 95%. You can then go to the person and make your peace.

Be careful you do not tell the person that s/he hurt your feelings or made you upset. Most psychological modalities say to do this and clear the air. This is abuse. My experience is that more often than not, this results in the other person becoming defensive, defers resolutions, and you get your negative payoff. Clear your feelings within yourself, then approach the other person for a resolution. If you find you are unwilling to do this and persist in gossiping and believing others made you angry, you will go to the next level.

**Four o'clock:** You will either start arguing or will withdraw as long as your programming dictates. Feelings are strong and the need to be right needs satisfaction. You have the testimony of all your friends you gossiped with that agreed you are right. You now feel righteous and justified in punishing the person. This is your last chance to return to the twelve o'clock "Good Life" with a minimum negative payoff as you can assume the person heard the gossip. Your thinking mechanism is barely functioning and you are almost entirely into emotion. You can turn this around by catching yourself, soften your voice and apologize. If you are withdrawing, become aware of it and tell yourself to speak and resolve the problem. Many times when you withdraw to the "Silent" role you believe that the other person knows that you are angry and the reason why.

Return to the twelve o'clock Good Life by giving up the righteousness. Be still and breathe deeply. Say to your self, "I am into something where I am not acting too sanely. I want to stop and discuss it in an hour or so and settle it. I value our relationship too much to do this to us." Know your anger has nothing to do with the other person and find a way to resolve it within yourself. At this point, if you do not go back to twelve o'clock, you will be programmed to go on to six o'clock. You will have your confrontation and argument and you will both receive your negative payoff. There is no return.

**Five o'clock:** Your need to be right, and your belief that others can make you feel bad comes over you. You then feel justified in having a confrontation and experience the "Negative Payoff" which is forthcoming. You cannot return to the "Good Life" without a payoff. There is little or no logic, and your ideal thinking process has stopped. The emotional right brain has taken over and you are a lamb leading yourself to slaughter by an unconscious dictate. Feelings of hopelessness overcome you for this is your Formula For Failure where there are no resolutions. This is where you genuinely feel it is the other person's fault and unaware you are following the negative dictate in your own head.

You will fulfill your need to punish yourself and the other person emotionally, mentally and physically. This is when you satisfy an addiction such as drugs, overeating, alcohol or tranquilizers, and blame others for causing it. When your emotional self takes over without your common sense, your primitive self acts itself out.

**Six o'clock:** Here's the payoff as you fulfill the need to retaliate. Your reasoning and righteousness entitles you to do this. You will display your hurt by pouting or not speaking to show others what they did to you to induce guilt in them. You may be punishing yourself for your own feelings of guilt. It is important to watch for the following items to determine the health of a person, couple, family or business.

### The Degree Of The Payoff

To reiterate, the payoff at six o'clock is in First, Second or Third Degrees. Fortunately, most cycles stay in the First Degree or lower levels of Second Degree.

- **First Degree:** You will withdraw, blame, yell, get drunk or slam out of the house. No one gets physically hurt. It is dealing with hurt feelings, which usually blows over in an hour or a day, a week, sometimes even longer.
- **Second Degree:** This level involves active retaliation that may result in physical violence with injuries that are reversible. A lesser Second Degree can involve a divorce or getting depressed according to what emotion you are feeling. This

type of punishment can last days, years or a lifetime but is reversible.

• **Third Degree:** Payoffs are permanent and involve suicide, homicide, or lifetime insanity. It is irreversible. Just think how few of these we experience in a lifetime.

Check the degree of your negative payoff when you are at the six o'clock position. If it is First Degree, review what happened that put you in this state. Decide that the stimulus that created it will never bother you again. Start eliminating all First Degree annoyances. The more you give up what you believe, think and do is right about minor, unimportant events, the less negative payoffs you will receive.

## Frequency Of The Payoff

In addition to determining the degree of the payoff, check the frequency with which your Negative Payoff occurs. This is an excellent way to measure the health of a person, partnership, marriage, office or organization. At a First Degree level once or twice a month, you have a pretty healthy relationship. If you are nitpicking, experiencing irritation or depression, and criticizing on a daily basis, you know it is an unhealthy relationship.

## Length Of Time In The Payoff

It is vital to become aware of how long you stay in the six o'clock negative payoff. It is another gauge to determine how healthy you and your relationships are. Do you stay angry for an hour? Week? If you stay angry for an hour, you are fairly healthy. When it extends to being angry and not speaking for a week or you go to second and third degree, you are now displaying deeper emotional problems.

You can make a decision on how long you wish to stay angry. I recall my grandson saying to me, "Grandma, I want you to know how much I appreciate you. No matter how angry you get at me, you apologize within five minutes." That is the time I set for myself many years ago and was surprised when he brought it up.

The **Degree** of the game, the **Frequency** with which you play it, and the and **Length of Time** you spend in the payoff, is an excellent clue to your mental and emotional health. This applies as an individual, a couple, a family, an office or a corporation.

**Seven o'clock:** Amazingly, after you received your Negative Payoff the first feelings usually experienced are relief and release, not remorse, sadness or depression. The purging is over and you have paid your dues. You can now relax and know you can once more be happy. You have either had your needs fulfilled, or made the other person suffer in some way because they did not fulfill your needs. There is a type of elation and smugness here that defies our sensibilities.

**Eight o'clock:** Logic starts to return with your need to patch the damage done. This is where you start to feel guilty and remorseful. You want to make amends and find yourself feeling rather awkward. There is a quiet period and you move around each other with a little nod of the head. You start having your first stir of a friendly feeling but may speak abruptly. You may even buy a gift for the person to show you are sorry. This can be from a magnanimous position where you are willing to forgive even though s/he was wrong. If s/he spurns your gift do not be surprised, as s/he may still be at six o'clock and feeling angry and feels you are admitting you were wrong and that s/he deserves appreciation. S/he may not show any appreciation, and if you get sensitive, you can go back down to the payoff section again.

**Nine o'clock:** Your logical side has returned. At this stage of the cycle, your discomfort is obvious. Your speech is tentative, apologetic, and hesitant as you try to make contact and become friends again. This stage alone should be a deterrent to going through this cycle again. Do you realize how differently you speak here as opposed to twelve o'clock when you use your beautiful, loving tone of voice. It also is far different from when you are at four o'clock when you are angry and in your critical role. An example is: At twelve o'clock you say, "Honey, will you please pass the salt"; Four o'clock "Tell your mother to pass the salt."; Nine o'clock, "Do you mind, er, if you, uh, can you pass the salt."

**Ten o'clock:** You are friendly with a twinge of reserve and self-consciousness. There is definite avoidance of discussing what happened since there is enough residual emotions from the six o'clock payoff. The memory and fear of returning their lengthening or repeating the cycle again is too close. This is how you want to think at three and four o'clock, and avoid the payoff. Emerging from the ten o'clock position, you are usually able to start feeling more comfortable and are appreciating being together again.

**Eleven o'clock:** You are at the door of the 'Good Life' again. The level of discomfort is almost completely diminished. You are laughing together and contemplating good sex as you go back to the "Good Life" at the twelve o'clock position hand in hand. Neither person is totally comfortable yet.

**Twelve o'clock:** Once you are back to the "Good Life," this is the time to discuss what happened. Make ground rules to avoid starting up the cycle again. Stay with your logical and caring self, which is combining your left/right brain functioning. Determine that you will listen to each other. Stay out of your negative critical parent role by accepting that there is no purpose or need for anger to get what you want. Decide that you will use Love to teach, instruct, provide information, correct and resolve situations.

Unconsciously using your Process is the journey around the clock over and over again. Process is any behavior you use to achieve an end result whether it is positive or negative. Where you use your process is the content. It can be mate, job, child, car, etc. The process remains the same for any content.

### Dr. Benjamin's Clock To Failure

To give you an idea how The Clock works, I have mapped my own process for my Formula For Failure Clock in Illustration 4. I am very familiar with my process, and although I have tracked it for years, I still go for a negative payoff occasionally. I delight that it is a rare occurrence rather than daily as it was years ago. The earlier in the cycle I catch myself in negative thoughts or feelings, the easier it is to reverse my adverse negative payoff and return to the 'Good Life.'

When I leave my twelve o'clock position, it will be toward someone that has done some trivial act that has annoyed me. One annoyance I use to leave the "Good Life" is incompetence. As illustrated,

# THE CLOCK

## YOUR FORMULA FOR FAILURE

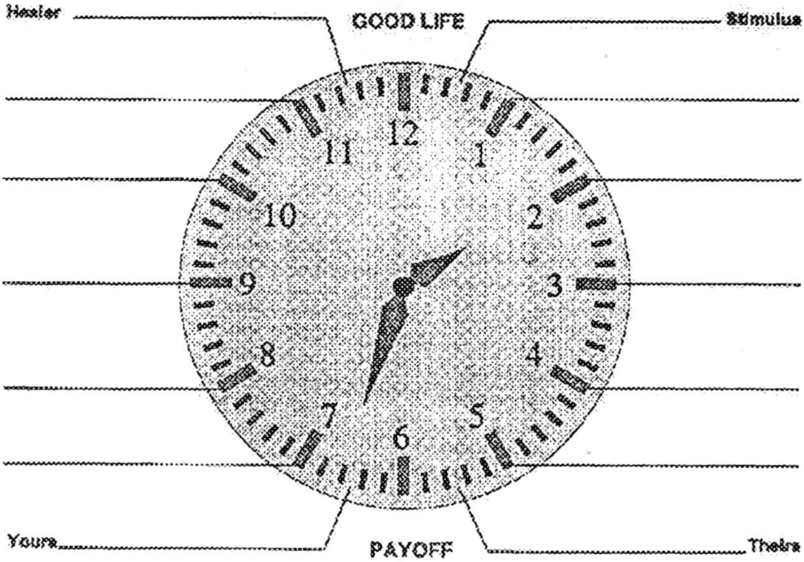
Healer
GOOD LIFE
Stimulus
12
1
2
3
4
5
6
7
8
9
10
11
Yours
PAYOFF
Theirs

Frequency ______

Intensity: First Degree ______
Second Degree ______
Third Degree ______

Length of time in the Payoff position ______

Illustration 4: The Clock To Failure

my secretary, Lisa, did not center a letter to my satisfaction. I look at a brief letter typed at the top of the page, leaving three-quarters of the page blank. Being a left-brain visual personality with all its negative ramifications, I start criticizing internally. I think, "For gosh sakes, can't she see what that looks like?" I just slipped into the one o'clock position leading to my Formula For Failure.

This is my first clue that I'm getting into a big deal over nothing. When I catch it here, I walk around my desk, shake my hands vigorously and say to myself, "Theresa, leave her alone. Go out there and simply say, "Will you please drop this down and center it on the page? Thanks so much." I practice this until my voice has lost its sarcasm and go out and do it lovingly. I have now reversed the process to the negative payoff, gone back to the "Good Life" and got what I wanted. Now this is sensible and no one got hurt or upset.

However, if I have a need to use Lisa to be rid of my anger, I will go on to two O'clock where I start feeling resentful. As a result, when Lisa comes in to tell me something, I am a shade cooler than usual. She asks, "Is anything wrong?" I now know I already started my negative payoff. Yet I say, "No, why?" She shrugs and leaves, not certain. I have a choice here of going our immediately and saying, "Lisa, I want this letter centered. It's not important. Just drop it down, and I am sorry I cut you off." If am too annoyed to do this, I usually go and sit in a quiet place, the beach when possible, and wait for peace to return.. I accept that my annoyance if First Degree and petty. I then look for the real annoyance within. When I am calm, I go back and tell Lisa I value her as a person. I tell her I do not want to make such an unimportant issue important. The person is important, not the issue.

If I fail to do this, I automatically go to Three O'clock that is the gossip stage. When my bookkeeper arrives, I shut the office door and show her the letter. I say to her, "Look at what Lisa did." My bookkeeper is smart. She says, "She will want to know that so she can change it. You know how conscientious she is about her work." However, my emotions have obliterated my brain and I'm off and running. So I take the letter now and show my friends. I feel good. They agree with me that anyone would know to center the letter. Now I still have the option to say to my friends, "Don't pay attention to me. Lisa is a good loyal worker and doesn't deserve this. Just let me gripe for two more minutes." When I do this, I can still reverse the negative payoff and go back to the "Good Life." There will be some residual of payoff here as she is bound to hear the gossip I created.

The alternative is to keep building my case, using the support I got from my friends. I also become judgmental and righteous and determined to prove I'm right. As a result, at four o'clock I now feel justified in confronting my incompetent secretary. My approach is defensive and adamant. I will tell her this is the tenth time I reminded her, (my need at this stage to exaggerate is overwhelming). With awareness and determination I can break my journey to a negative payoff by intercepting my own monologue and stop. All I need to do is say, "Lisa, I am sorry. You do not deserve this. I am angry because I did not settle a real problem I have elsewhere and using you." Before Lisa leaves for the day, I see that a small gift is on her desk. Now, if I persist in telling her off, I automatically move to five o'clock. This is where we both nurse our wounds and tell others what a difficult day we had with the other person. We will both look for the payoff to give to the other.

This puts us at six o'clock. The punishment arrives. We are either not talking, she is giving notice, or I am firing her and we are extremely emotional. Both of us believe the cause was the other person. The length of time spent at the six o'clock position varies. The punishment can go on for hours, days, weeks or months. When I have suffered enough or made the other person suffer enough, I will then be able to leave the six o'clock position. Fortunately, even if I do get in a position where I reach six o'clock, I do know I will not stay there. Almost immediately I make the first move and mend the damage I have inflicted, hoping this is possible and reversible.

Amazingly, at the seven o'clock position, there is relief that it is over. I now know the worse. I got my anger out and I accepted my punishment. I can now take a deep breath as I feel the release of negative energy and repair the damage. I will be finding a new secretary, an excellent distraction to not to deal with the real problem that could be elsewhere or I simply wanted to get rid of Lisa. No matter how negative the experience is, there is a reason and a positive benefit behind it. I am learning to get the positive benefits in a positive way without needing the negative journey.

## Summary

If you take responsibility for your part in the cycle and payoff, it will prevent this cycle or reduce its usage. Otherwise you will go through this same cycle (your process) all your life with other people and others (which is your content). If you believe the other person caused it, then you will repeat the process again. It is not important to know why you need a negative payoff. What is important is to know what it is, how to stop or reduce it and become a resolution-oriented person. Sometimes it is as simple as learning assertiveness and communication skills. Give yourself a gift and give up the need to be right. Become aware of your negative pattern that results in your Formula For Failure. Learn and change it to your beautiful Formula For Success. Remember, this clock is your life ticking away so make it good, make it happy and make it productive.

*Chapter Nine*

# Our Two Selves

Right and left brain awareness begins when we speak of our two selves, in which it helps to have background on the functioning of the right and left-brain. When we use just the left side, we become aggressive, too talkative and turn off our feelings and compassion. If we use only the right side, we get emotional, withdraw and become passive. Loving and lasting resolutions are achieved when you are assertive and use the Love from the right brain and the common sense from the left-brain. Balancing the traits of the right and left-brain makes us fully functioning people that achieve resolutions. My belief is that we all are basically good people and want to use this process to achieve resolutions and handle situations effectively without anger.

Roger W. Sperry and M. S. Gazzanign of the California Institute of Technology researched right and left-brain functions. They studied the behavioral and psychological effects of separating or "splitting" the brain in two. The corpus callosum, is a tract of nerve fibers connecting the right and left-brain. Their research involved severing this corpus callosum to prevent seizures in people with severe epilepsy. Remarkably, severing these fibers did not affect the subject's behavior or personality. However, they did learn that there is a dominant side and a non-dominant side that accelerates the chaos we sometime experience in making decisions. Knowing what is going on in the non-dominant side of the brain is vital in learning about self. It also revealed that each half of the brain has its own perceptions, sensations, learning experiences, and memories. In addition, it displayed its own unique strengths, neither side being stronger than the other. Some of the differences they found are:

| Left Side (Dominant) | Right Side (Non-Dominant) |
|---|---|
| Controls the right side of the body | Controls the left side of the body. |
| Sensible and rational. | Emotional and sensitive feelings. |
| Gets right to the point. | Deviates from the subject. |
| Has language. | Lacks language and uses abstract symbols. |
| Is a talker. | Is a silencer. |
| Thinks analytically, Computer-like. | Thinks intuitively, ESP and psychic abilities. |
| Social and extroverted. | Within self and introverted. |
| Processes information fast and analytically. | Processes information Slowly and methodically. |

It is difficult to know how each of us selects to be right or left-brain personalities. It may be our subjection to particular environments or an innate choice we have no say over. In either case, my observations show this is established early in life. I observed this at the mall as a man walked by me pulling two little boys in a red wagon. The one sitting in front was about four, and the one in the back about two years old. As they went by, the two-year-old rolled out of the wagon on to the floor. The four-year-old followed. The father turned around and said, "Get back in the wagon." The four-year-old jumped back into the wagon with alacrity. The two-year-old looked up at his dad and said, "I don't want to. I want to walk." The father yanked the child by the arm and dropped him into the wagon. He immediately rolled out again. The four-year-old bent his headway over as though praying the other child would not get dad mad. This time the father spanked the child who was yelling. "I want to walk." Obviously, the commotion and crying was a most unsettling experience for the mall's customers.

The last I saw of this little family was the father carrying the child on his hip. He was still yelling, "I want to walk." as he was trying to wriggle down to the floor. The four-year-old sat frozen, with his head bent and his hands over his ears. These signs clearly showed that the four-year-old exhibited right brain traits by withdrawing and being silent. He did not want to make waves. The two-year-old showed left-brain traits being more extroverted, volatile and talkative. Were these traits of right/left brain innate or from the environment or the way parents treated each individual child?

We all have an ideal self that strives to succeed and creates positive and effective results which is our Formula For Success. We also have a primitive self that will fight when it feels it is at a survival level such as physical danger, or to reproduce itself for survival of the species. It can also be put into effect in minor areas that your primitive self believes is important and your common sense self knows is silly. It is the natural desire to do what it thinks it needs to survive and where you fight to be right.

The "split" in yourself also reflects the split in a relationship and a form of survival to offset your excesses. You have often heard it said that opposites attract. This is truer than you realize. This split invites you to select a mate that takes the opposite role whether it is in a friendship, marriage or work. Say, for instance, that as a child you were beaten and you made a decision to never beat your children. If the part of you that wants to do the same thing to your child that was done to you is strong enough, you may just marry someone that will do it for you. In this way you affirm that you are not like your mother. You will show how you are a victim, helpless and beyond blame.

Right brain and left-brain personalities are automatically attracted to each other. That is why we see couples where one is the Talker and dominant and the other a Silencer that is submissive. The more extreme you are as a right brain personality, the more extreme left brain personality you will select as a partner, or vice versa. They balance each other out and become a checkmate for his/her excesses in either area. If you do not balance your right and left-brain within, you will select someone that will balance it in the relationship. When used to get negative results, which generally occurs when under stress, this will become the basis of your "War Games."

Here's an example of how to use the right and left-brain successfully. Using my process to create the marquetry pictures of inlaid wood, which involves inlaying hundreds of hand-carved pieces of wood to create a picture, I saw how I used my right and left-brain. The Love of creating these pieces of art came from my right brain and created the subject I wanted, by selecting the types and shades of wood to use. I carried this creative vision around in my head for weeks getting the picture exactly the way I wanted it. I had to Love it and needed it to feel right to get my nod of approval to make it up.

If I left my creation at this point, it would never come to life. I had to go to my analytical left brain to do the practical work that my right brain created to locate and purchase the materials needed, measure the size of the picture and calculate how to carve and fit the pieces together. I had to depend on my industrious left-brain to bring the creation to fruition. I went to my right brain to see if my creation was okay each step as I progressed through to the completed works. By using the both sides of the brain positively, the Quality emerged and it brought in the Money I wanted that enabled me to go to school.

You can make changes in areas you do not like in yourself. Take the analytical side of your brain and apply its common sense to the emotional side. It is the ability under stress to shift from right or left-brain at will. This produces resolutions and is true freedom. The emotions you feel prevent you from incorporating these common sense ideas. The more emotional you are, the more analytical brainpower you lose. That is why you resolve other people's problems so easily as you do not have the memories that cause you emotional involvement.

Start locating your own problems and resolve them. Decide that the next time you are emotional, you will stop and bring one part of your thinking self into the conflict. Start this process with a simple awareness that a conversation, whether it is with yourself or others, is going nowhere. Bring your thinking self in and deliberately stop the conversation. You can say, "Let us take a thirty minute break to cool ourselves and come back." To make "friends" with your emotions and feelings, you need to acknowledge them. You may say, "I'm feeling pressured right now. If you wait a minute I'll be able to listen to you." If you listen while pressured, you will not hear as you are in your right brain, and will not respond and distort what you hear. If you are in your left-brain, your answers may be sharp and abrupt. You will add the feeling of resentment to the pressured feeling. When balanced, you resolve issues with yourself and the other person without anger or chastisement.

When I first came to California thirty years ago, my next-door neighbor was eighty-four years old. We became fast friends even though I was only 20 years old. The wisdom she extended included this poem she gave me just before she died. I do not know who the author is even though I have searched. It so clearly states what I want to convey to you about our two selves; One that is ideal and Loves and the one that is primitive and retaliates.

> *There is a little tyrant and touch of the critic and martyr in all of us.*
>
> *There are moments when we want to dominate, to tear down and to make others suffer.*
>
> *These traits, however, can be and must be subordinated to the total goodness of the personality.*
>
> *Many people are miserable because they think that occasional destructive feelings necessarily make them a terrible person.*
>
> *But, one Swallow Does Not Make Spring.*

## Saints And Devils

My experience has been that when two people meet and develop a relationship, they always have the same level of anger. They just act it out differently, and will play the role they assigned to themselves.

The basis of all games, have the two personalities I refer to as Saints and Devils, which we revert to under stress. We have the Devils who are blatantly angry people and arguing to prove they are right. The complimentary role is the quiet, often beautiful Saints that are so willing to take the abuse and suffer.

In my marriage, I was the Saint and my husband was the Devil. Meeting my husband today, I would not take the first verbal or physical abuse. In fact I would not date him at all as I no longer have that kind of anger. To communicate effectively you need to own and give up your anger as well as the guilt. The thrill of knowing I had accomplished this occurred with a telephone call from my ex-husband after an eighteen year absence. I answered the telephone and heard a very annoyed voice say, "Are you aware how aggravating it is to try and call someone and they are never home." It was amazing that on hearing a voice from the past how quickly I reverted back to explaining my whereabouts. I caught myself, stopped and asked, "Who is this?" He said, "Stewart." I said, "Stewart who?" and heard an authoritative voice say, "Your husband."

*"Saints" need "Devils" to confirm their saintliness of how good they are. In dysfunctional families, you will find a martyred "Saint" taking abuse and a "Devil" giving abuse. These personalities marry each other to justify their mutual anger.*

I laughed and I passed this stage of defending. He wanted to visit the children and I assured him there was no animosity in the home and I never put him down to the children. When he arrived, the first thing I did was say, "Sit down Stewart, I have something to say." I turned and looked straight at him and said in a soft, kind, loving voice, "Stewart, I'm not the same person you left. I do not allow anyone to talk to me the way you did on the telephone." He stared and said, "What would you do?" I made it clear he would not be allowed in my home again. He said, "You mean it don't you?" I assured him I did and we were able to remain friends until the day he died. He was no longer my Devil and I had no need for a Devil in my live, as I was no longer a Saint. The roles of Saints and Devils, is the basis of all games and often marry each other.

Devils are scapegoats that Parents teach from birth how to be abrasive and abusive. The Devils allow the Saints to use them to expiate their righteous and saintly anger that is at an unconscious level. Both are equally responsible for their role in the game as each created them from within, no matter how it may appear on the surface. There can be no Abuser without a person programmed for abuse. An interesting aspect of Scapegoats is that if you have one in your life, be it at office, home, group, etc., and s/he elected to leave, it is only a matter of time before you replace her/him with another scapegoat. In a family of four daughters, mother and father, the father was the Scapegoat. The mother and all four girls believed he caused all the unhappiness. He was a true Devil's advocate and made them miserable. After a divorce, all was peaceful for these Saints living together with no Devil. In a matter of months, the second oldest girl was the Scapegoat. She filled dad's shoes and made all miserable until she left home. I cautioned them to watch what person they would use next but they were not convinced. After the youngest girl was established as a Scapegoat and a true Devil, they were convinced that the Saints needed Devils in their lives as surely as the Devils needed the Saints to be happy with.

It is difficult to grasp that a part of you wants to be loving and successful, and another part stops you. Regardless of what games you elect to play, all are used to keep you from getting what one part of you wants. Many people are convinced that these games prevent them from achieving success and getting what they want. The reality is that they are using these games to prevent their level of success from exceeding their comfort level in Love, Quality and Money. Up to these levels, they are happy, loving people on a day-to-day basis. Accept that you are a good person and changing, evolving and growing is a lifetime learning process. It is no different than learning to read at age five and improving your reading skills to understanding Shakespeare and Plato. It is a daily process lasting a lifetime and is not to be used to keep your self from being happy with yourself the way you are, or being afraid to make mistakes.

### Summary

It is well established that our belief systems and the need to stay within our comfort level of Love, Quality and Money is what we use to keep and Love, our problems.   It definitely is the basis for our Formula for Failure, which is a process, or cycle, used in all games.

This consists of anger at something you don't like and then gossiping to others about it. This justifies retaliation since you are convinced you are right. After your anger blows over, you feel guilty and your Formula For Failure is complete. It creates the non-resolution person and is played out by the Devils and the Saints. When you know this cycle within yourself, acknowledge and intercept it, your perception will automatically change and the games will cease.

*Chapter Ten*

# The Genesis Of All Games

Minding other people's business is the foundation and primary purpose for all games is to avoid exceeding your Love, Money, or Quality levels that were set at age ten. These levels are maintained by playing games. The genesis of all games is making other people's business your business, criticizing them and then helping them. The helper in the game is easier to see than the player that plays helpless and invites others to make it their business to intervene. The helpless person often creates situations to force the helper to help. When treating families, one of the most difficult concepts to convey is that what other's do is not anyone's business if it does not harm self or others. This is especially so when there is dissension and it does not involve you. You need to mind your own business whether it is your parents, your friends, neighbors and, most of all, your children. When you do not mind your own business, you will fall into numerous games where everyone loses. To stop games, learn how to mind your own business and give up the need to fix people or situations. It will not do any good anyway if they do not wish a resolution. You believe you want a resolution, however, a part of you will not achieve one for whatever reason exists in your head.

*To stop distancing myself to avoid intimacy, when troubled, I have a CONVERSATION in my head, make peace with it and avoid a CONFRONTATION. This is a powerful tool to stop playing games.*

There were two incidents that helped me see the wisdom of minding my own business, and also showed how traits are passed from one generation to another be they positive or negative. The first happened when I was nine years old and I put it into effect forty years later with my grandchildren.

As a child, I learned from my mother, a very practical and sensible person, who knew when not to help. My sister came running home several months after her marriage crying her heart out. She started to tell my mother how her husband upset her. My mother dramatically flung open the back door, threw out my sister's coat, overshoes, mittens, earmuffs and hat and loudly proclaimed, "Go home and solve your own problems. If I agreed with you that he was no good, and you two are kissing tomorrow, I would then be the one that was no good for putting him down today." She knew when it was none of her business. What a powerful message for me to learn at a young age.

*My own saying is: "Being nice and doing for others can be downright neurotic. It takes a lot of wisdom to effectively help another human being and know when to stop."*

Forty years later when my two grandchildren were seven and eight years old, they came to me to settle a disagreement. Both told their stories. I said, "I know you both believe you are right and I know you don't lie. Yet, your stories are different. Here I am feeling very unhappy. If I pick which one is right, the other one will be mad at me. That is not fair when I am an innocent bystander."

It is none of my business who or what is right or wrong, especially since it is First Degree. Both are equally responsible. I would lose that innocence once I choose to take a side as I have now involved myself. I told them, "Resolve it between yourselves and settle it for the whole day. When you do, we can then go and have fun." They did settle it but it was funny to have my grandson take me aside later. He said, "Grandma, really and truly my story was the real story." I said, "Sure, John. Sure it is. Don't you know Leslie feels the same way?"

To break the helping game, you need to learn how to mind your own business. You cannot win. You can only end up with one or both parties angry with you. You also may be told to mind your own business or the situation may end up costing you Money. I recall a friend asking me why my daughter had Texas license plates on her car after being in California a couple of years. I said I did not know and would not ask unless I wanted to take the responsibility that it might result in me paying for them.

I applied this same concept in business. A doctor called and said she had two employees that spoke to her in private without the other employee present. Both told the doctor they were having trouble with the other employee unaware that all three were gossiping. Each was requesting the doctor let the other employee go or she would resign from her job, as each truly believed she was right. I had the doctor tell them what I had told my grandchildren.

This was, "Look, you are both creating a condition where I will have to judge a person on intangible evidence. I stand to lose in either choice. I am going to give both of you two weeks to iron out your differences. Your emotional feud has no place in my business office. Gather some tangible documentation for me that will demonstrate what is affecting each other's job and what is needed. Work toward a solution, or I will discharge both of you." The doctor made both parties responsible for their actions. There was an entirely different atmosphere on my return visit to that office. The two employees were friendly and congenial.

Keep in mind, being in Love or in a relationship does not give you license to tell the other person what to do. You believe the closer you are to someone, the more say you have in what s/he does. Loving someone does not give you permission to talk any differently than you would to a stranger. Watch that you do not go to the other extreme and say, "I don't give a damn what happens to them." This is still keeping the problem.

Criticizing people is the ultimate method you use in making other people's business your business. In the process to learn how to mind my own business, and leave others alone, I decided to stop criticizing anyone. This means quietly inside my head or out loud to another person. I have succeeded to a great extent. It is still there; I have only become a little cleverer at hiding it. I know now it is never the other person. It is my need in my head, to criticize, distance, or punish myself for some reason. Otherwise, I can easily handle something I am unhappy about and resolve it.

Your belief that every little event in the other person's life is of your concern can create much unhappiness. However, it only creates day-to-day squabbles that corrode the Quality of a relationship. This is especially true with your children. You believe because they are yours you have the right to tell them what to do and it is your inherent right to help them, ask personal questions, walk into their home at anytime, etc. It is difficult to grasp that you do not have that right. I have learned to apply these concepts and philosophy with each human being I know regardless of the relationship that Kahil Gilbran put so well in his book, *The Prophet.*

> *The children are not your children.*
> *They are the sons and daughters of Life's longing for itself.*
> *They come through you but not from you,*
> *And though they are with you yet they belong not to you.*
> *You may give them your Love but not your thoughts.*
> *For they have their own thoughts.*
> *You may house their bodies but not their souls,*
> *For their souls dwell in the house of tomorrow, which you cannot visit, not even in your dreams.*
> *You may strive to be like them, but seek not to make them like you.*
> *For life goes not backward nor tarries with yesterday.*

You also need to know how far a person will accelerate his/her behavior to force you to make his/her problem your business. You need the wisdom to know when to intercede and how to handle situations. When someone manipulates you with the extreme behavior of threatening to harm her/himself, to get you involved, you need to know and make a plan on what to do to extricate yourself. Even children know how to manipulate and gain power over others by getting them involved in their business and then manipulating them.

A ten-year-old girl in therapy had three teenage sisters, and felt as though she had four mothers. She had many ways to have power over them. She was sitting in one of my rockers and started to swing her leg up and down. Her sister, Linda, said, "All right Suzy, we see you. You have our attention so you can stop." Instead Suzy swung her foot higher and wagged it at her sister who got even more incensed. Linda yelled, "I said you have our attention and you can stop." I said, "Linda, will you please picture a string from Suzy's toe to your mouth. Anytime she wants you to get upset all she has to do is wiggle her little toe up and down. The string will make your mouth and feelings get out of control." Linda admitted she did not like the thought of that happening. I said, "Cut the string and mind your own business."

Look for ways to resolve the issue and stop scolding and criticizing and mind your own business. Love is respecting the other person's value system. It is accepting that s/he has the right to believe what s/he believes, not what you think s/he should believe. Love is asking the person what they need to resolve the problem for her/himself. The need to help and involving yourself in their business is the basis of all games and the ultimate in inviting your Formula For Failure. When you stop helping and mind your own business, games between people, especially loved ones, will drop dramatically. The goal is to drop the addiction of criticizing and complaining and putting your nose in other people's business. Learning how to live each day instead of dying each day is a giant step in this direction. Starting today, develop an addiction to creating and enjoying life each day.

In the following chapters, the most prominent relationship games our outlined. They are listed by the degree of severity starting with the most severe, "The Game of Living or Dying" which exists in all games. The most severe, physically, is Abused vs. Abuser.

*Chapter Eleven*

# The Game Of Living Or Dying

Freud was one of the first pioneers in exploring our two selves. He made this clear in his explanation of libido and mortido. The libido is our drive to live and mortido is our longing to die. As I see it, libido and mortido have nothing to do with birth or death but with the process of living or dying on a daily basis.

*Each day or our life, we decide whether we will use it to live or die. The ultimate aspect of living is creating and striving for perfection like a piece of art.*

One of the existing theories is that this split occurs as the result of the trauma we experience at birth. When the baby is entering the world of air and oxygen, s/he needs to expel the fluid from the lungs. If the person delivering the baby cuts the cord prematurely, the baby's libido gasps for air. The fear of mortido occurs when the water is still in the air passages and prevents the air from entering the lungs. The child is now experiencing the need to live and survive and the fear of dying simultaneously. Throughout your life you have this split. During each incident you experience in life, you will be living life or dying. When you are living each day, you go to work, have new experiences and expand your knowledge. You raise your children and strive to be successful in your career. Life is exciting. Learning to sail, ski or dance is living. In other words, you are creative and happy.

Peter Paul Rubens, a Flemish painter, was explaining the exquisiteness of the luminosity he achieved painting women's skin. He casually said, "I was fortunate. It only took me twenty years to get the effect I wanted." He had a goal and his technique was growing and improving, and in the process he was creating. That is living. Being positive and creative is living until you die. Dying is having what you do deteriorate and you go nowhere. Your world gets smaller and smaller. You have less and less new and different experiences. You narrow your world with physical or mental illnesses. You lose your Money, your memory thus your motivation. You see this happening with older people. They reach a certain age and make a switch. The mores in our society invites this switch. It goes so far as to make it look good. We call it retirement. Over the years, I have treated many depressed people after retirement. Working with the servicemen at Camp Pendleton, I observed a high rate of alcoholism occurs within one year after their twenty-year retirement. Society encourages us to retire, collect Social Security and go on Medicare. What this invites is having someone take care of you, thus slowing down or stopping living and creating. This is dying until you die.

I lived across the street from a retired couple. Chester was eighty-years-old, had black lung disease and was incontinent. Visiting one day, he said, "Theresa, if people ever tell you that you live until you die, don't believe it." "You die until you die." I replied, *The present system in the* "Chester, either live until you die or have the *United States accepts* decency to die." This upset Chester to the ex- *that retirement is an* tent that he threw a book at me. This prompted *open door to dying until* me to go over and hug him. "Chester, I tell you *you die for a majority of* that because I Love you." He said, "What can I *people instead of living* do? I can barely get around." He had led a very *until you die.* interesting life working in the Utah mines and won a middleweight boxing title. I told him to tape his memoirs for his family. I gave him my extra tape recorder and said, "Start talking and I'll type it up for you." Two weeks later, his wife brought the tape recorder back and I knew Chester was going to die. A week later, I awoke in the middle of the night to find all my clocks stopped at one o'clock. The next day coming home from work, my next-door neighbor came over. She said, "Did you know that Chester died?" I asked what time and she said, "One o'clock this afternoon." That was twelve hours after my clocks stopped. It's possible that was Chester's way of saying, "Goodbye." He decided to die when he had enough. It is possible that we all decide when to die by curtailing our living. Dying until you die does make it easier to go when your time is up.

An indication of whether we are living or dying until we die is what we discuss. Living is discussing something you are excited about that you are doing today. Dying is discussing the past or worrying about the future, and what older people revert to. An excellent example of what we discuss when living or dying is shown in the following two poems. A fourteen-year-old yearning to live free, but being told to start dying, wrote the first one. The second poem was by an eighty-three-year-old woman that says, "The next time around I'll do more living and less dying."

### Lament For The Soul

*I would like to run up to you and shout, "I Love YOU,"*
*But I can't, because it would be unethical.*
*I would like to kneel in morning grass and*
*Praise a God who does not require*
*Doxologies and hymns with words I do not understand,*
*But I can't, because it would be sacrilegious.*
*I would like to run in bare feet through*
*Endless sands and grassy hills*
*Throw my face up to the sun,*
*But I can't, because it would be insane.*
*I would like to live my own way and not bother*
*About the rules society makes up*
*To protect themselves from themselves,*
*But I can't, because it would be illegal.*
*I would like to roam through meadows of grass*
*And pick daisies hand in hand, naked with you,*
*But I can't, because it would be immoral.*

*And so I stay in my own little shell,*
*Quite ethical, quite religious, quite sane, quite legal, and*
*Cramping my soul because of a decree of society's*
*That to be myself would be wrong.*
                    Janice Harder, Age 14, Picton, Ontario


## I'd Pick More Daisies

*If I had my life to live over,*
*I'd try to make more mistakes next time.*
*I would relax.*
*I would limber up.*
*I would be sillier than I have been this trip.*
*I know of very few things I would take seriously.*
*I would take more chances.*
*I would be crazier.*
*I would be less hygienic.*
*I would make more changes.*
*I would take more trips.*
*I would climb more mountains, swim more rivers, and*
*watch more sunsets.*
*I would burn more gasoline.*
*I would eat more ice cream and less beans.*
*I would have more actual troubles and fewer imaginary*
*ones.*
*You see, I am one of those people who lives*
*prophylactically and sensibly and sanely*
*hour after hour, day after day.*
*Oh, I've had my moments and, if I had to do it over again*
*I'd have more of them.*
*In fact, I'd try to have nothing else.*
*Just moments, one after another,*
*Instead of living so many years ahead each day.*
*I've been one of those people*
*who never goes anywhere without a*
*thermometer, hot water bottle,*

*a gargle, a raincoat, and a parachute.*
*If I had it to do over again,*
*I would go places and do things*
*and travel lighter than I have.*
*If I had my life to live over,*
*I would start bare-footed earlier in the spring*
*and stay that way later in the fall.*
*I would play hooky more.*
*I wouldn't make such good grades*
*except by accident.*
*I would ride more merry-go-rounds.*
*I'D PICK MORE DAISIES!!*

Nadine Stare, 83 Years Old

These two poems so aptly describe the span that we live out in our lifetime. It shows the ways we stop living and start dying with no-no's and false and negative belief that create our Formula For Failure. When you live aggressively, left-brain, or die passively, right brain, you are creating an environment to play games. Either role will lead to a form of dying, and both parties are fully responsible. Games are your dying process where you cut off the intimacy of Love, the Quality. These are the payoffs to dying whether it is passive or aggressive. When you live and create, using the positive sides of the right and brain, you receive the positive and loving payoffs you deserve. Remember, most of the time we are here is good and beautiful. Look and find a way to stay in the beautiful here and now for longer and longer periods of time to ensure you will live until you die.

*Chapter Twelve*

# The Games Of Life

The Abused vs. The Abuser are participants in the most abusive game there is; between the Abused and the Abuser is the threat of physical harm. Many factors contribute to people playing one of these roles that primarily are modeled by the parents. This is created by the negativity the parent exposes the child to. There are many areas in our society that teaches us to be the Abused or the Abuser personalities. We see it modeled in today's movies and television. The modeling of our politicians does more than anyone can suspect.

*Beliefs of being physically or spiritually destroyed are on the child's mind and based on primitive survival issues that affect how we handle daily situations that arise.*

Much negative connotation comes from the Bible. A depressed young man involved in his religion, brought in his Bible for me to read. I wrote down 123 negative words and phrases in the first fifty pages. They included evil, sinful, perish, wickedness, deceit, shedding man's blood, sex disease, selfish, etc. The saying alone, "An eye for an eye" teaches abuse if there is enough justification and righteousness. There is no excuse for abuse. No action warrants it as we then become the Abuser.

I made an interesting observation in treating the children of the Abused and Abuser personalities. A young man had been beaten and Abused by his father. As an adult, he then consciously and

openly directed his hate and anger toward his father for the abuse he
meted out to him, his brothers, sisters, their mother and friends. It

*Society supports the* was only when under hypnosis that it became
*"Abused" martyr un-* quite clear that he was unconsciously angrier
*aware of the couples se-* and harbored far more resentment toward his
*cret and unknown* passive mother who allowed the abuse. She had
*alliance. They are both* relinquished the responsibility of protecting
*acting out their* her children from an abusive environment. The
*pre-ordained roles set* court regarding child abuse cases where the
*by their parents in* mother did not do anything to stop the abuse
*childhood.* approached me. I found that in prosecuting a
parent that is the Abuser, the prosecution overlooks the Abused parent's responsibility to protect the child. Both parents are equally responsible for protecting themselves and the children. This view is
now starting to hold up in a court of law.

While working with policemen, I found that many times when on
a wife beating call, the wives attacked the policemen when they at-
tempted to stop the husband from beating them. They took the husbands' side when the policemen arrested the husbands for assault
and battery charges. The Abused wife would protect the Abuser husband and withdraw the complaint. The police do not like to take
these cases as there is a lot of work involved writing the cases up,
taking them to court and getting no results.

Abuse is on the increase, especially regarding children. Research
shows that in 1974 there were 60,000 reported child abuse cases. In
1991, there were 2,700,000. In 1971 there were 3,000,000 single
families as compared to the 8,000,000 in 1991. This increase could
have stemmed from the increase in single families and the stress of
survival it created.

***The Abuser Personality*** The "Abuser" personality has the macho
syndrome and believes they are in command as they boss spouse and
kids around. The Abused personalities can be male or female but are
generally attributed to the male because of their macho leanings.
These traits are passed on from generation to generation and are very
difficult to intercept or change.      The Abusers have deep-seated

desires to do to others what was done to them. They are unaware they have become what they hate and are just as helpless as the Abusers that modeled the abuse for them. This is one of the places where men that do not display some of the Abusers' traits are looked on as Wimps and women that become Abusers, are called Bitches. The Abusers are definitely left brain personality at their negative self.

***The Abused Personality***  The Abused personalities play the roles of the Martyrs to perfection. They are the picture of saintliness that is belied by their ability to passively allow someone to be physically, emotionally, verbally or mentally abusive. Almost without exception, they truly believe they have no choice. They will sit quietly with their hands in their lap with bowed heads. At times you will see a faint glimmer of a smile while accepting the abuse. Abused people rarely make eye contact. This role is generally played by women but has been played by men.

*When you Love someone enough and accept s/he without rancor, it invites change of his/her destructive behavior. Loving a person unconditionally does not mean taking verbal, physical, mental or emotional abuse.*

The Abused personalities are like the passive listeners of gossip. Accepting abuses and listening to gossip, they are as responsible as the people doing the abusing or gossiping. At some level, all parties involved want it. The passive acceptance is approval and permission. Many of these women that allow the abuse believe there was nothing they could do about it. I asked one woman, "What would you do if a stranger came into your home and beat you and your child the way your husband did? Would you cook and serve him dinner and spend the night in bed with him making Love?" The Abused adults use the excuse and belief that they were in fear of the Abusers. They truly believe there is no way out and no place to go. They are unaware that healthy people would be terrified to live under these conditions.

There are many subtle ways people invite the abuse without knowing they are doing it. Looking how they do this and stopping it may have the Abusers accelerate their need to abuse and any movement could provoke them to hit the Abused personalities. A raise of an eyebrow would be enough provocation. The Abused personality uses these subtle forms to aggravate without any conscious awareness. Outsiders viewing a couple like this, automatically blame the Abusers.

***The Abuser Solution***   The Abusers needs to know they can change these destructive and negative traits. It takes awareness that the Abused personalities will use any ploy necessary to get the Abusers to hit them. It's difficult for people to grasp this concept thus making it difficult to resolve or change it. To know there is no blame and work with the knowledge that both parties are responsible in every game goes a long way to achieving a lasting solution.

A young man, Enoc, was in therapy because he had physically abused his wife and children for years. After hearing me lecture, he called and wanted to stop being an Abuser. He became aware of the control his wife, as the Abused, had over him. He was unaware that she could only have this control with his permission. I told him to be aware to what extent his wife would go to get him to hit her. He said, "Dr. Benjamin, you are wrong on this one. She told me if I stopped hitting her and the children, we would have a perfect marriage."

When Enoc starting gaining confidence that he could give up the role of Abuser, Timi accelerated even more. She actually pursued him trying to get him to hit her. He brought it up in therapy. He said, "Dr. Benjamin, I work diligently at not ever hitting anyone again. Timi has gone off the wall and pursues me. She sticks her face into my face and shouts, "Hit me, Hit me. I dare you to hit me. You have gotten chicken lately," as she's pointing her finger at her chin. When I finally hit her she leaves me alone. It makes me wonder why I don't just hit her the first time and get it over with. To prevent himself from doing this, he made a decision that each time she provoked him to hit her he would calmly leave the house and in this way eventually conquered his game.

***The Abused Solution***   The most difficult areas to resolve Abused people's need for abuse is to have them accept that there is a solution. They are not "stuck." They do have say and support to stop being abused. It is true, they will not get as much attention as being abused provides them. When they bypass this need for support for a negative problem, they will then start talking and meaning what they say to stop being abused.

When Abused personalities mean what they say and not stop making idle threats, the Abuser will know it. When they tell the Abusers three times, at most, that they will not accept abuse and have not acted on it, it is not only an idle threat but an out and out invitation to continue the game. Research in abuse has shown that usually abuse stops when the Abused personalities decide never to accept abuse again and prosecutes the Abusers. A research done by the New York Police found that when the Abused personalities prosecute the Abusers, eighty percent of the time the Abusers do not hit them again. Abused people need to use the support available to them and are found in almost every city in the United States. There are centers to stay at, police to protect them and family members to help. In utilizing these supports in a positive way, they resolve the problem of being abused for life.

***Summary*** The game of Abused and Abuser, like all games, indicate that they are using their Formula For Failure to limit their Love, Quality and Money in life. Becoming aware of the games, intercepting and replacing them with their Formula For Success results in the abuse stopping for the both of them.

When someone fears being in the presence of another, it is common sense to leave immediately and get help. That is what healthy minded people without that kind of anger do. They do not subject themselves to that kind of treatment nor allow children to be abused. I saw this in myself and somewhere in my depths I refused to let it happen. My husband "spanked" my son who was three years old. I saw the black and blue marks on his body while giving him his bath. It broke my heart and I took my stand. I also accepted my responsibility that I allowed it. I went out to my husband, and said, "You have lost the privilege of being a father. If you touch or reprimand that child again, you will have to kill me first.

One morning I faced my complicity in this, and I said, "Enough. You are going to get out." I had no Money, no friends in California, and no parents on either my side or my husband's side of the family.

I headed for the mayor's office in Los Angeles with my children who were one and four years old. I sat in his office and demanded aid and protection. I no longer needed the abuse.

I went to an attorney and instantly earned his respect. He asked me if I had food or Money, and I said, "No." He lent me ten dollars. I assured him that I would pay it back with interest. He said, "I know that or I would not have lent it." I do not know where I got the wisdom to act on this. I do know I have never allowed that kind of abuse again to this day. I subjected myself to physical abuse the first twenty-four years of my life and no longer had any need for it for myself or to put on others.

When Abused or Abusers decide to change their abusive pattern to maintain the relationship, both need to change simultaneously. If only one changes, the other accelerates the behavior to bring back the relationship to the status quo of Abused and Abuser. If only one changes, the relationship will dissolve, as the other party still needs to play. Both parties unconsciously agree to play this game from the first day they meet. We are responsible to communicate what we will or will not allow.

This game of Abused and Abuser like all games can end. The goal is there when both parties take responsibility to bring it to a close forever. One way is to squarely and honestly look at what it is doing to children, and use the Love within to make the change. This is when their Formula For Success takes over and they prevent passing these negative traits on for another generation. This is true Love and Joy.

**Front Seat Drivers vs. Back Seat Drivers**

People who are at war need to act it out some place. Many times it is with children, as in the Abused vs. Abuser Game, or Money as in the Givers vs. Takers Game using them as weapons or ammunition in the battle. The battle can reach immediate dangerous levels when the war is brought into a car. This is a method to act out the opposing roles of the game within the relationship. I was surprised to learn how common this game is.

This was verified for me when I saw the cartoon, *Non Sequitur,* by Wiley in the Washington Post Writer's Group. It shows a couple in an airplane in the middle of space. The man said, "No, I don't want to pull over and ask directions. But if you'd learn to read a map, we wouldn't have gotten lost!" At the bottom of the cartoon it says, "When NASA sends up husbands and wives."

When I have a couple in therapy playing the Front Seat Drivers vs. Back Seat Drivers game, I check carefully to see if they are merely aggravating one another or if it involves physical harm. I use the standards I set for First, Second and Third Degree payoffs in a game. The degree of the pay off is a clue to the depth of the person's anger and the danger of their game. I ask how many tickets and accidents the Front Seat Driver has had and the amount and degree of injuries. In this way, I determine the seriousness of the game for First degree and negotiate. If it is Second or Third Degree, where there is harm, I have them agree to take separate cars until they have made peace and stopped the game.

The Front Seat Driver vs. Back Seat Driver game between Linda and her husband, Delman, went like this. They were driving along enjoying the scenery when Delman takes the wrong exit. He then acts disoriented and does not know how to get back on the freeway. He makes a wrong turn and has to turn around. He backs up and bangs into a post, makes an illegal U-turn and gets a ticket. If Linda tells him where the turn off is or where to go, Delman gets upset. He accuses her of "starting it again." He says, "If you didn't get on my case, I wouldn't get so tense." However, if she doesn't tell him, he misses the turnoff several times. In fact, he misses them until she starts instructing him again. He also gets angry with her for not telling him he was passing the off-ramp.

This is the essence of the Back Seat Drivers vs. Front Seat Drivers. They can't win when they are in the car. The Back Seat Drivers are at the mercy of the Front Seat Drivers who are unable to relinquish the power they now have over them. Like all games, this is a power play that developed when the Front Seat Drivers made the first frightening move and experienced the power over the Back Seat Driver.

***Front Seat Driver Personality***  The Front Seat Drivers are usually passive, aggressive personalities that act out their aggression behind the wheel of a car. The power of this position for passive personalities far outweighs the power in any other game. It renders Back Seat Drivers, who are the aggressive personality, powerless in the most blatant way. The Front Seat Drivers get in the car in a most affable manner with no sign of their game.

I recall a gentleman, Maurice, calling me for dinner. Getting in his car he was open, friendly, bright and articulate. Once in the car he was disoriented, drove erratically, speeding and slamming his brakes and missing his turn-off several times. I thought of all the patients I had that have Front Seat Driver vs. Back Seat Driver games. I decided to remain silent and noticed that this made him miss even more turnoffs and drive more erratically. I asked him how long he lived in the area. He said, "Fifteen years." So he did know the area and had no reason to be missing turnoffs. When I got home safe and sound, I gently asked him, "When we go out again, will it be OK if I drive my own car?" What I did here was to not play Back Seat Driver with my aggressive personality and resolved it to not occur again.

This man's driving in an erratic manner is pretty blatant, and it is easy to recognize it is a game. However, sometimes the Front Seat Driver and Back Seat Driver games occur so subtly it is difficult to know if the Front Seat Drivers are really lost, or playing the Front Seat Driver vs. Back Seat Driver game. Getting lost while driving can happen. Asking for information openly, does not constitute nor is it indicative of Front Seat Driver vs. Back Seat Driver game. However, if disorientation is evident, I investigate if it is real, an invitation to the game or if the person has a serious disturbance.

On my third date with a man, we went out to dinner. Almost instantly, I picked up the change in his driving. We were discussing a very interesting subject when he started to act distracted. He stretched his head forward peering intently out the window. In very rapid succession, he stepped on the brake, started to turn right, then left and stopped at a green light. He muttered something about what way to turn having come to a stop in the middle lane. He then eased over to the left lane to turn in that direction. The light changed from green to red then green again without him moving and he acted totally lost and disoriented. He then made a harrowing right hand turn across three lanes of traffic.

Up to this point, he showed no signs of disorientation or loss. He was a capable and responsible man, and was now acting extremely immature. I remained silent through it all. The turn he took was the wrong one and we went around in circles for a while. He finally asked for help. I intuitively knew this man has played this game for a long time. I gently told him, "Don, I do not give directions to a driver unless asked for it straight. Pull into that gas station. They will help you." This led to a discussion that lasted through dinner. He denied it was a game. I agreed he was probably right, but in case it was a game it would stop here. And so it did! This is what happens when Back Seat Drivers are willing to speak up lovingly and invite the Front Seat Drivers to look at their game.

***Back Seat Driver Personality*** You will recognize a "Back Seat Driver" as they are an aggressive personality. They sit up straight in the seat as if they are driving and swivel their head a lot. They look bright and alert and when annoyed or late, insist on a fast, aggressive driving. If you get in their way they roll down the window, yell at you or give you the finger. This is the typical left-brain action of Back Seat Driver personalities. You can see how annoyed they get when the passive slow Front Seat Drivers are driving and acting lost and helpless.

Linda's role in playing the Back Seat Driver went back to the early days of her marriage to Delman, fifteen years ago. She is a highly critical person and difficult to talk to when she pulls her righteous act. Delman's defense was passivity. He acted this out by playing dumb and lost although he is a successful businessman with a fine mind. He discovered a perfect way to get back at Linda by exaggerating his passive role behind the wheel of a car that dares her to accelerate her Back Seat Driver role.

Typical Back Seat Drivers find it impossible to stay out of the game. They are caught into "making" the Front Seat Drivers see their incompetence and change before they are killed. The Back Seat

Drivers scold, direct, correct, and say anything that comes to mind to get the passive Front Seat Driver to succumb. Back Seat Drivers cannot accept they are powerless in the face of Front Seat Drivers.

***Front Seat Driver Solution*** To resolve this game, Front Seat Drivers need an awareness that was obliterated when this game started. To play the Front Seat Drivers game, it is necessary that they shut down their common sense, their fear of an accident, or the anxiety it creates in another person. To bring this game to a halt, they need to access their responsible, intelligent self and bring it with them.

They also need a plan on what they will do or what they want others to do when they slide into the Front Seat Drivers behavior again. Without this awareness, they will continue it all their lives. The Back Seat Drivers know Front Seat Drivers are not stupid or irresponsible and find it difficult to believe that they do not know when they slide into the disoriented Front Seat Drivers' act.

Front Seat Drivers need to bring this awareness to mind such as putting a note on the dash, stopping the car when they make a wrong turn and determine to bring their good driving selves back into the car. When Back Seat Drivers starts reprimanding Front Seat Drivers, the Front Seat Drivers need to immediately apologize, make the shift to awareness and drive sensibly. They can tell the Back Seat Drivers what word or phrase to use to make them aware that they are playing Front Seat Driver again. This needs to be said in a calm, loving supportive manner and discussed openly and honestly. There are many options, but the most powerful one is a decision to stop the role forever before someone is harmed.

***Back Seat Driver Solution*** The most powerful stand Back Seat Drivers can take is to be quiet. When compelled to speak, do it in a soft and loving way. Since you are the talker, be the one that initiates a resolution. It is vital that Back Seat Drivers do this from a sensible and non-judgmental place and not in a car.

In the case of Delman and Linda, they were both willing to look at their game. However, it was Linda, the Back Seat Driver who took the initiative to address it. In therapy, they began to learn how to settle this Front Seat Driver vs. Back Seat Driver game. I asked Delman, "Do you or do you not want Linda to instruct you while you are driving?" He said, "Yes, if I am missing a turn off." Linda asked, "Then why do you get mad when I do?" I then instructed Linda to ask Delman, "How am I to know when you want me to tell you what to do?" When he was unable to answer this question, they agreed that Linda would not say anything, or she would take her own car. When Linda kept her word and remained silent, Delman's driving got more erratic. He accelerated his disoriented act. At one point he almost had an accident when he got lost and pulled out in front of another car. They finally arranged an agreement in writing of what to do if Linda did get in Delman's car and he acted lost and disoriented. She would either drive the car herself or get out and take a taxi, if possible. If the game still continued they would take separate cars or she would drive until they were sure they had given up this game.

***Summary*** This is one of the most difficult games to bring to a halt. One is never sure if Front Seat Drivers are really lost and disoriented or playing at it. The Back Seat Drivers are unable to stay out of it and find that any corrections or help is useless.

*When you do not speak up and say how you will resolve an issue the first time it occurs, you have automatically given permission to play the dangerous game of "Front Seat Drivers" vs. "Back Seat Drivers."*

Whether they are "real" games or not is irrelevant since the goal is to not start them if there is a possibility of one existing. This game, like all others, plays out our Formula For Failure. This consists of a stimulus that creates anger, which can be at someone that is driving in a disoriented manner or anything that has occurred recently that upset you. When they know this cycle within themselves and acknowledge it, their perception will automatically change and the game will cease. This process is especially vital in Front Seat/Back Seat driver's games where someone can be seriously harmed.

Once the game is accepted at the beginning of the relationship, without awareness and intervention, it is on for life. They need to make it known the first time the game shows itself whether playing the Front Seat or Back Seat Driver's role. It either stops at that point or there will be no relationship. Fortunately, most drivers on the road stay out of this game however, it is far more prevalent than we realize. My observation has shown it is usually played out at a First Degree level. When both parties look at what they are doing and find a solution, the game stops.

### Givers vs. Takers

The games of Givers and Takers are the most frequently played games and disrupt our lives more than any other game on a day-to-day basis. Other games may be more violent at the Second or Third Degree levels of a problem. However, Givers and Takers games, are played out at First Degree levels most of the time. It is the game that we fight the hardest to prove we are right and end up investing the most time, energy and Money. The Takers are created from the moment a child is trying to tie his shoe and the parent takes over and does it for him.

The traditional relationship role dictates from birth that we have to care and do for others to the extent of being responsible for each other's happiness. This inundation to do for others starts with our parents making us relinquish our favorite toy to a friend. Then society, teachers, and churches carry the belief on. It is just expected that we will be generous and give and help others at the expense of ourselves. This is expounded again and again, adding the guilt of being greedy, selfish and even sinful when reluctant to help someone. All fail to convey that people need much wisdom to know when to help and when to stop helping someone. No one teaches us at what point we may be contributing to making and keeping other people helpless.

The word "care" has many dimensions in the game of Givers and Takers. When care is given and taken sensibly, for a particular reason and with set limits, it is healthy. When we don't care if someone's black, a homosexual, short, or slow, that is healthy. When care is Love, hugs, listening, that is healthy. Our belief systems on Love and caring are the strongest ones we have, so I wish to elaborate on the confusion that surrounds it. Too often Givers are trying to prove and show their loving and caring selves and start doing for others and become Givers.

In essence they are saying, "I am a true and loving person and care for you, and I want to help you. I don't understand why you push me so far which forces me to keep helping you or abandon you."

Takers are saying, in essence, "You have got to help me. I can't help being where I am at and you shouldn't have any expectations of me in this position. If you were truly, loving, you would understand this." At this point, both parties start to believe, "Nothing will ever change. Nothing I do works." In this way, they re-establish the status quo by giving and accepting help again and once more the game is on.

These two personalities are either family members or marry and blame each other for the roles each play. Both are unaware that together they form a perfect union for the game and are equally responsible for the role that was chosen early in life. Each of them would get an idea how ingrained these roles are by deciding to reverse them. It is impossible for the Taker to become the Giver and the Giver to become the Taker. The power of their belief systems dictates their behavior and makes them a slave to their roles.

***The Giver Personality*** The Givers are co-dependent personalities that are constantly at the mercy of the Takers of the world. As Givers taking care of the Takers, a co-dependency develops that keeps Givers continuously involved in relationships with troubled people. The Givers' self-worth, self-esteem and purpose in life come from assuming the responsibility for people's feelings and behavior. As a co-dependent personality, Givers need troubled, needy, or dependent people to validate their existence. Their personalities are inexplicably drawn to those that are perpetually troubled be it a minor disturbance, a serious problem, or a chemical or drug dependency problem.

*My mother used to say, "When you do someone a favor, you are lucky if they don't kick you."*

No matter how much they wish to deny it, when they help someone, they are conveying one of the following messages. "I am more capable and responsible than you are." "I have more knowledge than you do." "I have more Money than you do." "I'm a kinder and nicer person than you are." This ends up alienating the very people they most wish to help. Being Givers and doing for others gives them a feeling of power and control over another human being and is often difficult to relinquish. To experience the power it has, if the Givers stopped today they would feel the pull to keep helping and believe they have no choice and they are "stuck" to help. However, when they encounter people that do not want their help, they often view them as ungrateful. They go so far as to tell people that do not want help that they should learn to accept help.

Without awareness, when Takers decide to change, Givers, or co-dependents, will sever the relationship. At first they will feel a sense of relief. It will be a load off their back. However, in time they will either lure the Takers back helping them again or find other troubled people to start the helping cycle all over again. True Givers look for every opportunity to do for others regardless of whether they want it or need it. They take over cleaning someone's house or helping him/her out of trouble. They are giving of their time and Money. It is as natural as breathing to them. They simply cannot mind their own business. In many families, Givers create irresponsible members; it can be financially, emotionally, physically ill, mentally ill, or a good old scapegoat in the process of helping them.

*There is a difference between being nice and being good. When doing a good act, rarely is it mentioned or made known to anyone. When you are nice, you make sure your acts are known and want recognition at some level within.*

In interviewing employees who are "key" workers in an office that volunteer all sorts of tasks, they often feel frustrated and unappreciated. The knowledge that their help may be annoying to others wipes them out. As a secretary using this gung-ho approach during my St. Theresa phase, I did any work that was on anyone's desk. I helped whoever needed help, as I was a true Giver in every sense of the word! One day I walked into the coffee room and heard, "That Theresa is a pain in the neck." It hurt to hear this so I started to slink away but I decided to go back and face them. I told them what I heard and asked what it was that I did to annoy them. They told me that I invaded their territory and desks because I took it upon myself to file their correspondence, type their dictation or make telephone calls for them. This stunned me as I believed I was helping them. They said, "You do help, but at least ask. We don't always want you to help us."

Society defines Givers as generous, nice, kind people. Years ago, my therapist, Dr. Don Hanley, asked me, "Theresa, could you ever be altruistic?" In all honesty, I had to admit I could not. If I wanted to do for others in its truest altruistic sense without any recognition, I would simply put cash in an envelope and mail it to a needy person. I would also be sure I left no fingerprints on it and never tell a soul as long as I lived. I must admit, when I do a good deed, I need to let someone know, somehow or sometime, and eventually have an expectation of praise for my generous gesture.

Even when Takers do want to return the favor, it is difficult to know what will be a return of equal value for what the Givers have in their head that will truly compensate them. When Givers do for others, they are rarely aware they expect anything in return. They are unable to acknowledge this even to their deepest self, that they want at least a "Thank You." Takers, prepare yourself for the day that Givers remind you of the help or tell others about it. When this occurs and the Takers say, "I wasn't aware you were expecting me to return the favor," Givers will instantly say, "No, of course I don't. That's not what I meant." Givers need to check if they have a residual of doubt that Takers will never appreciate their help and repay their kindness. Most likely, they will be asking for more help next week. It is the Givers responsibility to say, "I will not do what you ask without having an expectation. I will end up getting on your case. It will not be fair to you or me."

Perceiving themselves as selfish or feeling guilty for not helping others will mar the Givers' Love for the Takers, the Quality of the relationship and certainly Money. It definitely curbs the potential and ability to make the Money for the Givers and the Takers, or keep it when they do make it. This is often used as a reason why Givers can't continue helping. Givers may start fretting that others may perceive them as greedy and selfish, which is a distorted perception. Those that feel selfish can change their perception by asking themselves, "Are people who keep helping people until they become helpless, generous or kind?" There is a book for those of you who are sensitive to others' opinion. The title alone impacts much wisdom, *What You Think of Me is None of My Business* by Terry Cole Whittaker. This sensible thinking reminds me of Ralph Waldo Emerson's thoughtful comment that "All sensible people are selfish."

People may appear to accept their giving roles, but no one knows if Givers are carrying resentment in their souls and desire to be compensated for years of giving. Certain events, like a divorce, oftentimes bring these resentments to the surface. This occurred when a patient came in for therapy and truly did not know she had expectations. She did kind acts all her life and was a true Giver in every sense of the word. She served her husband faithfully helping in many areas including working in his office. Her resentment made itself known when she learned he wanted a divorce. She recalled every good deed she did saying, "I gave him my time, did his bookkeeping, gave him my Love, devotion and loyalty and my paycheck when I worked." I informed her, "You did not give anything. You lived it. If you gave it, you would not have remembered the good deeds for twenty years. They would have been just part of living, not giving."

*My mother used to say, "When someone says they are doing something for you for your own good, run for your life or pay for life."*

Givers internally record every deed they have done for others. Therefore, isn't it possible she only lent it to collect the loan when she needed it, such as her husband leaving her? Givers can check out if they have an expectation by going within their own minds to ask, "Is there any part of me that wants some kind of recognition or return if I do this? If they listen very carefully, a voice will definitely respond. If they do hear a nagging voice, they need to clearly state this expectation to the Takers by saying, "I'm willing to do this for you, however, I want you to pay me $75 or your help in cleaning my back yard." In the bible, Jeremiah 22:13, states:

> *Woe unto him that buildeth his house by unrighteousness, that useth his neighbor's service without wages, and giveth him not for his work.*

Givers who help people financially over time, start to feel there is no place they can stop. Rarely will they hear, "Thanks for helping me but I can't let you continue." On the contrary, the longer Givers have helped the more upset and angry the Takers become when the Givers cease helping. Most of all, Takers invariably believe that anytime Givers decide to stop giving Money is when they most needed it, and the worse time they could have picked to stop. They are unable to see the whole picture and will put themselves in this position again and again. It is difficult for them to fathom that their actions are for the express purpose of getting others to pay for them. They believe they want the Money because of the circumstance, and it is impossible for them to see that they created the circumstances to get the Money.

*My mother used to say, "If you do people favors once or twice and stop, they may be annoyed or not notice. However, if you have helped them twenty times and stop, you'll get your kick."*

To stop helping someone financially, Givers usually say, "I don't have the Money," or "I would help you but I have to pay for mom's nursing home." The Givers also create problems in their lives where they actually lose Money to justify not helping others. This can be getting fired or losing Money in investments. Most management books say that when people quit or are terminated from their job, they have been unconsciously planning it for some time. Many times to relieve the burden of helping, Givers will become physically ill or mentally depressed. They justify not giving the Money. They also hope the Taker will recognize the situation and not ask for any more Money. This rarely happens.

***The Taker Personality*** In spite of the teachings of parents, church and society to be Givers, and to do for others, there is a segment of the population that plays the opposite role as Takers. There can be no Givers without Takers and vice versa. There is a possibility that Takers are here to accommodate the Givers and give meaning to their lives, or the Givers created them to give themselves purpose.

The Takers convey irresponsibility by playing stupid, dumb, helpless, dropping things, shrugging their shoulders and numerous other signals to invite the helper to jump in and help them. As adults,

Takers may not hold a steady job or may become alcoholics, drug addicts, develop a physical or mental illness or just generally be unhappy and troubled to maintain the Takers role of being helpless.

My Italian friend, Roberto, has a fine mind, is well read and can match me in any conversation in philosophy, psychology, etc. He has a big investment in not being successful on any job. Even though he is quite capable, he has been fired many times or worked himself into a state that he felt he had no other choice but to quit. The process he used to achieve the result of not working was to play dumb. He used a wide-eyed look, shrugged his shoulder, outstretched his hands and said, "What's going on." One day when he put on his famous blank, helpless look, I said to him, "Roberto, how did you get the "Dumb Italian" look down to such perfection?"

When my gardener left, I offered Roberto a job to do my yard. I did not believe that he would pull the "Dumb Italian" act on me. He was aware that I knew how intelligent he was. Within two days of hiring him, he pulled many flower plants I loved thinking they were weeds. In quick succession, he left the water running, broke a water line and set the sprinkler system for an hour thus flooding my yard. It was disastrous and I had no recourse but to fire him. His act was so perfect that I almost doubted my own perception of his intelligence. This was in spite of the fact that I had known him for eight years. If I had viewed giving him a job as helping him because he needed work, I would have assumed he didn't appreciate it. His need to fail was greater than the excitement of finding a job. He was a natural Taker and used his dumb and helpless role to have others help him. He lived with his mother, a natural Giver, who was constantly giving him Money while he looked for the next job.

Takers make sure they never have anything to give. Many years ago playing my Giver role, I helped my girlfriend who consistently ran out of Money. I gave her food, made clothes for her or lent her Money. She always assured me that if she had it, she would give me the shirt off her back. Relating this to my therapist, he said, "Theresa, don't you know she will never have a shirt to give you." I got upset because it was hard for me to believe it was true. However, in the coming weeks, I noticed I purchased shoes for $10.95 and she bought a pair for $29.95. After purchasing these shoes, she still expected me to pay for lunch as she did not have enough Money. I then became consciously aware that I had no family, child support or help from anyone. She had her family providing clothes, sending Money and receiving child support. Thus, I learned that Takers never do have it to give. She did not do it purposely or was dishonest. She simply played her Taker role as I played my Giver role.

When parents are the Givers they often produce children that are Takers through constant criticisms. The child then feels that the Givers can't do enough for them to make up for the years of misery caused by their constant criticisms. They want other people to see the "real" Giver's personality and will create situations to get the Givers to start complaining or withdraw help. They then prove to others that you Givers are not as generous or loving as you wish to project. Know that when Takers become self-sufficient and happy, they are destroying the evidence that proves to others what a difficult childhood or marriage they had experienced from Givers. This is why Takers find if difficult to create a happy life. Any happiness the Givers may have, creates anger in Takers as they have an inner need to remind the Givers, and any one else, of what the Givers were really like constantly putting their nose in the Takers' business and then not helping.

I listened to a thirty-two year old man who was living with his mother berating her after she financially aided him for ten years and wanted to stop. She made an appointment to discuss how to end their Giver and Taker roles. He was to look at what he was willing to do to become self-sufficient and financially responsible. She was to present a plan on how long she will help and what she was willing to do to extricate herself from his complete dependence on her. It soon became clear that he firmly believed his mother should understand and continue supporting him. He declared he had not finished his education and had no way to support himself.

He soon discovered his mother's intent when she lovingly and repeatedly told him she was going to bring it to an end. She told him she would give him six months support to work out his problems and he lashed out viciously. He told all the abuses she did to hurt him that ruined his life. There was no end to the terrible accusations this man made and believed was done to him. I had made it clear to both of them that no matter what he said, she was to answer, "That must have been a terrible experience for you to go through as a child. You now need to decide how you are going to support yourself." The more she lovingly maintained her position that she would no longer be helping him financially after six months, the angrier and uglier he got until he threatened suicide stating it was his only way out. This is acceleration and pressure to get Money that he mistakenly took for Love and caring. To him, his mother's stand was in essence saying, "I no longer Love you."

Both Givers and Takers need to look at what solutions and options they can apply to extricate themselves from these negative roles that will last a lifetime if not brought to a halt.

***The Giver Solution***　　At some point, Givers need to take a stand and say "No" and be prepared for any response or action from Takers who are in constant need of help. They may accelerate to extreme levels to force Givers to keep giving and will apply so much pressure that Givers start believing they cannot extricate themselves. When Givers find themselves in this type of dilemma, they need to have the wisdom and temerity to stay with their decision. If they do not, they then need to accept the responsibility for contributing to the Taker's helplessness and find a way to live contentedly within the context of the game of Giver and Taker.

When people's lives are at stake, then Givers need to volunteer to support that person without complaint or martyrdom whether it is directly or hiring others to do it. It becomes irrelevant whether the person is actually helpless or deliberately acting helpless to get the Givers' help. If Givers believe Takers will commit suicide, they are in the same situation as parents taking care of a retarded child. Keep in mind, it is difficult to know when it is an act and when the person really is helpless, which is rare. If it is real or Givers elect to not take a chance, they need a plan they can live with. Parents of retarded children or fatality ill family members have this responsibility for a lifetime. The more they accept this fact and integrate it into their daily lives, the less stressful and unhappy they will be. This stops martyr roles and the Giver and Taker battle even though Givers are still giving.

Givers that show care by doing things for others, need to learn to inquire whether or not they have that privilege. Takers need to stop accepting help and learn to get care in positive ways and make a decision that they will never tell anyone they are in need of help. Learning when the help they are asking for is real or contrived is healthy. Takers or Givers were never taught when caring and helping goes negative. Refusing to play these roles takes awareness, tenacity, determination and Love. The most valuable information to gather to stop this game is to know the Giver and Taker personalities so you will rarely be deluded by either role. This includes knowing their motivations, needs and goals.

It is interesting that Givers can help with Love, and Quality, but it is the Money that is requested and given. Givers need to say to Takers that constantly borrow Money in a loving way, "I have the Money and I'm electing not to give it to you." This is a powerful stand for Givers' freedom. The usual stand is to lecture in a whiny voice, "This is the last time I'm helping you." It does no good. Takers have heard it all. Saying "No," lovingly reverses the role of Givers.

One of my assignments at school was to say "No" to the next person that asked me for a favor. I was not to give any explanation. A few days later a friend called to tell me her car was broken down about five minutes from my house. She asked if I would come to pick her up. I immediately thought, "This is different. It is not a favor that would put me out." I did not allow myself to be deterred from my school assignment and said my simple, "No." There was a long silence on the other end and she finally said, "Okay." It is near impossible to explain the range of feelings within me. It was an incredible experience. The response I gave felt cold and hard and she did think I was angry at something she did. My feelings of anxiety were intense and only subsided when I could tell her it was an experiment and assignment for school. This taught me a valuable lesson. Saying "No" without Love and understanding was the same problem as over-giving. I concluded, when you do not feel like doing something for someone, you need to refuse with Love, gentleness and firmness.

Bertrand Russell said, "A sense of duty is useful in work but offensive in personal relations."

To break the addiction of being Givers, they need to take into consideration and apply the following elements. These are things which are important to know:

• Caring and helping others requires the wisdom to know if you are giving genuine help or whether you are rendering the person helpless.
• Ask the person's permission to help her/him with set rules and guidelines for repayment.
• Helping someone is a privilege and not your righteous duty as a Giver.
• When you help, have no expectations in return other than those requested.
• What plan you will give to the Taker if s/he doesn't repay.
• Listening to a problem beyond a certain length of time helps the Taker keep it.
• When it is none of your business and time to lovingly step out of it.
• You will cease any interference or criticism into the person's problems.
• You will lovingly say, "I trust you will find a way to resolve it. Your problems in a positive fashion."

Givers change by examining their beliefs and thoughts on giving to others. They need to check out the exact point they start feeling resentful. This is difficult to detect since they do not believe they are the type of person that resents doing for others. They rationalize it is because the Takers expected too much from them and were unreasonable. The earlier they detect the resentment or irritation of helping someone, the easier it is to stop it. When Givers learn to say, "I am feeling resentful and prefer not giving you a loan. Feeling as I do,

I may berate you or talk about you to others. It's not fair to either one of us." This goes a long way toward stopping the game.

***The Taker Solution*** The Takers first issue to address is giving up their independence and autonomy. Both are vital elements to a healthy outlook in life. These elements of responsibility and independence have a direct influence on feeling fulfilled, and give life purpose and meaning. With meaning and purpose they will not expect others to help them. Without meaning and purpose they will feel empty and expect others to fill the void within them, which often is fulfilled when someone is helping them unaware that it only relieves them temporarily. They need to grow and become happy by using positive methods within.

*When you want a resolution to a problem, you will find it with or without help. If you do not want a resolution, no help will ever reach you.*

Takers believe others should help them when they are down. They go into rages when Givers says "No." It is the Takers' responsibility to lovingly say, "I appreciate the help you gave me and I have decided to resolve my problems on my own." Are you aware that the chance of Givers surmising that this sounds ungrateful upon hearing it is very high? They may also feel discounted and upset when the Taker says, "No." This is taking away their purpose in life to help others. The Takers' role changes when they examine their beliefs and thoughts that had them adopt the role. Taking the responsibility to become self-reliant, helps the process. They need to feel the humiliation of taking from others year after year. To break the addiction of being Takers, review and apply the following concepts and know you will:

- Cease asking for help.
- No longer put your self in a position to need help.
- Give up saying, "I can't help it, it's not my fault."
- Hold your head up and use the natural pride of self and lovingly say, "I will find a way."
- No longer make your problems known to anyone except for a resolution.

- Repay help you ask for, when a true emergency requiring help arises.
- Trust that you will take the responsibility to resolve any problem by yourself.

Takers can change the game by concentrating on not asking for help, refrain from letting others know they need it and refuse it when it is given. They may hear, "I was only trying to help you," which is an often-heard phrase. When Givers offer Takers something, the Takers need to look the person in the eye and say, "I prefer taking care of it myself." If they got in too deep and need the help to survive, they can present a plan on how they will repay them with a set date. When Takers actually pay the Givers back, they have taken the first step to changing. Takers, need to check if they genuinely want a resolution to break the Takers game, if they are willing pay for the necessary information to resolve it and if they will use it when it is given to them.

***Summary*** Givers or Takers need to learn how to break the game and plan how they will do it. If both of them decide to change and grow, it is a bonus and it is much easier. However, if one refuses to change, the other needs to break the game without the person's cooperation. To do anything with the purpose of changing other people is self-defeating. When the change does not occur, both parties have created another area of dissension.

It is vital for Givers and Takers to look for ways to resolve the issues. Both can avoid scolding or criticizing others and to mind their own business by not giving or taking help. Love is respecting other peoples' value systems. It is accepting they have the right to believe what they believe. Love is not what either parties think others should believe or feel or how to live. Love is asking people what they need to resolve their problems. It takes wisdom for Givers to help others positively and for the Takers to know when to stop taking. When Givers give something, it's not their business what the Takers do with it.

An example of a Giver having an expectation occurred when I gave my son an expensive wristwatch for Christmas. I believed I was giving it in the truest sense of giving. When he opened the gift he said, "I'd like to give this to my friend, Gary. Are you comfortable with that?" I had a range of emotions because I wanted my son to have it. When I told him this he said something that was so profound. He said, "Well, you did not really "give" it to me to do as I please. You gave it to me to do what would please you." And, of course, he was right. It took me four months before I could completely give him the watch without any negative feelings. I called him and said, "Of course you can give it to Gary. It's your watch."

*Givers: trust yourself and risk taking a stand of not being a "Giver" and helping someone. Takers: Love yourself enough that you can give up being a "Taker" and help yourself.*

To know the true addiction of the roles selected as Givers or Takers, they can play the opposite of what they are. Takers can become Givers and Givers can become Takers. In this way, they will learn what is really involved in the two roles and expand their limits in Love, Quality and Money. In other words, reverse the role. Givers learn to ask and accept help, act as though they can't do it and don't know what their going to do next. They can bumble or lose their job. This is inconceivable to Givers.

Takers can play the role of being independent, lovingly and confidently refusing to accept help and feel the humiliation of acting helpless and accepting and expecting others to give to them. They can speak up and say, "I prefer handling this myself," and mean it and do it with no excuses. They can start giving and helping others. This is inconceivable to Takers. Oftentimes, we think the Givers are right and the Takers are wrong, however, when they connect with each other, neither one of them are willing to let go. It is a destructive game and both are responsible. When either party thinks it is the other party's fault and believe that under those circumstances they do not need to do anything to resolve the problems, then the game will continue to enhance their problems.

I found all games are stopped when the person starts creating something. It can be a family, a business, or a new job. They can create a piece of art and find their worth and purpose there rather than playing the Giver vs. Taker games to find purpose and go on to expand their limits in Love, Quality and Money. If neither party is willing to change their roles or want a resolution, there is nothing anyone can do. Both parties believe if they meet the right people, their problems will be solved. The truth is that when they are ready to solve their problem they find the teacher who will provide the direction.

### Frigid vs. Impotent

*It seems that our Creator made babies but the "Devil" made sex desirable.*

The main ploy in the Sex Game is to withdraw sex by playing Frigid vs. Impotent. There are many variations of this game you bring to bed. When you withdraw sex by getting Frigid or Impotent you are using the strongest weapon that exists to retaliate against another person and still be in First Degree. Generally, women, in their traditional virgin role, used frigidity more than men used impotency. Impotency usually shows itself later in life. It is as though the man said, "You denied me all my life, now I deny you." This usually occurs when women no longer fear getting pregnant and as they develop a more liberal attitude toward sex. Today, with the liberated sex attitude in women, impotency is on the rise and frigidity is on the decline.

The passive Frigid and Impotent players generally need an aggressive partner. These roles were derived from the numerous "No No's" received as a child, regarding their body and sexuality. They learned very early in life to become ashamed of their genitals and bodily functions whether it was sexual or not. Any show of them was followed by a reprimand or gales of laughter. Any discussion of sex was considered bad, very serious or funny with ribald joking. How can we grow up and feel comfortable about these functions? These reactions also taught you just how powerful it can be to use, abuse or deny anything to do with sex. As an adult, people are still outraged and reprimand you or laugh at anything sexual. The fact that you dare not make a sound or let anyone guess you are engaged in sexual intercourse certainly establishes the "No No's around it. We can shout and yell at a baseball game, or laugh loudly at a movie to show enjoyment. Can we with sex? Never! We must be quiet or abstain at all costs.

Many subverted messages creating guilt and negativity regarding sex, comes from the church. The ultimate message is having a child without sexual intercourse that is demonstrated with the legend of the Virgin Mary. Then we have priests and nuns that are not permitted to have sex. There has been much controversy in Jesus as celibate. The lamas in Tibet went off to meditate in caves for years away from all women. Think of the message subliminally conveyed to humans that have to populate the earth with this lowly act to produce God's most precious creation? The message was that if they had sex, they could never reach the higher limits of consciousness.

Another variation of sex games is using the Frigid and Impotent roles to justify interest in someone else. This is where they have an affair or flirt with others implying sexual involvement, which I call a "Dry Love Affair" and is used to make the other person jealous or angry. If the game gets heavy enough, they may actually have an affair, fall in Love, or ask for a divorce. This implies, "I don't have a sex problem with others, so it must be you."

When the Frigid and Impotent personalities have an affair to retaliate against their mates, that is not the real crime. The real retaliation is letting the other parties know it. This is done in three ways. The first is "Telling them on purpose" which is a confessional to have a clean start in showing their honesty and how sorry they are. However, if it hurts the other person, it is their true intent at some level and an act of hostility for a previous infraction they feel was done to them. It takes a lot of wisdom to know when a confession is good for someone's soul.

The second way is by accident such as leaving a hotel ticket in their shirt pocket. Knowing their wife will find it is an act of hostility and again, their true intent. The three most prevalent excuses are, it was an accident, I made a mistake or I forgot.

The third way they hide their ability to retaliate is to provoke someone to tell the person. If a woman is going with a married man and wanted his wife to know, it will happen. My friend, Delia, confided her affair to Nora, a neighbor, who disapproved. Nora was provoked and in her righteousness, told Delia's husband, unaware that this is an act of hostility. Her true intent was for Delia to be punished by her husband by berating her or even breaking up the marriage. This format is the result of the early training women were given to punish other women. They rationalize, "It was for her/his own good. I would want to know." This is all part of the sex game.

A man I was involved with mentioned he ran into a classmate of ours and invited her to dinner. Upon her arrival I knew instinctively they were having an affair. This was his way of letting me know and I elected not to say anything. I was aware that if I did not respond, he would find another way. Using a process of elimination, I calculated how he would manage to do it.

Reviewing the three ways you retaliate, I thought about his confessing. His passive personality prevented a confessional method. Bringing her to the house was as close as he would get to a confession. I thought about his provoking someone to tell me and negated this method. He had too big an investment in his good guy image and would not let another person know. Therefore, I went on the premise that it would be an accident.

It would not be in his closet, dresser drawer or office. He knew I would never think of opening or prying into any of these places. I thought about him leaving some piece of evidence in his car. I put this on "hold" as a possibility. However, it was a little too blatant. I then thought of his attaché case and fantasized how he would leave it behind one day. I pictured him calling me and requesting some information he needed out of the case and there would be the evidence. Of all the ways he could do it that was the one that felt right. He would do it accidentally.

I waited four weeks. One morning, entering the living room, there by the front door sat his attaché case. I slowly opened it and right on top was a Love letter from this woman. I closed the briefcase and pondered on what I to do and decided to let myself take over and trust I would handle it well. When he came home that night, I simply told him about my waiting for him to leave the case behind to let me know what he did.

I made it clear that the subject was not open for discussion. I did not wish further pain by listening to a confession. I liked myself too much for that kind of game.

These are the various ways we play the game of Frigid vs. Impotent. Let's explore what makes up these personalities and the solutions to apply. Keep in mind, the games, especially this one, are ways we use to avoid intimacy above our comfort level.

***The Frigid Personality***  The Frigid Personalities are usually strongly influenced by the traditional values of being a virgin. This gives women permission to play Frigid and view sex as dirty or a man's perversion. They rarely felt comfortable with sex and often did not move a muscle during intercourse. This attitude was prevalent in "traditional" marriages where women who enjoyed sex were viewed as depraved. I learned this at eleven years old when I went to live with my sister after her husband died. Every night her girlfriends would come over visiting. They would sit in the kitchen drinking tea, eating Ritz crackers with cream cheese and discussing men. I would be in the den doing my homework quite fascinated by their views of sex.

One evening they got into an especially raucous discussion about how to get out of having sex with your husband. They kept getting sillier and sillier. Eventually, they reached an ideal solution. They discussed how they would wait until their husbands were undressed, tell him someone was calling at the window and leaning out, he would lay his penis on the windowsill and they would then slam the window down. Never had I heard such laughter as they sputtered and groped for control at this abusive fantasy.

The Frigid game is also played when women want to retaliate. This can occur when a man has gone out with another woman. The Frigid personality will go through all kinds of trauma and crying and elicit a promise from her husband to never go with another woman again. Once this is elicited, the woman "pays him back" by not responding sexually. She may say, "I can't help it. I just think about that woman you were with", and completes the punishment and retaliation. Generally, women, in the traditional sense, were not permitted to say they enjoyed sex even when they did. Currently, women are still accustomed to playing some form of frigidity but it is changing.

*The Impotent Personality*  Once again we have the passive personality. Being impotent is a powerful way of doing nothing. The men are convinced beyond any reasoning that they can't help it, when often it is precipitated by anger, jealousy and fear. Impotency is not as common as most people believe. When it is caused by a medical problem or the natural process of aging and not used as a game, it is devastating and difficult for any man to accept.

As in the case of the female Frigid Personalities, the impotent personalities also use impotency to retaliate against some kind of perceived crime or neglect. This is not as prevalent as it is in women since the primary reason for impotency, that is not medically induced, is to be taken care of. That is why in many marriages, the women end up taking care of a sick and impotent husband.

The retaliatory part is often anger at women in general rather than one woman that betrayed them. It is generally what all women did to them including their mother. They believe women can't be trusted and may say, "They're all whores." This is more the impotent personality that had been aggressive before becoming helpless and playing the passive role. This shows in the passive body language where they are seen walking slowly, tentatively, with rounded shoulders and bent to some degree. They have a lost, vacant or disoriented look similar to the Front Seat Driver or the Abused passive personality. This is a far cry from the aggressive males' strut, shoulders thrust back, talking loudly. Some males keep this stance and will do anything to not convey their personality of impotency.

*The Frigid Solution*  The Frigid Solution is locating whether women are more strongly influenced by their traditional beliefs of society and religion, or are angry at all men in general. If it is caused by the indiscretion of one man, the problem is usually temporary.

Once it is established that Frigid Personalities are caused by beliefs or anger at men, the most effective method to turn it about is to change their perception. Women that hold the Virgin Mary as an exemplar of womanhood need their perception changed to reflect reality. Marilyn brought this up in the sex workshop and related her shame around anything sexual. She explained this by saying, "Even the Virgin Mary had a baby without sex." I asked her, "Who made sex and for what purpose." She instantly replied, "But God made sex to have babies, not to enjoy." I asked, "Then why did he create the pleasure derived from sex?" "Oh", she said, "That's to ensure that the existence of man would continue." My reply finally led to her reassessing her belief. I said, "Why didn't God make wanting sex like an itch that needed satisfying rather than pleasure." The last item I told her was to examine her belief of what God planned as we approached over-population. This started the change in her belief that sex was dirty and she was instructed to accept her sexual self and start displaying her sexuality. This was with the body, language, the clothes she wore and being her loving selective self.

When there is a general anger toward one man, frigidity is usually temporary. When anger is directed toward men in general for being promiscuous, peace needs to be made with the past. Learning to trust they can handle whatever arises helps stop the jealousy often found in frigid women who become suspicious and convinced men can't be trusted. Trusting yourself, leads to trusting others.

Changing perceptions and beliefs, making peace with the past, trusting and accepting your sexuality as beautiful, opens a whole new world of Love and mends many of the troubled relationships of today. If sex is an expression of Love, why withhold it?

***The Impotent Solution***   One of the first ways the impotent personalities can start improving his sexuality is to literally take on the macho, aggressive role. They need to make a decision to give up the passive role, which is a way to ask to be taken care of and have no expectations in marriage around sex. A masculine, he-man strut, talk and posture will not fill his need to be taken care of which often includes impotency. The primary reason impotency rises as men get older, is because their need to be taken care of increases. They genuinely feel it is their turn to collect.

When impotency affects men that are aggressive, it is usually caused by a devastating loss of a woman they Loved and wanted. It's a blow to their pride and a defense to not get involved and hurt again. It also is caused by the fear of losing their maleness and thought of as a wimp. Whatever the cause, it is devastating and with Love, patience and acceptance by all, can be turned around most times.

When Max came to one workshop he had had an impotency problem for several years. He displayed the typical posture, soft voice and slumped shoulders of the passive impotent personality. One of the psychotherapists in the group started a conversation with Max and deliberately took on Max's mannerisms, talk and eventually slumped into the same posture. Everyone but Max noticed what was going on. The therapist then had Max get up, stand straight, put life and vigor into his body and voice and to take long strides like a "man". This started breaking his, "I can't help it," poise he adopted over the years that strongly influenced his impotency role. Over the years, I watched the positive affects this exercise has in helping men become sexually potent again for those who did not have a medical basis. This exercise was combined with probing of the inception of the impotency and the belief systems.

My friend, Ally, and her husband, Hugh, went through such an episode. Ally was highly sexual and had an excellent relationship with her husband for many years. When Hugh turned forty years old, he began to play Impotent. They talked about it; they argued about it, Ally threatened to get sex elsewhere and Hugh was bewildered that she didn't understand. He felt it was something he couldn't help even though it was ascertained it was not a physical problem. The more she pursued him and discussed it, the more he played Impotent.

After much discussion with a therapist, Ally learned that the only way to help Hugh with his impotency was to not pressure him for sex. Ally made it a point of going for body work and massages to fulfill her need to be touched. Slowly but surely, the tides turned and he made the desired sexual move. That was many years ago and this problem has not returned. It may be that he needed her total support, which she gave. In essence, she said, "I Love you and want you no matter what. Sex is not as important as our Love for one another."

***Summary*** All games are a derivative of the sex game with a different arena or theme. They are either a continuation of the roles played in the "traditional" sense. This can take the form of adhering to them or defying them. It is playing the female silly chatter role or the stoic strong male role. The goal is to recognize it is a game and change it regardless of the role the other person plays.

The easiest way to change it is to decide you will never contaminate your sex life. When you think of the utter beauty and closeness sex brings into your life, know you will keep it pure. The enjoyment, the laughter, the touching and feeling of another life that close is enough of an incentive to keep any game out of my bed. I will not contaminate the Love in sex by withdrawing it, going with someone else, implying I am interested in someone else or having sex without the full beauty of it. I will not accommodate others and have sex with someone under pressure or desire to please. I want to feel the desire for sex and Love to my soul and know its beauty and depth for another human being. When you see and experience sex like this, there will be no games in bed. Learn it, feel it, and taste it to the extent that all your five senses will enjoy.

## Talkers vs. Silencers

The brain split is often seen between the right brain Silencers and the left brain Talkers. Silencers have a powerful position and drive Talkers insane. Talkers rarely win because they cannot talk as long as Silencers can remain silent. Talkers' power in a situation is blatant and obvious. They appear as a troublemaker and are blamed for being a loud mouth. Silencers appear helpless and a victim of Talkers. This makes it difficult to detect their part in the game and usually elicits other people's support.

I searched in vain to find how Talkers and Silencers are established. However, I did find that once established, it is a survival issue and if not adhered to, they just may die. Several years ago, I asked my sister, Edie, a question. "How, as a child, could you possibly regain serene and quiet when the whole family was fighting." She would sit in a corner with her hands folded and a smile on her lips. To my astonishment she answered, "I was afraid Ma would kill me." It was difficult for me to believe that she really thought my mother would kill her. Then she said, "I need to ask you a question. How could you yell back at Ma and fight with her when she was beating you?" To my surprise I answered, "I didn't care if she killed me. I could not stand for her to kill my spirit." Both were survival issues even though one created a Talker and the other a Silencer.

Like all games, Talkers and Silencers are drawn to each other. This provides lifelong tools to prevent getting resolutions and avoid intimacy. Silencers play the martyr to perfection taking on tasks and duties and being good little boys and girls. As a result, everyone believes they are meek, innocent people badgered by a big bully. As a friend put it, "Talkers are drawn to Silencers and then both are drawn and quartered." Silencers get society's sanction since people are unaware of the power of this role that makes Talkers appear in a negative and disruptive light.

I recall a demonstration in my psychology class years ago. Our instructor selected an aggressive male and a passive female. He had them stand up and face each other with the palms of their hands pressing against each other. He instructed the aggressive male to start pushing the passive female around the room. It took all of us some time before we realized the helpless female was in reality leading the aggressive male. The two partners involved weren't even aware that this switch had occurred. In discussing it, neither knew when they changed from the left-brain pushing the right-brain personality and to the right-brain pulling the left-brain personality.

There is also role reversals when Talkers are silent and Silencers rage on. This occurs when the battle reaches limits where Talkers feel justified withdrawing and be silent and Silencers feel justified to blow up and yell. Being a Talker, I recalled being enraged to a point where I was unable to speak. My children used to say, "Mom's okay when she's ranting and raging, it's when she is quiet that we worry."

To make myself speak, I took long breaths, relaxed and quietly said, "Everything in me says to not speak and I do not want to do that."

***The Talker Personality*** Talker-type personalities are usually typical left-brained individuals that have not learned to keep their mouth shut. The more stressed and helpless they feel, the more words come tumbling out of their mouth. There is a sort of panic to it and belief that, "If I only can explain what I mean, you will understand." These personalities are unable to grasp that the Silencer has long ago turned them off. In other words, they do the very thing that does not have others listen to what they so desperately want heard.

Another way Talker personalities do not get heard is their tone of voice, persistence and critical remarks. Talker personalities are not listeners and do not know how to be heard.

If Silencers do speak up, Talkers say hurriedly, "Let me tell you one more thing." Talkers invariably urge Silencers to speak up. When they do, Talkers find countless ways to silence them. They may get angry or scold when Silencers don't make their point quickly. Talkers also consistently disagree with what Silencers say, act impatient and interrupt. Talkers will correct the Silencers' grammar or the validity of information presented to insure Silencers' reluctance to speak up again. This maintains the necessary role for both parties in the partnership.

***The Silencer Personality*** Silencer personalities are the ultimate in passivity on a day-to-day, lifetime basis. It is one of the strongest survival issues that we have. However, they will pursue Talkers when the Talkers elect not to speak. For a school paper, I chose to write on this subject. I lived with Randy, a Silencer, and I was the Talker. As part of my assignment, I studied the speech patterns, phrases and timing that Randy used. I started on a Friday evening to remain silent. In less than an hour, Randy started asking me if I was mad. I assured him everything was fine and I was not angry. I used the same phraseology and tone of voice he did. In a matter of five days, he was beside himself. Even when he went to his office, he called every twenty minutes to check if I was angry. At night he talked and asked questions in a way I never experienced from him before. My silence agitated him extremely.

The intensity of the pressure within me to speak made it impossible for me to go the full week as I planned. An interesting aside is that I usually sleep six to seven hours a night. The energy it took to keep silent had me sleeping ten to twelve hours a night. I finally told Randy what I had been doing all week. I asked him, "Randy, why did you keep asking me if I was mad? Is that what your silence means?"

It is interesting that a few months later I chose to write another paper employing the opposite role and pursuing and accelerating my aggressive behavior on Randy relentlessly. I accelerated my critical parental role to where I complained about everything Randy did. This included the way he talked, walked, did the yard, drove his car, etc., etc., etc. He sat there more passive than ever. The acceleration included me putting him down in front of our friends and family. Everyone was getting angry with me and telling me to, "Please leave poor Randy alone." I pursued this for six days. After completing this assignment I discussed what occurred and asked, "Randy, how far would you have let me go before speaking up? Was there a point that you would have said, "Theresa, that is enough." He thought about it for a time and sadly said, "I don't think I would have ever said anything." This was inconceivable to me as a Talker but did show the powerful position the Silencer wields.

I recall a couple coming to group therapy. One of their problems was the wife's annoyance with her husband who took several minutes to answer a simple question. In one session, I brought up that my daughter wanted to sit in on a session to write a paper for school and were there were any objections. Everyone was answering and debating except Jim. I watched him closely. He would look up to the ceiling for a while. Then he would look down on the floor to the right and cock his head as though he were listening. He shifted his eyes to the left and looked up again. After about five minutes he slowly said, "I don't care if she sits in. You can put what I say on the front page of a newspaper." I could not help laughing and said, "I know Jim. There is a definite reason why you do not worry about what you say getting in the newspaper. It is because you never say anything unless you check it out in your head until it is a perfect answer. You check if it looks and sounds okay to others and picture what they may think and say. You then check how you feel about it. You keep this process up until you get approval in your head. That is why it takes you so long to answer a question." This is the Silencer's process and it is difficult to give up the support they get from it. Silencers get full support and Love from everyone around them for their suffering. Remember, it is as difficult for Silencers to speak up as it is for Talkers to remain silent. The more of a Talker you are, the more of a Silencer you will select and vice versa.

***The Talker Solution*** Like everything else, there's a solution to all things. With this in mind, I approached my Talker self and said "What can you do to balance your role as a Talker." This is when I learned that Talkers go into their aggressive role and Silencers go into their passive role. I asked myself, "What is the middle role?" It was being assertive, of course. So start the change of roles by using assertive measures to get what you want with Love, patience and common sense. This means without being aggressive or passive and using both sides of the brain. My Talker role is intensified when I am nervous.

I then asked myself, "How can I switch to being assertive at will?" Eventually, the answer came as they always do when you have made a decision to resolve or change an issue. I learned to check when I was talking if I was really saying something or rattling on to keep others from talking. I became aware how quickly I became bored when a Silencer spoke. "Why?" says I. The Silencer is right brain and a slow, methodical thinker and talker and I get impatient. I then learned to slow myself down, remember how much I loved and valued the person, and made myself calm to really listen. Find a technique that works for you. A mirror does wonders for me. If I'm bumbling on, I excuse myself, go in a bathroom, stare in the mirror and say, "Theresa, listen calmly and with Love."

High up on Talkers' priorities is defending. They cannot seem to stop explaining. I overcame this by changing my perception of defending by saying, "Theresa, where is your pride?" I would then immediately keep still and ask the Silencer, "How did I upset you?" Look for ways to be still and patient. Enjoy and accept the Love and intimacy that is there for all of us.

**The Silencer's Solution**   Silencers need to recognize when they are being silent in a negative way. Silence can be beautiful when listening, praying and meditating. It's when it goes passive that the game is on. When Silencers become aware of this switch to the game of being a Silencer, they are on the first step to assertiveness. The other is their decision to give up the game and finding what they need to talk under any conditions. They can remember how much they Love others and speak up when not playing the game. They can check if the relationship got too loving, happy and intimate and they withdrew into their silent world.

They can practice in front of a mirror talking non-stop as they play the Talkers' role. It is healthy when they start laughing as they know they are now lightening up. All roles are heavy. They can refuse to be a prisoner of their silence and accept it may be a retaliation coming from inner anger. They need to check if they accept verbal abuse to prove to others how beastly Talkers are. Last but not least, they need to explore if it is worth it and start living assertive, healthy lives.

**Summary**   Talkers can learn to recognize that right brain Silencers give information in a slow methodical manner. Talkers need to slow down their speech or risk overwhelming Silencers. Silencers need to learn when conversing with left-brain Talkers to be brief and to the point. Talkers processes information very rapidly and become easily impatient or bored. Learning about each other's speech patterns and processing will produce better communication and resolutions. Talkers need to learn to wait patiently and lovingly and allow time for Silencers to gather their thoughts and answers. Silencers need to learn to speak up and ask Talkers to slow down their speech and allow time to process the transfer information.

Both the Talkers and Silencers are responsible to stop the games. One way is to reverse their roles. Silencers can catch the next time they find themselves withdrawing and being silent. They can stop and ask themselves, "Do I want to do this the rest of my life? Can I speak up and tell the other person, 'I'm going to get a glass of water and I'll be right back.'" The same goes for Talkers who find themselves raging on and everybody has a resigned look on their faces. At that precise moment they can stop and say, "Here I am talking up a storm again. I'll go for a walk and come back in a happier place." This is *powerful!*

### Waiters vs. Laters

The Waiters vs. Laters game is one of the mildest games we play to keep Love and intimacy at bay when someone gets too close. Even though no one is tangibly hurt, it can guarantee to ruin an evening, vacation or a marriage. Like all games, it was developed in childhood by our belief systems and early decisions. The game of Waiters and Laters in a relationship involves time that affects the Quality of life. It provides a built-in war and retaliation tool. The Waiters are always on time or even ahead of time. The Laters are late for everything.

*Whether you are a "Waiter" or a "Later," the belief system of which one you select is set early in your life. Without conscious awareness and intervention, you will obey this belief regardless of the consequences.*

What people do with their time and with whom they spend it can be used as an expression of Love or anger. When time is used for positive living, they are making their lives work and improving the Quality of life. When they use it negatively, it is a weapon and ammunition in the war with their loved ones. It is a powerful tool to withdraw time from people that want to be with them. This is where the Waiters and Laters game comes in. It can be anywhere from waiting five minutes for someone or an emphasis to change the Later to being on time since it is only right. However, the basic reality is that right or wrong, it is just as difficult to change a role. Once again, it will help to learn how difficult this is by switching roles. Waiters can imagine the anxiety they would experience being late and keeping others waiting. Laters can experience the tension and anxiety of being on time.

Waiters believe they are right and unaware of their cooperation in this game. Such as staying out all night without explanation. This fills a relationship with doubt and contaminates it.

They conclude that Laters ruined the dinner, the first half of the play is over, and everyone waiting is tense. Yes, Laters wield a lot of power. The more power Laters wield, the more difficult it is for them to give the role up. You deal with what is, not what it should be. Learn to understand both sides. It is just as difficult to change either role.

*The Waiter Personality*  Waiter personalities were good little boys and girls as children. They cannot imagine keeping people waiting and are unable to understand the rebellious nature of the Laters. It is of the utmost importance for them to do everything right and proper and can't understand why Laters can't see or do this to the world's satisfaction.

There is a lot of resentment toward Laters who are viewed as irresponsible, inconsiderate and uncaring. Waiters get everyone's support because the Laters are not doing what they are "suppose" to do. Waiter personalities have a parental attitude toward Laters, who slide into the child role whining, "I couldn't help it." This pushes Waiters to telling everyone of the Laters irresponsibility again and again.

*The Later Personality*  Later personalities experience all kinds of anxiety being on time. Even though they are aggressive by nature, this is their passive way to retaliate. Consciously, they feel the anxiety of being late, but unconsciously they fear arriving early as they are rebellious by nature. Their thoughts run to, "I'm early, I wonder if I should go in." "What shall I do while I am waiting?" "What if someone sees me in the car. Will they call the police?"

Laters are high-energy people that can't tolerate idle time, such as waiting, that they feel is being wasted. They truly believe they can get one more task done before leaving the house. It is interesting that they are genuinely shocked that the time went by so fast and they are late again. It is inconceivable to the Later personalities that they are deliberately late at some level within. There is resentment at the Waiters for not understanding it isn't their fault. It is also inconceivable to

Laters that they keep Waiters waiting to retaliate for the anger they feel within for being told over and over that they should be on time.

I am a Later who worked with a Waiter. To live in good faith with him, I diligently worked at being on time. My goal is to arrive early. Right now I am putting my energy into just being on time. I found myself doing chores that I did not have to do. It was most difficult to stop

*Yes, there is always a memory to everything you do especially when you face an issue in yourself.*

these distractions, get dressed and leave. When I finally managed to be on time for a business trip, I experienced severe anxiety and stress. I have always felt anxious and stressed being late. Now I found I was in a double bind feeling the same way, if not more, being on time. I asked myself, "Why?"

This brought up a memory of my mother who would run to each place we children went, such as school or playground, and time herself. We had to do it in the same time or be beaten for dawdling and had to confess where we went. It is interesting how some of my brothers and sisters became Waiters and some became Laters under the same conditions. The second memory was my husband repeating what my mother did. He timed himself going to the grocery store and expected me to do it in the same time. He instructed me to not dawdle and visit my friend. How did he know my mother's pattern? How did I convey it? I can't recall telling him about it, yet conveyed it to him somehow. I'm fascinated how our belief systems recreate childhood patterns!

*The Waiter Solution*   Waiters can learn to step out of their games by taking the importance out of being late. So you missed a plane, first part of a play, etc. No one was harmed, and it is First Degree. Taking the negative energy out of the game gives them their power back. Waiters instantly lose all power when caught up in the agitation and upset that Laters create. Strive to accept it without rancor. Know that you are angry because being late is an irresponsible act and these Laters should know it and change. It is your helplessness that creates the rage toward Waiters.

I am a Later by nature and taught my daughter, Lorri, so well that she became a Later too , but I became a Waiter whenever we were to meet. Here is how I resolved the Later game with my daughter. I decided to give up fretting over First Degree problems, such as waiting, and learn how to resolve them. Lorri keeps me waiting anywhere from one to four hours whenever we are going someplace. Over a ten year period I told everyone that would listen to me how she inconvenienced and kept me waiting again. This gave me a wonderful opportunity to use my favorite line, "She did it again." This got me all the sympathy I needed since I was the one that was right. I complained to Lorri how pressured I felt with patients due, etc. Nothing ever changed. My anger exceeded the crime of her being late. I thought, "Theresa, aren't you sick and tired of the same conversation for ten years. She's not going to change, so give it up."

After realizing it was First Degree and caused no harm, I decided her being late would never again bother me. When I was to meet her, I read a book, did some work and made sure I had no other appointments. That was eight years ago. I knew I gave it up because I never had any compulsion or desire to tell another person or have a need to discuss it with her. I'd rather be happy with her company when she is late than be right and unhappy that she should be on time. I took the responsibility, gave up the need to be right and resolved it for myself.

In relating this story to others I found many times I would receive the same reaction. They felt that I was giving in and encouraging irresponsible behavior. This is not the issue. The issue is that she is not going to change. I want to know what to do in the face of that. It is facing you are powerless to change the person, but have the power to change yourself. It is not "giving in" and it is not approving of the act. It is simply making a choice. I can stay angry and attempt to change her. I can stop speaking to her, and make the day miserable when she shows up late. Or I can simply accept that behavior as part of our friendship and enjoy the day. You need to deal with what is, not with what should be.

An interesting aside that arose from this little tale happened when my daughter was entering this into the computer for me. She wrote a note back and asked me to write about my being late. Of course, where else would she learn it so perfectly! I kept her waiting many times when she was little. This bears out my contention that what bothers people is usually one of their own failings within themselves, or fear that they may develop becoming a Later, or are angry because they cannot retaliate the way Waiters do.

***The Later Solution***   Laters need to take a long hard look at the role they play and ponder the need to be irresponsible and childlike. This is especially important when they are quite responsible in other areas of their lives. First they need to see if they are willing to forfeit and give up this perfect rebellious power. To give it up, they will need to learn what they use to make themselves late and take on the responsibility to change it. Writing down all the excuses they have ever given for being late does this. It helps to carry a piece of paper and write down their new excuses as they relinquish their old ones. They need an awareness that when they find themselves giving an excuse and defending being late, to jot it down instead of saying it. This helps stop the defending.

Whenever Laters hear themselves thinking, "I'll just make a quick telephone call," they need to stop and run out the door. When leaving, it is vital that a realistic time is set to leave. Be ready to go out the door fifteen minutes earlier. This needs to take into consideration having the house all locked up, the keys in your hand, and your coat and purse in the car.

My patient, Andrea, was a Later. She was a schoolteacher and very responsible. She was jeopardizing her position and hurting her marriage. We did two things. First she changed the behavior that caused her to be late. When she found herself clearing glasses off table instead of going out the door, she stopped herself, placed the dishes on the floor by the door and immediately walked out. The second area addressed was being late with her husband. My notes showed a pattern that if she and her husband were getting along for several weeks, there would be an episode of lateness that created an argument, thus the distancing. She became aware that waiting for the happiness she experienced with her husband to end created more anxiety than bringing it to a halt by being late. Looking at the behavior that made her late, and the reasoning used to be late, contributed to her rarely being late today. Look for the purpose in being late.

Laters can gracefully accept Waiters complaining about being late without defending or giving an explanation. Defending and excuses creates anger in Waiters as they have heard it all and rarely have experiences that make them late. Defending, results in Waiters chastising Laters and Laters giving eternal excuses. If the end result is our true intent, is this what Laters want? If so, is it to be punished because they feel they deserve it or are they are angry with the Waiters and punishing them? It could also be anger at existence itself.

We hold onto our games with a tenacity that defies all reason. Laters can take full responsibility that something is going on in their head, be it retaliation or wanting someone to take care of them, and do not defend in any way by giving explanations, excuses or alibis. Remember, these ploys will work only when Laters take on the responsibility, want to change, give up this retaliatory tool and have made a determined decision to be on time no matter what.

*Summary*  Laters need to take full responsibility to give up their late game with no excuses. Waiters need to make a decision to give up being annoyed and never mention or refer to the Laters being late again and give them so much power. With persistence and awareness, Waiters and Laters can overcome the game.

*Chapter Thirteen*

# Formula For Success

Love is the first healer, the most powerful tool for change and learning how to act rather than react. Love yourself the way you are now. Loved people change and there is no more effective Love than Self-Love. When you have it, you can give it. In fact you will actually emit Love just Being rather than waiting for an external event or person to express it. You need Love and support from yourself to change, not chastisement, anger, criticism or wishing you could get rid of that part of you. These create the opposite effect. Love somehow mysteriously conveys itself.

I recall a friend that went to his den after work with a glass of wine and newspaper. His children knew not to bother him. One night, he decided to test the power of sending waves of Love. When he got home, he set aside his newspaper and wine. He then concentrated and thought about loving his children. After a while, both children came into the room and climbed in his lap. They had never done that before.

We all have a Little Beastie within us that is rebellious, emerges without warning and upsets others. It will make remarks that you cannot perceive saying when you are in your ideal self. Learn to accept and Love this part of you. It is the only way you are going to make peace with it. Little Beastie is the five-year-old child within that reacts to what someone said or did. What does a rebellious five-year-old child want? Of course, it wants Unconditional Love and acceptance. I know my personal five-year-old child so well that I call it affectionately, "My Little Beastie."

As a result, when a problem arises, you can choose to shelve your own feelings and listen to the other person. This enhances communication immediately. For example, in a work situation a patient or customer is angry. If your Little Beastie within feels angry in return and can't express it, then acknowledge Beastie's feelings. Say lovingly, "Little Beastie, you are feeling angry. However, I'm going to shelve your feelings right now so I can take care of the situation I find myself in. To show my appreciation, I will buy you a hot fudge sundae this afternoon." Then do it. This prevents build-up of resentful feelings when you are doing more than you want for others. This is Empathy, and a powerful tool in healing yourself and those around you. Not compensating yourself eventually builds up. Beastie creates a big blow up and you hate yourself for not being more patient and loving.

While lecturing at St. John's Hospital in Santa Monica, I looked over the audience and pondered how many religious people may be in there. Knowing what My Little Beastie might do, I said, "I have a Little Beastie within me that is extremely rebellious. She has a propensity to swear in front of religious people. However, today, she is sitting beside me being very good because I promised her a hot fudge sundae this afternoon." The audience's response was immediate and all understood and got in touch with their own Little Beastie. I also know it is important to make sure Little Beastie gets that hot fudge sundae or next time around Beastie will not sit quietly. It will swear. So make your peace within. Learn to do it before Little Beastie acts up by giving it unconditional Love and go for your win. Otherwise, it will feel the guilt, retaliate and accept abuse for acting up.

Loving yourself as you are, is a learned process and prevents you from taking abuse. You can do this by hugging yourself, listening to what you want and recognizing and acknowledging your feelings. Tell yourself you understand this other self who has a life of its own, and does things you don't like. Listen to your inner voice to learn what that part of you wants, and tell that part you will take it up for consideration. Negotiate with it.

When you learn to communicate successfully and resolve problems within yourself, you will then be equally successful at resolving issues with others. This is one and the same process. When you handle situations well, you like yourself more. The more you like yourself, the better you handle situations that end up win/win. The words you use when thinking and talking about yourself, also affect Self-Love. Many books and psychotherapists advocate saying affirmations in order to feel good and change your thinking. They may be, "I am a good person." "I will be responsible today." Rarely mentioned is how you negate these affirmations in hundreds of ways every day with confirmations of your shortcomings or faults. You can say affirmations from now to doomsday, however they will not be effective if you spend one tenth of the day negating them. This can be by saying, "I'm not very good at that." It can be by the way you talk, walk, look, act or handle people and problems. Throw away the words "good, bad, wrong, and right." Instead restate the situation as effective. If it was not, ask yourself what do you want to do about it to make it effective. Decide to discuss the resolution in your head, and not the problem.

In the book, *Transactional Analysis in Brief* by Stanley Woollams, M. D., Michael Brown, Ph. D., and Kristyn Huige, M.S.W, state:

> *It is generally true that people do not Love as strongly as they hate, so a moment of hatred may over-shadow hours of Love or caring.*

Self-Love is not allowing anyone, including yourself, to talk to you in a critical or harsh way, nor accepting abuse physically, emotionally, or verbally (First, Second or Third Degree). You may feel angry with the person that abused you, but some part of you will be angrier that you allowed yourself to take it. You only allow people to talk to you the way you talk to yourself. Also know that when you talk to someone else critically, it will have the same negative effect upon yourself. Self-Love is also paying attention to your body and what it is telling you. Are you tense, nervous or in pain? The physical reaction to anything that happens to you, is often the forerunner to such emotions. Learn whether you feel the emotions before or after criticizing others, and learn where in your body you register the stress. When you do become aware of the emotions and tension, relax your body and breathe slowly and you will experience a reduction in that emotion. You cannot keep anger if your body is relaxed.

Watch when there is a conflict between what you say and your body language. The body language is usually more truthful. An example is saying, "I'm not angry." However, you find you are clenching your teeth. The truth of the matter is that you are angry.

To build your self-esteem and increase Self-Love, give up defending yourself. Know you do not owe anyone an explanation. It is humiliating and demeaning to your self. When you do volunteer an explanation in your defense, prepare yourself that the other person may not accept it. Almost anyone can dispose of a defense easily as being irrelevant to the subject. Defending stops all communication and prevents resolutions and you lose your power. You have relinquished it to the other person.

I recall working in an office building that hired a new telephone receptionist. I was instructing her on telephone office policy and she got upset and refused to follow it .I finally said, "Keri, if you do not wish to answer the telephone according to our office policy, I will pick it up in my office." For weeks she refused to speak to me. Each morning I said, "Good Morning," with no response. She would not relent, and I was pulled in by her silence and said, "Come on, Keri, stop acting like a damn two-year-old." As a result, she called the owner of the building and complained that I swore at her. The story got blown out of proportion and my friend asked me what happened. When I told her, she said, "Is that all that happened? I am going to tell everyone the truth." I said, "Joy, you are my good friend and I am asking you not to defend me. It will all blow over." In time, Keri was on someone else's case creating another furor in the building. I felt good that I did not defend myself and liked myself a lot better.

Becoming aware of your feelings gives you the option to express them or not. This is the basis of true empathy.   By learning how to acknowledge your feelings as they occur, gives you opportunities to achieve resolutions as problems arise. This will prevent build up of feelings, which makes it difficult to handle dissension. The longer you are happy and feel good, the more you build a reserve of good feelings and are able to resolve issues in Quality with Love.

*To achieve resolutions, the next time you are annoyed for any reason, remember that it is not important to be right. Give it up and go for what you want with Love.*

One of the most destructive methods of breaking off Love and caring, is to complain and criticize anyone for anything. This also includes criticizing yourself, which creates the anger within you. It is corrosive and prevents any resolution except a temporary one where the person will adapt, and then retaliate later. If you genuinely want to resolve an issue, you will not use this system of putting another person down. Start today to stop criticizing and complaining whether it is about others or yourself. To tell others something you wish them to change or improve, you need their permission. You will not get it unless you demonstrate Love, gentleness and assurance that they are perfect the way they are. Only then will you know that you genuinely want a resolution at all levels within you. That is the true essence of Love and the first step in your Formula For Success.

When you use the full power of Love in your being and you have made peace with your existence with everyone and everything in it, you will reduce any and all problems in your life. Those that do arise will be easily and quickly resolved. Effective communication will be at the tip of your tongue ready for use under all circumstances. Keep this power in your conscious mind at all times, and especially, when you want to use its energy to move you from your Formula For Failure to your Formula For Success. This prepares you for the attitude that is necessary for all effective communication that leads to success in Love, Quality and Money.

### Attitude — The Second Healer

The next item necessary for clear, positive communication is to approach the other party with a resolution attitude. Removing preconceived perceptions, judgments, assumptions or conclusions about the person or the problem does this. Approach the person with Love, an open mind and a desire to resolve the issue. This is more effective than having your mind set to prove you are right, and the other person is wrong. When this occurs, you will not listen and when a person relates a problem in an attempt to resolve it, you will correct their English. This is an attitude of non-resolution.

When you project a certain attitude to a person, it invites a similar response. A positive attitude more often than not, invites a positive response. A negative attitude invites a negative response. It is like a stone dropped into a pond. Its effect reaches into infinity be it in time or memory. When you give a person a warm smile and sincere compliment, s/he passes it on to the next person s/he meets. Your actions are contagious, and you are the only one that can choose to have them be positive or negative. That is what makes up your day and your life. Often, you are unaware of the ways a negative attitude can affect your life.

I recall my friend, Kristen, saying how someone at work received several gifts from her customers. She remarked, "How come I never have anyone give me gifts like that." It reminded me of passing one of our clients at the post office. One day I said, "Good morning, how are you?" He frowned and grumbled, "What's good about it." I was reluctant to address him again. Several months later, the man I worked for asked me to make up a list of certain clients to send Christmas gifts to. It was only in introspect that I realized that when I saw this man's name on the list, I did not include it to receive a gift. It would be difficult for him to perceive he did not get a Christmas gift because of his negative attitude months before.

A negative preconceived attitude of the other person's guilt is another way you affect a relationship. No matter how cleverly you think you are hiding it, you instantly convey it at some level. Once the other person perceives it, there will be an attitude of instant defense. This became apparent while consulting in an office and turning the Rolodex file containing patients' names. I saw certain names had black Avery dots next to them. I questioned the receptionist who replied, "Oh, those are 'Turkeys.'" I learned this meant they were difficult patients. I asked her to remove the black dots. I explained that anyone seeing that black dot would have a preconceived idea about the patient before arriving. As a result, they would greet this patient accordingly, and most likely receive the expected negative response.

Once you have a preconceived idea that the other person is difficult, the adverse effect will create a breakdown in effective communication. With a healthy attitude, the more difficult a person is, the more important it is to develop an understanding and caring attitude. To greet an antagonizing person with an entirely different approach than s/he expects, disconcerts her/him. The next time someone approaches you in a confrontational mode, respond as you would in a normal conversation. This will change the entire tenure of the exchange. The difficult person likes the power to upset other people. Your change in attitude to accepting and understanding takes that power away from him/her.

My experience is that once you have disarmed and understood a difficult person, s/he will often become your most loyal ally. Applying the change of attitude to perceive "Turkeys" caused surprising results. The difficult patents became a wonderful source of referrals of friends and relatives to the practice. This proved to be the case in many of the offices I applied this management concept.

*I improved my communication breakdowns by recalling my mother saying, "Theresa, if someone gets mad at you, that's sad. If two people get mad at you, that's too bad. If three people get mad at you, look into yourself."*

An excellent example of giving a different response to a difficult person occurred when I was seventeen-years old and selling hosiery in a department store. A woman approached the counter and requested hose that were 29" long. As I took the box down she abruptly said, "How can I be sure the hose are really the length you quoted?" I said, "I will measure them for you." As I opened the box she said, "Now don't snag them." I assured her I would not. "Now don't stretch them. It won't be the correct length." I replied, "I'll be careful. We have had excellent training in handling hosiery." She didn't like anything I showed her and she said, "Is that all you have?" I assured her I would go to the stock room and get more. She said, "Do you expect me to wait around here all day while you are dawdling in the stock room?"

At this point I felt a rush of anger. By some miracle, there followed a resolve that this woman was not going to upset me no matter what. This shift in attitude created an entirely different response from what I felt was a justifiable angry retort. I replied, "No, I would not expect you to do that. I know what you want and will ship them to you." She was a little taken aback and said, "And what if I don't like them?" I looked at her calmly and answered, "I'll pay for them myself."

Amazingly, within an hour she was back with a large box of Fannie Farmer's candy and said, "Thank you. You made me see myself." This resulted in her being responsible for making me the highest paid salesperson in the store, although I was the newest and youngest. I transferred to cosmetics and at Christmas time she referred all her wealthy friends and family. That is the power of setting an attitude that conveys you are going to get a resolution with or without the other person's cooperation.

Change the attitude that creates the breakdowns in communication by systematically letting go of past associations with negative results. This means with your parents, friends, children or mates, whether they are still in your life or not. This is making your peace with what was, what is and what will be. In the meantime, prevent new associations and friends from becoming negative. Take responsibility for creating the problems and examine the communication process that alienated your family and friends in the past and resolve not to use that formula again. Know you have the power to create a new attitude for success. Keep in mind that all negativity, including a non-effective attitude, can only manifest itself by turning off your thinking self and defending what

*Accept that the end results you are now experiencing, are your true intent at some level within, no matter how negative they may be.*

happened. You will maintain the attitude for effective communication if you use it with the power of your Love, the knowledge you can change anything you want at anytime, under any condition and have fun doing it with your Formula For Success.

## Communication — The Third Healer

As a child you did not have much say, and you were not responsible for the breakdown in communication. As an adult, accept that you contribute 50% percent of whatever happens between you and another person. This is the first step of taking responsibility to communicate and to change. To communicate effectively and achieve the results you desire, you need to know what your true intent is at all levels within your head.

My contention is that if you put six tablespoons of salt in a cake, it will result in a salty cake. If someone tells you it is because you put six tablespoons of salt in it and you continue doing it, you want a salty cake. The same is true if you enter a conversation with a passive attitude and accept abuse, anger or blame, you rarely achieve the results you desire from your ideal-self. The way you feel affects results. When positive, both win. When negative, no one wins.

When placing blame, remember, that what you perceive to be reality may not be. The other person feels as strongly that what s/he remembers is also the true reality. Change because you want to change no matter what stance the other person takes or whether or not it influences or changes others.

*To build trust and have others hear you, make your words, body language and tone of voice congruent with each other.*

During any conversation to resolve an issue, model the behavior you expect to receive. If you want respect, you need to be respectful. I saw a mother in the grocery store hitting her four-year-old child for hitting his little sister Which is one of the most incongruent messages parents send to their children She was yelling, "How many times have I told you not to hit your sister?" Do you think this little boy will hear her words or copy    her modeling? Her modeling, of course; which has far more weight than any words she could possibly say.

Speak in a clear adult tone and avoid parental, whiny or angry tones. When presenting the problem, give information and request resolutions. The words you use lose their power over the tone of voice used. Too often, what comes back to you from children is precisely what you taught or modeled for them. If you model being adamant about how a child is to act, you just may be teaching the child how to be stubborn. Each person you meet mirrors yourself. If you smile, they smile. If you scowl, they scowl. These messages can be blatant or subliminal and deliver negative messages without intent.

In Disneyland, I noticed two attractive girls on the merry-go-round and two young men standing by watching them. One of the young men ingeniously threw a penny to the girls and yelled, "Since there is no gold ring, catch this." One of the girls smiled politely and sat on her horse rather frozen staring straight ahead. The other girl threw her head back and laughed and reached to catch the penny. Upon missing it, she scrambled off her horse and picked the penny up. The next time around, she threw the penny back to the young men caught up in the play. When the girls got off the merry-go-round, both the young men ran toward the girl that threw the penny back. The three of them were laughing and started a conversation. I noticed that the other girl looked hurt, and left out with a puzzled look on her face. She did not have any idea that she shut these young men out. She had not mirrored their actions back. This was as though she slammed a door in their face. They mirrored back what they perceived her actions conveyed and shut her out. All of this occurred at an unconscious level.

Be consistent in what you want. It is another way to build trust and have others hear you. Changing your story or mind indiscriminately invites questions and digressions from the problem at hand. You now create another new problem drawing you away from the one at hand. If you change your stand on a subject, state clearly what new information you received that warranted such a change.

Another way to improve communication is when you are sitting down to discuss a problem, be sure the distance between you is comfortable for you both. Some people like to sit close and talk. A sign of this is if they are leaning forward as though to hear you better. They usually do not like a desk or piece of furniture between you. Other people like a distance of at least six feet. They may lean back in the chair to achieve a comfortable distance if you are too close.

The same goes for eye level. When possible, keep them at the same level. Looking up to someone or down to someone affects all communication. Looking up may recreate your position as a child looking up at your parents. This invites a childlike role in the same way looking down on a person gives the perception of taking a superior parental position.

While watching a therapist questioning a patient in group therapy, I noticed every time the therapist asked a question, the young man looked up. He was unable to answer a question without looking up. The only way the therapist could stop this was by asking the questions and simultaneously placing his hand just above the young man's eyes so that he was unable to look up. It developed that the young man was looking inside his head for his parent's approval to his answers.

There are two methods I devised that show a break in communication. The first one is people's propensity not to answer a question directly. Over the years of listening to patients, I discovered that if a question went unanswered, I recorded it. When you do not answer a question directly, you are usually digressing. This will immediately break the continuity of the communication and all intents to achieve a resolution, disappear. People who were angry or in an argumentative place, usually do not answer a question directly. This point is made very clearly in the following question and answer:

*A man asked his wife, "What time is it?" She responded, "Where did you leave your wristwatch this time."*

Note, she did not say, 10:20 A.M. This opened my eyes. I have watched carefully when I fail to answer a question directly, or when someone will not answer my question directly. When this happens, I wonder what I am trying to avoid answering. The number of ways people devise to avoid answering amazes me. Because of this cleverness in digressing from the subject matter, I made up a policy. When I ask a question and do not receive an answer directly, I will "anchor" the question by putting my fingernail in my thumb. I hold it there until the person stops changing the subject and rambling around it and then ask the same question again. When repeated several times, I bring it to the person's awareness that s/he has the option to say, "I prefer not answering that question." That is an answer. This helps all parties to stay on the subject. When one digresses, it presents the opportunity to explore what you are avoiding. Not answering a question is the same as failing to ask straight, loving and professionally for what you really want.

As a result of these observations, I created the following list, "The Art of Avoiding Answering a Question." Review it and see if you can locate the ones you use. Check those off and see if you can turn them around for more effective communication.

### *The Art of Avoiding Answering a Question*
- Insist on giving more information.
- Change the subject.
- Laugh.
- Cry.
- Repeat the question, either aloud, or silently move your lips.
- Say, "I don't know."
- Ask another question back.
- Say, "I don't remember."
- Defend, rationalize, and justify.
- Get rescued or get a back-up to verify what someone said or did, i.e. "Ask Mary. She was there."
- Say, "But look how far I have come. I don't think I'm that bad."
- Admit to guilt immediately. Confess how wrong you are.
- Take any punishment offered and do anything but answer the question.
- Say, "What did you say? I didn't hear you."
- Answer using words like, "I'll be there early or late, or soon, or in time." This is open to interpretation.
- Be vague, inaudible, apologetic, babbling or nagging.

- Become angry— and show it.
- Call names and make accusations, i.e. "You did the same thing last month."
- Withdraw and refuse to speak.

My second list, "The Art of Not Being Heard," breaks down communication by learning how not to be heard. You speak or make a request and the other person has not heard a word you said. You often hear parents say, "You haven't heard a word I said." or "But I have told her a thousand times what I wanted." My first memory of learning "The Art of Not Being Heard" was when I was eleven-years-old and heard my sister tell her son to go to bed in one way or another at least fifteen times. She would say, "Chuck, will you please get ready for bed." She had perfected the "Art of Not Being Heard." Become aware of the actions and phrases that invite the other person not to hear you. Review the list and select the ones you use. Once you discover what they are, consciously decide to stop that particular behavior and learn to be heard when you speak.

*Listen to people as you desire people to listen to you. All of us crave to be heard, as parents invariably cut us off as children.*

### The Art of Not Being Heard
- Resolve an issue in a meeting and failing to follow up on it.
- Use an authoritative or whining tone of voice.
- Be intimidating and aggressive.
- Repeat yourself ("I told you ten times...").
- Fuzz out, act confused, blank your mind out, etc.
- Getting drunk. (Who listens to a drunk?)
- Shout.
- Avoid eye-to-eye contact.
- Avoid eye level contact.
- Withhold part of the information.
- Start in the middle of the subject.
- Mumble or talk too softly.
- Pick the wrong time for the subject.
- Pick the wrong place for the subject.

- Don't allow enough time.
- Make accusations and put downs.
- Express negative feelings and anger.
- Talk at the same time as the other person or talk while another conversation is in progress.
- Out shout each other.
- Withdraw and don't contribute to the subject.
- Hinting at what you want - rather than asking for it directly.
- Use a body posture and gesture such as finger pointing or looking like a child.
- Play helpless.
- Interrupt.
- Discount knowledge you have on the subject.
- Procrastinate ("I'll tell him/her later." or "It's not worth it.")
- Think that it's not important.
- Believe it's no use.
- Resign self to a barrage of words.
- Defend self with a barrage of words.
- Be indecisive.
- Don't follow through.
- Say, "I'm going to..."
- Speak to someone who doesn't want to hear or is unwilling to listen.
- Remain passive.
- Not ask specifically for someone to listen to you.
- Act as though you know more than the other person.
- Convey you are right and the other person is wrong.

A good listener usually knows how to get others to hear when s/he speaks. You know others hear you when you receive a direct action to a request to do something or a direct answer to a question. Communication is not only learning to listen, it is learning how to have others listen to you. The more times you ask a person for something, and do not get what you want, the more you have perfected "The Art of Not

Being Heard." The most difficult question to receive an answer to is, "How do you feel?" When the sentence, "I feel..." is followed by the words "I feel they, that, when, she, he, if, how, it, my, you, whenever, John is..." the question is not going to be answered.

To have effective communication with anyone, you need to be aware of two vital areas. The first is what is going on within you emotionally and the second is what behavior you use with these emotions outwardly. When you become aware of these, you will be to detect which ones you use for your Formula For Failure and which ones you use for your Formula For Success. In this way, you will be able to intercept your Formula For Failure and consciously change it to your thoughts and behaviors that constitute your Formula For Success. The earlier you catch your first negative emotion, the easier it is to stop the negative end results, and achieve positive results. When you are in a happy and contented mood, and handle situations and problems sensibly, you will achieve the results you want. Once negative emotions appear, your thinking self has gone to another planet. The more emotional you are, the less your thinking apparatus is working. Your emotions put you within the center and core of the problem. You cannot see anything else but the problem. You box yourself in, and concentrate your whole being on how you feel. You ponder how someone else hurt you. You have gone in that box with these feelings

*Making your peace with the past is more apt to happen when you settle the problems you are experiencing today.*

with the cover nailed down tightly, and you believe you cannot get out. You locked yourself into your problem with no escape. When you are in this position, you want others to hear you. You want to be given what you believe you have coming. You want the other person to make the moves and change any behavior so you can come out of the box. The reality is that the other person is thinking and feeling the same way. Neither of you is moving but waiting for the other one to emerge from her/his lonely box and coax the other out. You both put yourselves in a position not to be heard and lost all ability to communicate effectively.

*Empathy:* To develop a more effective method of communicating it is vital to learn to attend to the emotional issues within. Dr. Richard

Calabrese, Associate Professor and Chairperson of the Communications, Arts, and Science Department of Rosemary College, River Forest, Illinois developed the Process of Empathy, Illustration 5 on the following page. His research established that Empathy is an acquired skill and not something you were born with. The prevailing belief up to that time was that Empathy was innate and others were unable to learn it.

The Process of Empathy gives you the tools and know-how to get out of the box and look at yourself objectively. It is knowing how to take care of your own feelings. The Process of Empathy allows you to accomplish this. Donald A. and Nancy L. Tubesing of the Listening Group, described empathy as:

> *Research in the field of counselor education indicates that the single most significant dynamic in the helping relationship is empathy, one person really hearing and feeling of another and responding to them with understanding.*

Dr. Calabrese's process involves four steps; Tune Into Your Own Feelings; Express These Feelings; Tune Into The Other Person's Feelings; Responding To The Other Person's Feelings.

**Step One: Tune Into Your Own Feelings**    A surprising concept in Dr. Calabrese's study was when he said, "Before attending to the other person's feelings, take care of your own." He means acknowledging your own feelings before attending to the problem to become a resolution person. The next time you are upset about something, before approaching the other person, tune into your feelings. Once you do this, make up a plan by exploring specifically what you want, how to get it, and set a date for a loving discussion to achieve a resolution.

**Step Two: Express Those Feelings**    The second step is to "Express Those Feelings." Many modalities and therapists advocate going to the person and expressing your hurt feelings. This only expands the problem and is the only area I do not agree with Dr. Calabrese. It is more important to clear your feelings on your own then go to the other person and lovingly ask for what you want to achieve as a resolution; rather than saying what you didn't like

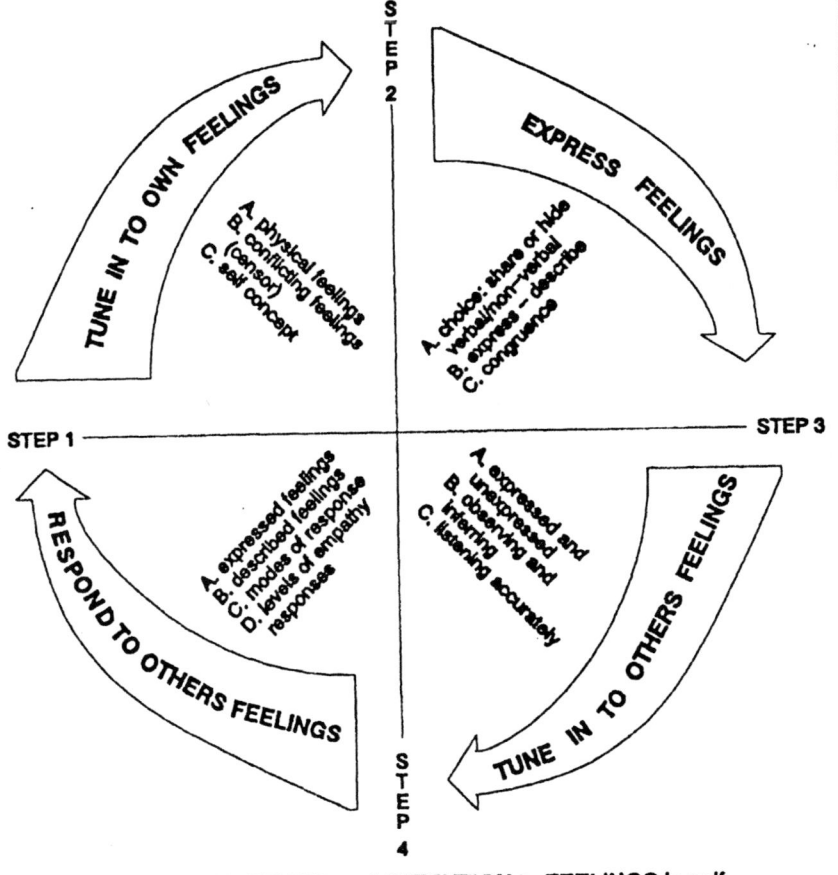

# THE PROCESS OF EMPATHY
## FOUR PHASES OF THE EMPATHY PROCESS
### The Process In One Huge Circle
### All Phases Occur Almost Simultaneously

STEP 2

TUNE IN TO OWN FEELINGS

A. physical feelings
B. conflicting feelings
   (sensory)
C. self concept

EXPRESS FEELINGS

A. choice: share or hide
   verbal/non-verbal
B. express – describe
C. congruence

STEP 1

STEP 3

RESPOND TO OTHERS FEELINGS

A. expressed feelings
B. described feelings
C. modes of response
D. levels of empathy
   responses

TUNE IN TO OTHERS FEELINGS

A. expressed and
   unexpressed
B. observing and
   inferring
C. listening accurately

STEP 4

At all times LISTENING and ATTENTION to FEELINGS in self
and FEELINGS "heard" from others Is absolutely essential

Illustration 5: The Process of Empathy

about them. This is not conducive to resolutions. It only starts a new argument of defense by the other person.

**Step Three: Tune Into The Other Person's Feelings**   Once you have taken care of your feelings and know you will pursue an effective result, then turn your attention to Step Three where you tune into the other person's feelings knowing you will attend to your needs once you have made a positive connection. To do this first, by being an active listener and attending to the person's emotions, is essential. After the emotions are attended to, then you can give common sense observations to resolve issues or to give proof of your Love and go for the win-win solution.

**Step Four: Responding To The Other Person's Feelings**   There is no empathy without a response that conveys you have heard the other person. Be the person to clarify her/his feelings and understand and accept them. When I use this process on children, they find it difficult to accept that someone is actually listening to them and inviting talk instead of telling them to keep quiet.

Listening to seven-year-old Matthew relating an incident, I said, "Now let me see if I have this right. You were walking home from school when John threw a rock at you and Philip. Is that right?" This gives Matthew the opportunity to correct my interpretation of what he was relating. He answered, "No, the principal blamed me for starting the fight." This special listening is saying, "I want to hear you and understand you. You interest me as a person. I care about you."

It is genuine interest that leads to understanding and generates warmth and trust in a relationship. This is Empathy.

Once you learn how to make peace with yourself using the Empathy process, look at how you convey the information. Your behavior, in speaking or body language, is the link between your inner you and the person you are talking to. Eric Berne's Transactional Analysis helps you to locate the behavior that puts these beliefs into effect. Addressing the inner thoughts and the outer behavior can result in resolutions to almost any problem.

*Transactional Analysis* Transactional Analysis helps you explore your "outer" self. To start your process of change, notice how you project yourself to others. Look for the positive ways you go about resolving issues and the negative processes you use to keep problems. Notice these same traits in others and learn how to diffuse them. Learn which ones hook your anger. Once you know what they are, you can then reprogram your responses. To recap Berne's concepts for your immediate use, he suggests you speak and act out of three different ego states. They are Parent, Adult and Child as shown in the PAC Ego States, (Illustration 6), on the following page. All are necessary in our life and each has a positive and negative side. The following outline will help you understand ego states, describes what the are and how they affect communication, positively and negatively:

### ...*Parent*

**Positive Critical Parent**: This is our conscience. It weighs what is right and what is wrong. Its strongest message is "Don't harm self or others." It knows all other messages are unimportant.

**Negative Critical Parent**: This ego state makes everything important. This is where you need to do everything right; how you eat, sleep, walk, talk, etc. The parent ego state does not teach you how to be happy. The message here is that it is better to be right than happy.

The Negative critical Parent never ceases its corrections and admonitions. The need to be right is so strong that happiness and Love will be forfeited to prove it. The time and energy to prove who's right results in never achieving resolutions.

Some of the traits of the Negative critical Parent includes a harsh, critical tone of voice, body language shows in rigidity and gestures such as pointing a finger or raising your eyes to the ceiling. These parental postures, gestures and tone of voice, alienate people and stop effective communication.

All the unimportant "No-No's" of your life generate from this position. They start with the first time your mother in the first months of your life, moves your hand away from your genitals.

**Positive Nurturing Parent**: The Positive Nurturing Parent ego state teaches you Love, and its strongest message is, "It is okay to be." You speak softly and gently and give hugs and kisses and learn how to be affectionate. This is where you support others.

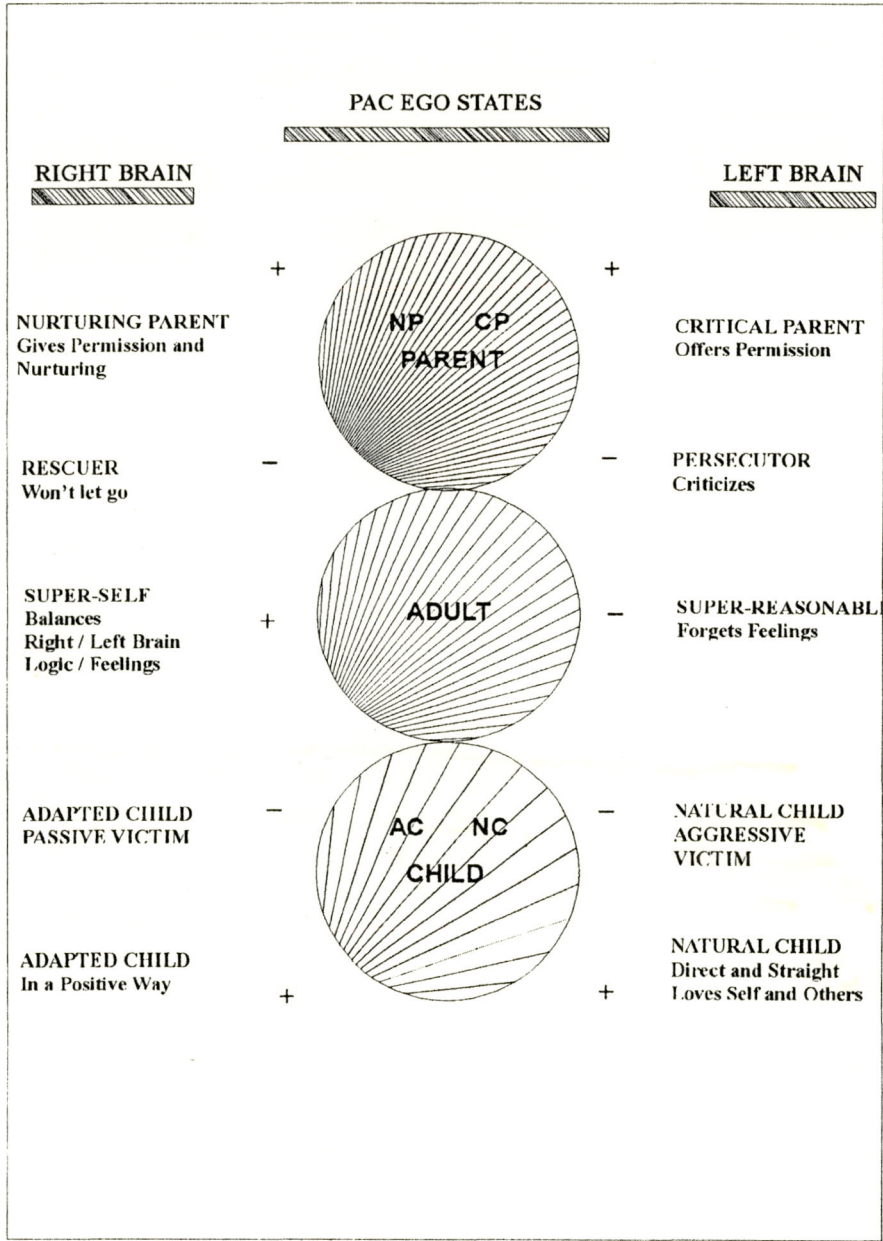

PAC EGO STATES

RIGHT BRAIN

LEFT BRAIN

**NP** **CP**
**PARENT**

+ +

NURTURING PARENT
Gives Permission and
Nurturing

CRITICAL PARENT
Offers Permission

− −

RESCUER
Won't let go

PERSECUTOR
Criticizes

**ADULT**

SUPER-SELF
Balances + −
Right / Left Brain
Logic / Feelings

SUPER-REASONABL
Forgets Feelings

**AC** **NC**
**CHILD**

− −

ADAPTED CHILD
PASSIVE VICTIM

NATURAL CHILD
AGGRESSIVE
VICTIM

ADAPTED CHILD
In a Positive Way

+ +

NATURAL CHILD
Direct and Straight
Loves Self and Others

Illustration 6: PAC Ego States

**Negative Nurturing Parent:** Your Negative Nurturing Parent gets so nurturing it is unaware of the harm they are creating in others by making them helpless. These are the givers of the world and helping is their purpose. You do not know how you create situations that require rescuing and you can't mind your own business. This is where the co-dependent personality stems from.

### ...Adult

**Positive Adult:** This gives straight factual information based on research, common sense and effective results. You use a clear firm tone of voice that conveys confidence. You remain cool and in charge in an emergency. You mean what you say and can implement or delegate without anger or frustration to achieve resolutions. You have a conversation, not the critical Parent's confrontation.

**Negative Adult:** This is close to the Positive Adult, but you overlook the emotional element in resolving issues. This type of person appears cold and uncaring to others, especially when support is needed. Not listening to the other person's emotional involvement can prevent getting resolutions.

### ...Child

**Positive Adaptive Child:** You will obey law and order, stop for red lights and fulfill requests from others. You will speak up if you feel something is unfair or if someone is taking advantage of you. You will be an excellent and trustworthy employee, will exercise initiative, and do what the employer wants without being monitored.

**Negative Adaptive Child:** With this personality you lose self. You will obey blindly with resentment that eventually builds up until you retaliate, in a passive-aggressive manner. Your voice can be sugary sweet or whiny, or withdraw completely and play helpless to perfection. Your feelings are extremely sensitive and you believe others do not understand you. You also have a false belief that says if you do what others say, they will know what a good person you are. You rarely give a "Yes" or "No" answer, taking a neutral stand where everyone loses as this personality creates anger.

**Positive Free Child**: When you are in your Positive Free Child mode you are the way you were the moment of your conception. You are the essence of Love, free and beautiful and uncontaminated by the negative messages of life. You are happy and joyful when you return to this ego state. You experience unconditional Love and have permission to enjoy sex. You have made peace with your self and your existence and know what life can be. Your laughter and goodness will be heard around the world as you have no expectations of how others are to be. You will lovingly tell someone they are stepping on your toes and will make him/her laugh..

**Negative Free Child**: Your Negative Free Child has fun at the expense of others. You do this by joking in a crass, sarcastic manner. You are a "Talker" and make threats and have tantrums. Your defiance and rebellious nature disrupts conversations and organizations. You love the power to make others angry.

### ...*Summary*

By keeping these ten parts of yourself in mind, you can learn to recognize where in your ego you are coming from. This gives you the opportunity to isolate these pieces of behavior and change them. Check out what ego state you rely on under stress. When asked to do something under an emotional situation, become aware of what ego state you access and know you have the power to come out and use the one you want to become successful.

Another excellent tool to intercept your anger and give a more favorable response is to change your body posture and gestures to emulate the Adult Ego State. Watch if you are pointing your finger (the Negative critical Parent). Check if your shoulders are drooping in a "poor me" stance which is the Negative Adapted Child.

The Adult sits straight, but not rigid, relaxed with feet firmly on the floor and hands in repose. When I have a child in therapy, I will physically arrange their body, feet, head and hands to an Adult ego state. I will then elicit an answer to my questions or talk about the problem.

When you can access any ego state under any circumstance, your success increases dramatically whether it is in Love, Quality or

Money. This is true freedom and what people call "control." The difference between a winner and a loser is that the winner has more options. Moving to a different ego state at will increases your options for resolutions. Choosing how you act under any condition or situation is using your Formula For Success.

You will have successfully achieved these two communication tools when you experience more positive results in conversations. You will answer a question directly, request pertinent answers to questions you ask, and people will start acting on any request you may make without resentment. This is an effective method of reducing emotionalism and stress in your life, workplace and relationships. Know what you will do when you make a request and it is not acted on. A winner always has another option to be heard and get a resolution that is favorable.

While in training, my tutor said, "There is no such thing as a resistant patient. You just have not learned to speak her/his language." As a result of this piece of wisdom, I created the form on the following page, Communication Preferred (Illustration 7). Knowledge of how each of you prefer having information given to you enhances your chances of receiving a direct answer and definitely assists you in being heard.

Take the responsibility to tell others how you want information given to you. Ask how others want information given to them. This prevents violation of each other. Some people like you to talk to them in private, and others are not concerned about you discussing it in front of others. Some prefer having instructions in writing, and others "can't stand those notes." Enter your name, the names of people in your family, friends, or office. Have them check off how they wish you to address them. Each person is given a copy to refer to before bringing up a subject that may be upsetting.

*To resolve the unhappiness within you, take a stand and accept the full responsibility for your life. Give up wallowing in the wrongs done to you or you have done to others. Enough is enough!*

## COMMUNICATION PREFERRED

Telling someone how to improve something often is interpreted as criticism. It is important to find our how they can best accept information and instructions by asking, "How can I tell you this without offending you?" Below are some answers received. Fill in the names of people involved and have each one check off or write in what will apply to them so that you will know how to approach them.

| Names | | | | | | | | | | |
|---|---|---|---|---|---|---|---|---|---|---|
| Written | | | | | | | | | | |
| Touch | | | | | | | | | | |
| Soft tone of voice | | | | | | | | | | |
| Direct eye contact | | | | | | | | | | |
| Tell in a factual manner | | | | | | | | | | |
| Be concise/brief, not repetitive | | | | | | | | | | |
| Need direct confrontation | | | | | | | | | | |
| Approach when making light of situation | | | | | | | | | | |
| When withdrawn need space | | | | | | | | | | |
| Tell at time it happens | | | | | | | | | | |
| Need time and space | | | | | | | | | | |
| Told in private | | | | | | | | | | |
| Other: | | | | | | | | | | |
| Other: | | | | | | | | | | |
| Other: | | | | | | | | | | |

Illustration No.7: Communication Preferred

## Motivation To Change - The Fourth Healer

Learning to intercept and change your Formula For Failure, and applying the concepts presented here prepares you to learn and use your Formula For Success. This is the time to discover what will motivate you to change your lifestyle, your way of thinking, and developing a resolution attitude. Stopping thoughts, words and deeds that are negative, opens doors and clears your head by making room for new ideas and creativity. At some point in your life you need to start integrating the information into your life that you have learned. Whether you are going to classes, growth groups, or psychotherapy, you need to say, "Stop! When am I going to apply all this knowledge?" The concepts in this book will provide you with the information needed to apply and achieve what you desire in life. You are either ready to apply the knowledge or you can go on learning more concepts. You can review and work out your past and vent your anger on your parents again. You can go back and vent one more time. To go from learning to integrating what you have learned is a quantum leap.

People around you start to perceive that you have no intention of using what you learned to be successful. You, in effect, become a "professional student/patient" always "going to" and never doing it. When my own children were little, they were not permitted to give the answer, "I'm going to do it." If I asked, "Did you clean your room?" they were expected to say "Yes" or "No" but not, "I'm going to." Allowing a child to say, "I'm going to," teaches and strengthens the negative act of procrastination in activities of day-to-day living.

*Find what motivates you. Make your plan. Extricate yourself from any problem you are experiencing and enjoy life. This is the blue print of your Formula For Success. We all have it, we just fail to use it at times.*

You not only need to apply these new concepts and accept full responsibility, you also need to locate what will motivate you to do this. Each person has a particular Love or interest that motivates s/he. Take the three major success areas: Love, Quality and Money, it soon becomes clear that all motivation fits into one of these three categories.

To create a healthy environment that will provide the ingredients to motivate you, associate with people whose lifestyles are complimentary to yours and have the same goals. Work in a healthy environment in a position that you enjoy. There are three motivators on a job. One is ideal hours that will allow you to be home with your family (Quality). If you need recognition to be motivated, take the responsibility to work in an environment where your work is appreciated and acknowledged (Love). Know in advance specifically what you need to feel adequately recognized and tell the person. If Money, motivates you, locate how much you want and go for it by asking what you need to do to get a promotion and a raise.

When I was raising my children, I was motivated to earn Money to create a better life for the three of us. My friend was leaving a well paying position and I told her of my intention to apply for it. She said, "Theresa, don't. He is terrible to work for. He never says, "Hello", "Goodbye", or gives you a compliment." You can see her motivation was verbal recognition, (Love). I said to her, "Peggy, you have a husband. He supports you and your family. I need the Money and I do not care what he says or doesn't say. I'm motivated by Money."

I applied for the job and was hired. The first day I worked, he came out of his office and slammed his dictation on my desk. I looked up at him and said, "Thank you, Sir." He was clenching a cigar out of the side of his mouth and said, "You won't be saying that for long." I vowed at that moment he would never upset me. I worked for him for five years and for as many hours as I could (Time). I made the highest wage in the company. He never said "Good Morning" or "How are you? I recall my last day working for him. He came out of his office as he did on the first day five years before. He slammed his dictation down and I said, "Thank you, Sir." He said, "You never quit saying that, did you?" I said, "Mr. King, what you are is you and your family's business, not mine. You paid an excellent wage when I

*Keep in mind that it is okay to have expectations of others. However, to have expectations from anyone that cannot or will not fulfill him or her, is futile, if not downright insane.*

needed it and it was my motivator. I want to thank you for making life easier for me and my children."

Discover what motivates you in Love, Quality and Money and create the atmosphere that will provide it. If you are waiting for another person to provide it or motivate you, a part of you may want to stay exactly where you are because of some reason in your head. It may be fear of success, losing someone you love, etc. One way to take the responsibility to motivate you, is to ask yourself two questions at the end of each day. What did I do or say today that I did not want to? What did I not say or do today that I wanted to? Go over the day's events and the areas you wished you had handled differently. Act out how you would prefer doing it next time. Know what results you want to end up with. Learn new and effective patterns by practicing how you will handle it in the future. Do this with self-care and Love and know all life is learning.

Certain messages during childhood, that made up your belief system, gave permission that makes it easier to change. I recall my mother saying, "Theresa, always pay yourself and have a few dollars put away that no one knows about." I still do that and it helped to know it was okay to have my own Money. It also contributed to me eventually becoming financially independent. This resulted in expanding my own Money limitation.

The other message she gave me was going back to school while in her fifties, to learn how to read and write. This motivated me to get my high school diploma after my children left home and led to achieving my doctorate. This eventually contributed to the overall Quality of my life.

Another area that enhanced the Quality of life for me was recalling very vividly the story of how my mother bravely made a stand with my father. She was sixteen-years-old when she arrived in the United States. She saw the slums of Boston and something within her needed some Quality. She insisted my father buy her a beautiful black mahogany Baldwin piano. It sat in the parlor where we gathered to play the rolls of music that came with it. They paid on this piano for thirty years. We had it for fifty years and it was a symbol of class and hope! We polished it every Saturday morning to keep the dream of better things in life alive. That symbol enabled our family to have the first white stove, a refrigerator instead of an icebox and a shower in the bathroom, which was an unheard luxury in our neighborhood. My mother's insistence on Quality in a drab life, motivated her to find a way to attain these things for herself under the most adverse conditions imaginable, which included bearing eighteen children. Knowing that you are never "stuck", and will never again make an excuse or blame anyone or anything for where you are, is living.

So look for the positive messages you received as a child that give you permission to resolve any problem in Love, Quality or Money and they will motivate you to rise above any circumstances. They are within you no matter what kind of childhood you had or you would not be reading this book. Once you learn how to resolve your problems, you become motivated. Take the responsibility to find a resolution and make the shift to accepting that you are rarely stuck in a problem.

Make a commitment to write out one problem at a time with several options to resolve it. When I was faced with numerous barriers to supporting my children and myself, I felt like it was a huge ball weighing down on me and I could not lift it off and escape. I said, "I can't do it all by myself." This was my whiny, helpless self. When it dawned on me that my children would have to go to an orphanage I was motivated to find a way. I said, "Theresa, there are hundreds of single women living with two children. Now move it."

I pictured pulling one of the problems off my big ball and resolving it. I wrote the problem on a piece of paper and underneath it wrote out a plan. One by one I unraveled this ball of problems and the weight started to lift. Oh God, what a relief. I knew then, that for the rest of my life, I would never burden myself like that again. Here it is thirty years later and I have stayed with that promise. It can be done. Find a motivator and stop expecting or waiting for outside help.

*Chapter Fourteen*

# The Clock To Success

The last step in putting your Formula For Success into effect is to track its path. The way you want to know your route for your Formula For Failure you also want to know specifically your Formula For Success that will replace it. There are two stages of "The Clock to Success." The first one is learning the pathway to solve a particular problem. This can be emerging from depression, resolving a problem in your household, office or work.

The second stage is: Stop creating petty problems and use the energy to increase your creativity to expand your capacity for Love, Quality and Money in your life. You are going to expand your limits of success all the way to infinity. When I have patients in therapy, I explain how we have a day-to-day health line we live by. When they go below the health line, they come in for therapy to go back up to the health line again. However, I encourage each person to not stop there but to go on and use their Formula For Success to go above the health line and reach undreamed of successes.

It is encouraging to see more and more people come to therapy to keep their current happiness and to strive for higher levels of Love, Quality and Money. This is exciting and one of the most positive moves I have seen in a long time. It is inspiring to see the difference it makes, especially to children, when they learn how to use corrections to create a better life rather than criticism when they do something

# THE CLOCK

## YOUR FORMULA FOR SUCCESS

Healer —————————— GOOD LIFE —————————— Stimulus

Yours —————————— PAYOFF —————————— Theirs

Frequency _____

Intensity: First Degree _____
          Second Degree _____
          Third Degree _____

Length of time in the Payoff position _____

Illustration 8: The Clock To Success

parents to not approve of. Knowing your "Clock for Success" will definitely help you to intercept and switch your journey through your "Clock for Failure" to your Clock for Success for a positive payoff.

In the Formula For Success Clock (Illustration 8 on the following page), is the process used by my patient, Yvonne, and her son, Winston. She left the Good Life when her son hooked her anger by returning the car with an empty gas tank causing her to run out of gas. The anger was her entry into her Formula For Failure. At one o'clock she immediately stopped herself and said, "The way to resolution is to use my capacity for Love sensibly." Her goal was to approach him with Love and an attitude that would bring about a resolution not alienation. This was quite a change as she usually used her Critical Parent in her Formula For Failure to berate him for his stupidity and for being inconsiderate. Clearing her head, she moved on to two o'clock where she adopted an attitude of resolution. She did this by centering herself, feeling the Love she had for her child and recognizing that she had far more anger than the situation called for.

Having conquered this, she then set herself to move to the three o'clock position. She had resolved to keep peace in the family, which motivated her to use her Formula For Success. However, her biggest motivation was to model the process for her son to learn, thus enriching both their lives. Keeping this in mind, she made a plan of resolution and mapped out a strategy to effectively communicate her wishes to her son.

She made an appointment with me for the specific purpose of reviewing her plan. We discussed the most effective way to approach Winston that would ensure cooperation. She decided to communicate the problem directly to him that would explore the options to prevent this from happening again. She did not discuss this with anyone else, thus avoiding the trap of gossip. A date and time were set to meet in a private place. She elected to invite him to lunch to coincide with my schedule so she could call me if the conversation became difficult.

At four o'clock, she set up the time and place and let him know in advance that the purpose of meeting alone was to get a resolution about running out of gas. The strategy included letting him select wherever he wished to go for lunch and eat whatever he selected without any remarks about his weight, the cost, etc. It was important to set an attitude of adult-to-adult conversation.

After eating their lunch and relaxing, she approached the subject, watching her parental tone of voice, avoided saying what he did wrong, and gently asked for what she wanted. This was done in a reasonable, conversational manner steering clear of any confrontational type of meeting. She practiced saying, "I trust you will return the car next time with gas in it or a note letting me know it is low on gas." She made a plan to leave $2.00 in the glove compartment so he would always have some Money to purchase the gas. She also asked him if he had any suggestions on making sure this would not occur again.

At one point as he started to defend himself about how he ran out of gas, she started to feel agitated and applied what we discussed in her plan. She left the table and called me to say she was starting up parental messages. Clearing her head, she went back and very gently said, "Winston, you do not have to defend yourself. We all do things like this and you are too good a person to have to defend yourself. If you have a need to explain, I am willing to listen, but I want you to know it is not important. It is okay. We will discuss how to prevent it from happening again."

She also took the responsibility of telling him she had failed to check the gas gauge when he returned the car, which probably was to emphasize the problem he created for her in running out of gas. This possibility arose in our discussion and I asked if she ran out of gas going to the gas station. She said, "No, I was in the middle of nowhere and could have gotten "attacked." I pointed out to her that to go 'to the middle of nowhere' without checking the gas gauge was as irresponsible as her son. She assured him she would check each time he returned the car, thus both taking responsibility as grown adults.

Both of them were now moving into the five o'clock position where the success of the conversation was calibrated to occur. The consequences for not taking the responsibility to return the car with gas, or a note was clearly outlined. She said, "The next time the car is returned without gas, you will need to start leaving a $10.00 deposit with me that you will forfeit if there is no gas in the car when returned. I trust you will not let it occur again since you are a responsible and trustworthy person. " She looked for all the areas she was able to compliment and thanked him. This built the trust and confidence Winston needed to do what was requested by his mother. In addition, she assured him she loved him and that was more important than anything else.

The positive, happy payoff at six o'clock was Winston's relief at not being put down, a feeling of being respected for his trustworthy areas, and that he could use the car again. Yvonne's positive payoff was she had built up trust with her son, the peace in the family was maintained, she felt heard and was pleased about using her Formula For Success to achieve a satisfactory resolution.

The seven o'clock position finds them both feeling the release and relief because they attained a resolution keeping their friendship intact. This is a lot different than the seven o'clock position in the Formula For Failure where the relief comes from the punishment ending.

At eight o'clock, they were able to laugh and hug, and go on to discussing other things about their lives. This also contributed to the building of a good relationship where each is heard by the other.

The journey back to twelve o'clock is more rapid than the long arduous journey of making up you go through in your Formula For Failure. Everyone takes responsibility for what occurred rather than all defending and explaining. There is pride in handling things well rather than the guilt and sorrow. The healers for both Yvonne and Winston were acceptance, Love, respect and trust.

Note that the problem was First Degree as it is a minor one where no one was hurt or lost anything which is Level 1. However, if the car is returned again and there is no gas in the tank, it has now gone to Level 2 as Winston is not going to abide by the agreement. This is where it is important to check the frequency of the 'crime'. When mother keeps giving him the car and he keeps bringing it back with no gas, there is war in the family. Usually, at this point, some professional help is suggested, as the problem is deeper than just running out of gas. It is a family problem that breaks down the needful levels of communication and resolution.

The Formula For Success was used in this instance to resolve a particular problem and it is very gratifying to see it work. However, it is far more exciting to use your Formula For Success to expand your success levels in Love, Quality and Money. When you resolve most of your petty problems or settle them as they arise, you can then put your energy into expanding your success level.

An example of this occurred during the final stages of writing this book while it was still in its primitive, unedited state. This came about when St. John's Hospital, where I was to lecture, called and requested I bring my book no matter what stage it was in. They were getting many requests for it since my last lecture. I guessed there was a reluctance on my part to go to the next level of success with my book when I rationalized that I was unable to print it because it was not completed and chances of a publisher rejecting it were high. The thought of having it printed caused me the experience all kinds of anxiety. I wasn't ready. Television stations were calling, organizations seeking me to lecture were requesting dates, and I was making Money selling the book on my own even in its unfinished state. I knew I simply wasn't ready for this success.

Thus, I started my failure process, which is procrastinating. I called a friend, my sister, my son, got a glass of water, etc. At times I found myself out in front of my house for absolutely no reason. I had no clue as to how and when I left the computer.

At two o'clock I said, "Go back Theresa. You are going to finish that book. You know you Love what you did. Go back. I typed in seven more pages and found myself asking Dr. Don Hanley to lunch. I enjoyed it as we critique each other's books. It was a legitimate luncheon. No, I definitely was not avoiding finishing the book!

Here I am at the three o'clock spot and I am going over what motivates me. Ah, this is better, I am motivated by knowing how effective my concepts have been over the years giving each person the opportunity to resolve her/his problems and map out success. I said, "Theresa, it is good. You saw it work. The positive

Formula For Success could change the tenor of the country from the negative stage it is going through when it is made available to the needy masses." So being motivated, I went back to the computer, finished it, took it to the printers and filled the 200 orders I had on my desk. The Money I'll make! And probably why I wouldn't finish the book. Was this just too much Money for a part of me??? It was difficult for me to comprehend that I would do such a thing and I delved deeper into my mind. I found it was also the fear that people would not accept or see the value in my concepts. It would be a rejection of a deep part of me and I felt vulnerable.

At four o'clock, depression set in and I went down the beach and watched the waves. I saw them roll in and then carry out to sea the doubts, fears and depression. I sat and over and over I made peace with what is. I reinforced that it is okay to have a lot of Money. It was okay to have success. It was okay to be well known. It was okay if people reject my ideas.... and slowly the peace came and I returned to completing the book. This process of stopping the game, going to the beach and making peace with existence is one of my greatest success formulas and I use it when I reach my 'stuck' place and thus I expanded my Money level once again.

I made a plan to write the last chapter. I set a date, took my telephone off the hook, went into hibernation with no dates, no telephone calls, no luncheons, and no procrastination. I sat at the computer and finished the chapter that brought the book to completion. It was apropos since the chapter was on success. Before finishing it, I ran a new copy of the book off and decided the section of "Givers" and "Takers" needed revision. Anything to keep me from completing this! I was working industriously taking the chapter apart, cutting and pasting like mad. All of a sudden I realized I had it all torn apart and did not know what I was doing. It was chaos. My Formula For Failure had taken over. I started for the bathroom to take my shower, stopped and said, "Stop Theresa, get your Formula For Success back." At this very moment, I felt a profound depression.

I thought, "Is this what it takes to expand your Formula For Success?" It makes no difference. Go back and finish the chapter."

As I walked back, I felt the power of my Formula For Success, which is tenacity. I took the chaos I created by all my cutting and pasting and page by page put them in sections by topic identifying each page and completed it. I became aware of the relief and happiness that flooded my being with no sign of depression. I felt I went through a sound barrier behind which I was pushing and straining to a breaking point and all of a sudden I was sailing free. What a high. I know my next expansion will be easier.

As I stated before, I love the mind above and beyond anything else that exists and my appreciation of watching it work thrills me. There is no end to what we can do. Success is here for all of us and goes on into infinity and they're for all of us. This may be the true goal and purpose of our existence that everyone on earth will be happy, content and partake of the goodness here. Becoming aware of your success formula enables you to apply it in the areas you are currently limiting yourself. Know, believe and accept that you have a Formula For Success. You have used it many times over in areas that you have permission in your head to be successful. We all have one. No one is exempt. Take the responsibility to locate it and put it into effect in all areas of your life.

Complete the Success to Infinity form (Illustration 9) on the following page, to see if you can gauge your levels of success and failure. Start with the Love success and notice how long you can go without an argument or doing something that will create a distance between you and a loved one. If you are upset with someone on a daily basis for a First Degree minor infraction, you're Love level will be about 20% above the base line. If you find that you are lonely and willing to do anything for the relationship, you will know you are below your comfort level in Love. If this has existed for a week or month, you may be 20% below the comfort level. If it is a way of life, and you are constantly giving in to someone for Love, you are 60% below your comfort level for Love.

Explore the Quality level next. If you have high integrity and honesty, you will be 60%. However, if you are critical of others and unhappy, you will be on 20% above the base line. The Quality of your life is when all things are balanced and you enjoy the abundance of life. There is no end to the improvement you can make in your life and this enhancement goes on to infinity.

At the Money level, write in the amount you are currently making on the base line. Write on the line above what you can and will increase it to within the next six months taking into consideration your potential. On the line above, write in the figure you want in two years. The line above, write in where you want to be at the end of five years. Keep your figures at a reality level. If they are not, you will stay at the base line figure all your life. Filling out this form already indicates you are ready to go up to another level. Do the same process to go below your Money comfort level. Are you able to go on welfare? This puts you down to about 40%. Realize that it is inconceivable for a person who has a high Money success level, even prior to earning it, to go there.

In filling out where the level of the negativity in your life is, enter if you reach the First, Second or Third Degree level. My findings have been that people rarely go beyond the first level of punishment. This will show you how petty your arguments and adamant stands keep you from succeeding in Love, Quality and Money.

When I went into expanding my capacity for success in Love, Quality and Money, I opened doors in my head. Writing this statement "Opened doors in my head" brings back a memory. I dreamt of doors for many years starting at age four. I was always trying to push them shut and lock them to no avail. The doors would keep popping open and terrified me. I could hear someone coming to destroy me.

After I learned how to open the limitations in my head, I had a most profound dream. I was standing looking down a wide corridor. It was about thirty-five feet wide with shiny marble floors that were a light toast color. The corridor was in semi-darkness and went on endlessly, as far as I could see. On both sides of the corridor, every ten feet, there was an open door with light shining through. The light was

| Success to Infinity | | | |
|---|---|---|---|
| | Love | Quality | Money |

| FORMULA FOR SUCCESS | Set your highest comfort level for Love, Quality and Money. At the baseline, write in the actual amount you are currently earning, and the actual amount you will be comfortable earning. | 100 | | | $_____ |
| | | 80 | | | $_____ |
| | | 60 | | | $_____ |
| | | 40 | | | $_____ |
| | | 20 | | | $_____ |
| | **Base Line for Love, Quality & Money** | Set by Age 10 | | | |
| | Set your lowest comfort level for Love, Quality and Money. | 20 | | | $_____ |
| | | 30 | | | $_____ |
| | 1° Minor Problems and Losses | 40 | 1° | | $_____ |
| | 2° Harm to self and others but reversible | 50 | 2° | | |
| | 3° Harm to self and others but irreversible | 100 | 3° | | |

**Failure to Infinity**

FORMULA FOR FAILURE

Illustration 9: Success To Infinity

glowing softly as it reflected off the marble floors. The grandeur and beauty took my breath away. I knew that in each doorway I would find another corner of my mind to explore. My dreams of doors and someone trying to destroy me never returned after this dream. It is possible that it is a metaphor of setting my limits free by opening all the doors in my head. This is true freedom and expansion of your mind. It leads to a full and successful life that we are all entitled to. Do not ask for it. It is there for the taking.

As a psychotherapist, I explore, expand and resolve issues and sabotages around these three successes: Love, Quality and Money. This has created happiness and peace we all search for not knowing it is right at our fingertips. As you have discovered through the many examples, to reduce one of these successes in your life is to impoverish your life. The formula to balance Love, Quality and Money, allows you to take full responsibility for the success in your life.

Success is within you when you use your ability to expand your horizons and be successful to unlimited levels and give up the need to be right. It is all the open doorways with the golden light inviting you to explore. Walk down the corridor. Take all it offers from the many passages of your mind. Learn to believe in abundance. Know it is limitless and will provide you the successes of Love, Quality and Money you deserve simply because you are here. And that is the ultimate in your Formula For Success!

Printed in the United States
31565LVS00009B/47